DISHING UP® MAINE

DISHING UP® MAINE

165 RECIPES THAT CAPTURE AUTHENTIC DOWN EAST FLAVORS

BROOKE DOJNY

Photography by Scott Dorrance

Storey Publishing

The mission of Storey Publishing is to serve our customers by publishing practical information that encourages personal independence in harmony with the environment.

Edited by Dianne M. Cutillo and Carleen Madigan Perkins

Art direction by Kent Lew and Cynthia McFarland

Cover and interior design by Blue Design (www.bluedes.com)

Photography © Scott Dorrance

Maine map on page 13 © David Cain

Indexed by Andrea Chesman

Blue Design gratefully acknowledges John Naylor and Scott Anderson of Rosemont Market and Bakery pictured on the front cover and on page 203.

Printed in the United States by Versa Press
10 9 8 7 6 5

Library of Congress Cataloging-in-Publication Data

Dojny, Brooke.
   Dishing Up Maine : 165 recipes that capture authentic down east flavors / by Brooke Dojny.
       p. cm.
   Includes bibliographical references and index.
   ISBN 978-1-58017-841-9 (pbk. : alk. paper)
   1. Cookery, American — New England style. 2. Cookery — Maine. I. Title.
TX715.2.N48D645 2006
641.59741 — dc22

                                          2006001422

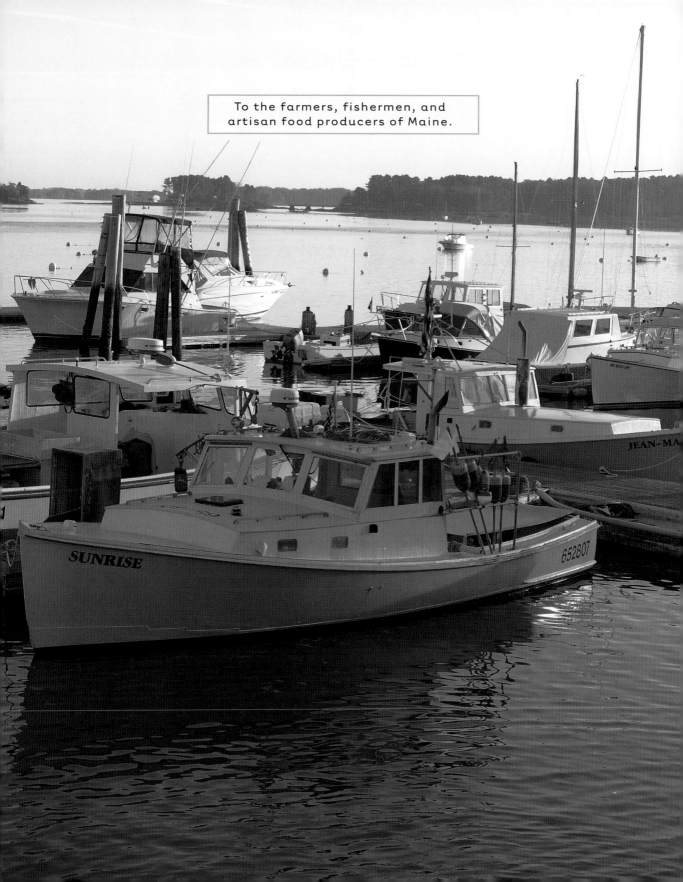

To the farmers, fishermen, and artisan food producers of Maine.

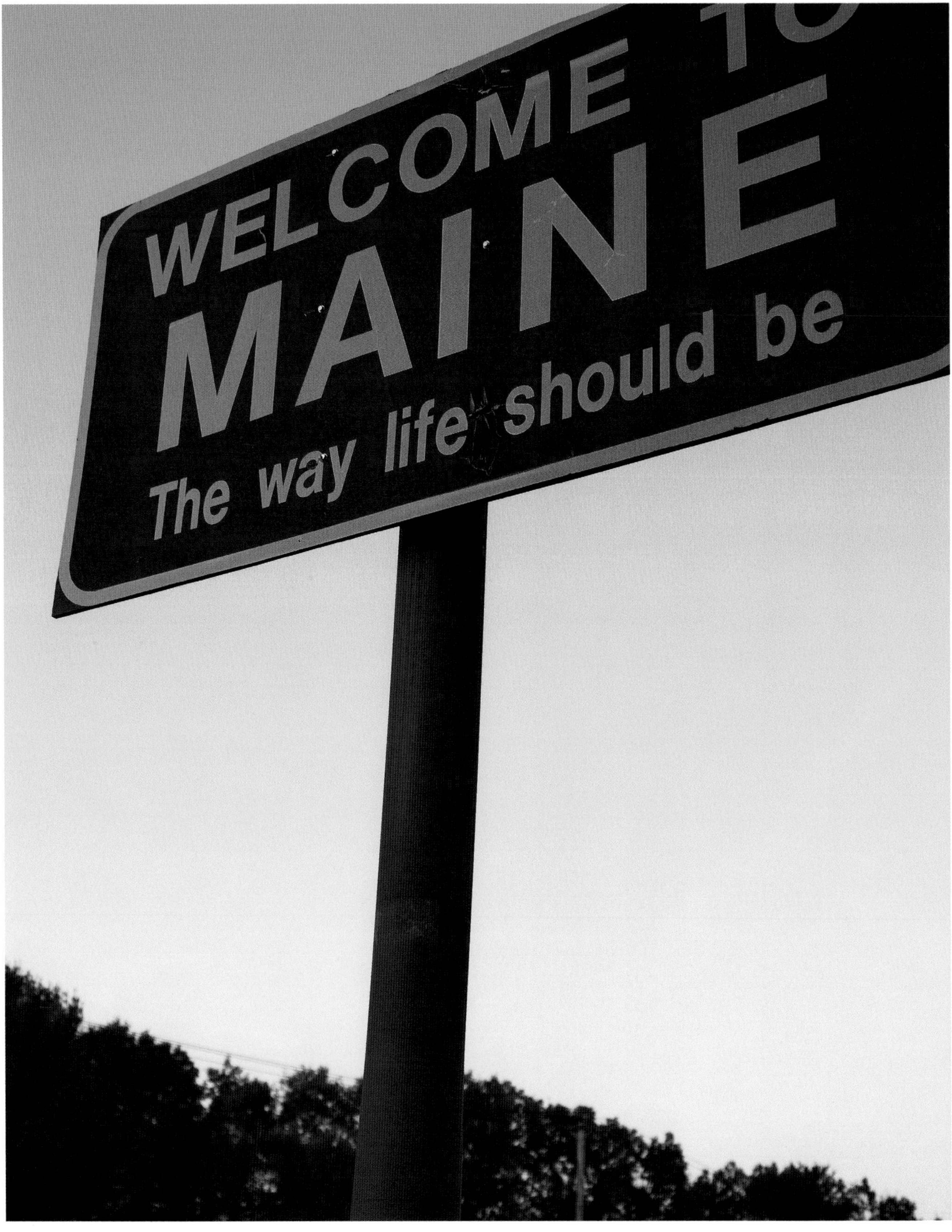
WELCOME TO
MAINE
The way life should be

CONTENTS

Acknowledgments

One of the lovely side benefits of researching this book has been meeting the fishermen, farmers, artisan producers, food professionals, and other dedicated people actively working to produce our wonderful food here in Maine. I thank them for so willingly sharing their knowledge and expertise — and their passion. I am also profoundly grateful for the constant support of old friends and family. Thank you all.

Kyra Alex
Ben Alfiero
Chip Angell
Karen Baldacci
Melanie Barnard
Elmer Beal, Jr.
Maurice Bonneau
Anne Bossi
Bob Bowen
Paul Brayton
Cindy Brown
Katey Burns
James Byron
David Chalfant
The Chase family
Eliot Coleman
Henry D'Alessandris
Paul Doiron
Roger Doiron
Matt Dojny

Maury Dojny
John Edwards
Adeena and Chris Fisher
Clark Frasier
Mark Gaier
Nancy Moody Genthner
Mike Giberson
Rhoda Grant
Mary Goodbody
Charlie and Susan Grover
Linda and Martha Greenlaw
Tom Gutow
Cary Hanson
Gary and Judy Hanscom
Abby Harmon
Janet Harris
Sam Hayward
Myles and Dick Henry
Brian Hill
Lee and Don Holmes

Rich Howe
Dan Huisjen
Caitlin Hunter
Melissa Kelly
Prescott Keyes
Steve Kingston
Elinor Klivans
Elena Kubler
Theda Lyden
Susan Maloney
Allison Martin
Rod McCormick
Anne Miller
Gretchen O'Grady
Sandra Oliver
Carolann Ouellette
Katherine Hall Page
Betsy Perry
Marty Perry
Herbert Peters

Brad Pollard
Mike and Libby Radcliffe
Sal Rooney
Bill Schmitt
Paul and Corinne Sewell
Pam and Ralph Siewers
Karen and Igor Sikorsky
Neale Sweet
Carolyn Waite
Doris Walton
Leslie Walton
Judith Weber
Martha Welty
Jasper White
Colleen Williams
Holly Williams
Susan Young

A few people have provided extraordinary help or inspiration: Anne Bossi, cheese maker; Richard Penfold, seafood smoker; Jen Schroth and Jon Ellsworth, organic farmers; Rich Hanson, scholar/chef; Deb Orrill, Maine foodie colleague; Barbara Keyes, friend and recipe tester; Joy Schmitt, who provided invaluable editorial help in the last stages of the project; Dianne Cutillo, editor extraordinaire; all the folks at Storey Publishing, including especially Deborah Balmuth, Sarah Thurston, and Carleen Perkins; and, of course, my husband, Richard Dojny, steadfast companion on all our journeys — culinary and otherwise. Thank you all.

INTRODUCTION

When I tell people that I moved to Maine for the food, I get some blank, disbelieving looks. The blank looks are not really all that surprising, because lots of people, even some who live in the state, take for granted the wealth of ingredients available in Maine and are maybe only vaguely conscious of the groundswell — now amounting to an unstoppable movement — of Maine artisans turning out some of the finest foodstuffs currently being produced in this country.

After vacationing in Maine for 20 years, and after 10 years of summer residence, about two years ago I found that it was time to leave Connecticut to live year-round in Maine.

Why has Maine life become so irresistible?

➤ Because of Mainers' deeply felt sense of history and of place, and the fascinating way that Maine's foodways fit into that context.

➤ Because Maine's climate and geography kept it somewhat isolated from the mainstream for so long that it developed its own unique culture and character as well as its own culinary history and food traditions.

➤ Because a good many of these traditions persist to this day. For instance, Mainers still eat molassesy baked beans on Saturday nights and make steamed brown bread or fluffy buttermilk biscuits to go with them. They still make simple, rich lobster stews and fresh-from-the-ocean haddock sandwiches (and don't apologize for their honest plainness), and they still bake hermit cookies and flaky lard-crusted blueberry pies because their grandmothers did.

➤ Because Mainers still eat, to a large extent, with the seasons. In winter, it's likely to be thick pea soup with smoky ham, vegetable-rich pot roast, rich and creamy seafood casserole, or cranberry-glazed meat loaf; in summer, thoughts turn to the likes of crab cakes, lobster rolls, barbecued chicken, and farmers' market pasta with Maine chèvre.

➤ Because, even though chain restaurants have started making some inroads into the state, Maine still has many wonderful, old-fashioned diners serving plainspoken, fairly priced Yankee fare.

➤ Because of the really top-quality restaurants opening in Maine, run by restaurateurs committed to cooking seasonally with local ingredients and passionate about supporting local farmers.

➤ Because I love the quirky names of Maine's dishes — whoopie pies, johnnycake (corn bread), Italians (grinders or heroes), graham cracker cream pie, frappes (milkshakes), pisser clams (soft shell clams), and the entire vocabulary surrounding lobster (chickens, culls, new-shells, shorts, selects, shedders, and so on).

➤ Because some of the best seafood in the world is fished out of Maine waters, and because seafood freshness is held in such high esteem in the state. Supermarkets, as well as small fish markets, take pride in selling extremely fresh (mostly local) seafood.

➤ Because farmers' markets grow in number and size every year, and who can resist the sight of mounds of ripe heirloom tomatoes or buckets of just-picked wildflowers?

➤ Because the artisan food movement thrives in Maine. Cheese makers; bread bakers; seafood smokers; fish, mussel, and oyster farmers; sausage makers; poultry and meat farmers, and specialty food producers (mustard makers, maple syrup producers, pickle packers, and so on) abound.

➤ Because of Maine's microbreweries. These enterprises, which now number about 20 in the state, range from Portland's relatively large and sophisticated Shipyard Brewing Company, which has been a leader in the national craft brew movement, to tiny Freeport Brewing Company, where two guys brew up small-barrel batches of seasonal draft beers in their barn.

➤ Because of Maine's wild blueberries — tiny, sweet-tart, and concentrated with the flavor of a northern summer, and beautiful to behold, spilling over in blue profusion from their cardboard pints and quarts at roadside stands, farmers' markets, and even convenience stores.

➤ Because of the roadside honor farm stands, which assume that the buyer is basically an honest sort, confirming our faith in basic human values.

➤ Because of the annual Maine Organic Farmers and Gardeners Association's (MOFGA) Common Ground Fair and all the other country fairs that showcase the mix of grand tradition and current innovations, from 4-H sheep herding to composting and from heirloom apples to French fries.

➤ Because of seasonal clam shacks, lobster pounds, hot dog stands, and dairy bars, scattered over the landscape, adding quirky charm (as well as great eating) to the Maine food scene.

➤ Because of Maine's food festivals, celebrating not only the obvious — clams, lobster, blueberries — but such obscure foodstuffs as Moxie (a soda pop) and ployes (a French-American pancake).

➤ Because of Maine's public suppers.

Maine Foodways Today

"Maine [is] the happening New England place to open a restaurant or start an artisan food business — a veritable Bay Area of the East," said Corby Kummer, noted writer and food critic for *The Atlantic Monthly*. Kummer, who made this statement in 2002 in the context of reviewing Sam Hayward's Fore Street Restaurant in Portland, cites Hayward as having much to do with Maine's current status as a culinary up-and-comer.

Hayward and a handful of other like-minded pioneers were attracted by the wealth of incredible raw ingredients in the state and found the Maine lifestyle to their liking. They broke new ground in the 1970s and '80s, opening restaurants in which they prepared Maine's raw ingredients with tremendous respect, cooking them with a minimum of fuss or embellishment. Others followed, and now, in addition to Fore Street, Maine has such award-winning restaurants as Street & Co. in Portland, The Arrows in Ogunquit, Primo in Rockland, Francine Bistro in Camden, and Cleonice in Ellsworth. The chef owners of these establishments have pledged to use fresh local ingredients in support of local growers, farmers, and food producers, and some are using the raw materials to cook innovative Mediterranean, Asian, and South American food, as well as creating their own versions of classic New England dishes.

At the other end of the spectrum proudly stand Maine's modest summer-only clam shacks and eat-in-the-rough lobster pounds. Here, you join us at a picnic table and scarf down some of the finest, freshest seafood this side of paradise. And, to complete the picture of Maine's restaurant scene, the state boasts several wonderful old-fashioned diners, as well as lots of family-run eateries serving honest, down-home Maine fare.

St. Lawrence River

QUEBEC

Fort
Kent

Saint John River

Allagash River

Presque
Isle

NEW

BRUNSWICK

Chamberlain
Lake

BAXTER
STATE
PARK

MT. KATAHDIN

Jackman

Moosehead
Lake

MAINE
FOODWAYS

Grand
Lake

Eastport

Rangeley
Lakes

Kennebec River

Penobscot River

Bangor

Waterville

Androscoggin
River

Brooklin

Bar Harbor

MT. DESERT ISLAND /
ACADIA NATIONAL PARK

Augusta

Penobscot
Bay

Rockland

NEW HAMPSHIRE

©2006 David Hall Cain

Lewiston

Brunswick

Sebago
Lake

Freeport

Portland

Boothbay
Harbor

N

Kittery

Fresh from the Land and Sea

The back-to-the-land movement started back in the 1960s in Maine. It was largely inspired by Scott and Helen Nearing of Harborside, on a rugged cape on the Blue Hill peninsula. The Nearings' work attracted young people with a willingness to commit to working the land and to *Living the Good Life* (the title of one of the Nearings' many books). While a good many of Maine's large family farms have disappeared, it is surprising and gratifying that, since 1997, the number of small farms (50 acres or less) has actually grown at a rate more than 10 times higher than the national average. These farmers are enterprising and entrepreneurial (many of them are dedicated to farming organically), and they are growing amazing produce of all types and in infinite and dazzling variety.

Eliot Coleman of Cape Rosier (see Farmer with a Vision, page 156) is one of the prime movers (some would call him the guru of this movement in the state),

Ed Behr, a noted food essayist, describes early Maine food and Maine people as "almost aggressive in their lack of pretension," but it might be misguided to fault the plainness of the cooking. Although the dishes weren't necessarily subtle, surely much of the cooking — especially when the cook was working with the superior-quality, in-season foodstuffs — was excellent. And, though some of the old dishes, such as coot (turtle) stew and switchel (a molasses-based drink sometimes called "haymaker's punch)," have dropped out of the culinary repertoire, most are still part of the continuum that is Maine food today.

and there are now dozens like him supplying farmers' markets, farm stands, restaurants, food co-ops, local grocery stores, and even chain supermarkets with fresh, in-season produce of exceptional quality. Mixed mesclun greens of superb quality and freshness, slender young leeks, perfect baby carrots and small purple and white eggplants, fat asparagus, skinny green and yellow beans, squashes of all types and all colors, apples, heirloom tomatoes, herbs . . . the list goes on and on.

And while Maine has produced some stellar food products for decades — mustard, pickles, sauerkraut, maple syrup, and more — a new crop of artisan food producers has arisen over the past 15 years. Today, Maine claims upwards of 600 small businesses that produce high-quality hand-crafted breads, farmstead cheeses, sausages, smoked seafood, microbrews, breakfast cereals, chutneys, and salsas.

But it's the seafood in Maine that still reigns supreme. Ninety percent of the *nation's* lobsters come out of the cold Maine waters, and other crustaceans and fin fish are still fished out of the Gulf of Maine in enormous quantities. Lobster and Maine are synonymous, and the timeless vision of tying on a bib and tucking into a shore dinner with all the fixings helps to lure visitors to the state by the millions every year. Lobsters boiled, steamed, baked, stuffed, simmered in a stew, or stuffed in a roll; sweet crabmeat made into cakes and crabmeat salad rolls; ocean-briny steamed clams, clam chowder, clams deep-fried and heaped in a bun; succulent broiled and fried scallops, fresh-from-the sea haddock sandwiches and milky haddock chowder; pristinely clean wine-steamed mussels; freshly shucked oysters on the half-shell . . . all this utterly dazzling fresh seafood, eaten in unpretentious little establishments in the midst of some of the most gorgeous scenery on earth. It's all absolutely fundamental and vital to the essential Maine experience.

— Ingredients and Cooking Notes ——————

Here are a few general guidelines about the ingredients and techniques in the recipes that follow:

➤ All eggs are "large."

➤ Unless otherwise specified, all-purpose flour is bleached.

➤ All seafood should be super fresh.

➤ Maple syrup should be the real thing — not Aunt Jemima's.

➤ I almost always use Hellmann's prepared mayonnaise (it's Best Foods brand west of the Rocky Mountains).

➤ Grainy mustard has more flavor than regular Dijon. I use Grey Poupon.

➤ When amounts of seasoning aren't specified — as in "before cooking, sprinkle the chicken with salt and pepper" — you should season judiciously to your own preference.

➤ Unless I call for extra-virgin, all olive oil in the book is just regular, off-the-supermarket shelf golden-colored olive oil.

➤ When cooking with wine, I usually use (unless otherwise specified) liter bottles of dry white and red wine.

➤ Get yourself a set of good-quality knives and keep them sharp.

➤ I stock my freezer with 1-pound bags of frozen corn kernels, peas, and spinach. Then I simply measure out the amount called for in a recipe and reseal the bag with a twist tie.

➤ Unless otherwise specified, salted or unsalted butter can be used interchangeably in non-baked recipes. For baking, I prefer unsalted butter.

➤ If a range of baking times is given, check for doneness after the minimum time. It's usually better to slightly underbake than to overbake.

➤ A good, heavy, wide (at least 11- to 12-inch) sauté pan is one of the most invaluable pieces of kitchen equipment in which you can invest.

➤ The internal temperatures for meats in these recipes is in line with traditional tests of doneness for best taste; however, the U.S. Department of Agriculture recommends 160°F for pork and ground beef; 145°F for other beef and veal; and 180°F for whole poultry (170°F for chicken breasts) to reduce the potential of contracting bacteria-caused illness.

➤ Similarly, the U.S. Food and Drug Administration warns that people with immune disorders and some other conditions should avoid eating raw seafood, because it may pose serious health risks.

Are you beginning to see why I had to write this book? After years spent gleaning blueberries from honor stands, buying live lobsters and crabs from the Sedgwick town dock, happily joining the lines at the Stonington or Blue Hill farmers' markets for everything from organic chickens and runny aged cheeses to maple syrup, and stopping at Carding Brook Farm in Brooklin to take our community-supported agriculture (CSA) shares in peppery mesclun, then making a detour for freshly baked bread and another for fresh nest eggs, how could I resist the urge to create a book that would showcase the bounty of the state?

Dishing It Up

Throughout *Dishing Up Maine,* I'll guide you through all the foodways of Maine, not only with recipes and techniques, but also with local stories, literary quotes, history, and lore. These pages are full of tested and updated recipes for such tried-and-true classics as homey chowders and stews, fresh and dried codfish cakes, creamy scalloped potatoes, sky-high biscuits and blueberry muffins and dark brown bread, old-fashioned baked beans, sparkling cranberry conserve, and such traditional Maine desserts as wild blueberry pie, dark and sticky gingerbread, raisin-studded hermit bars, and custardy grapenut pudding.

You'll find information on everything you ever wanted to know about lobster cooking and lobster eating, plus classic and new ways to enjoy fin fish. But the book is much more than a comprehensive resource on traditional Maine foods. I have also developed dozens of recipes using the wonderful array of fresh and artisan products in new and interesting ways. So look for the likes of Limed Lobster and Melon Skewers; Winter Salad of Oranges, Radishes, and Basil; Pan-Fried Haddock Sandwich with Jalapeño Mayo; Grilled Spice-Brined Pork Tenderloin with Heirloom Tomato Salad; Seared Duck Breast with Cumberland Pan Sauce; Seafood Primavera Salad for a Crowd; Roasted Whole Striped Bass with Lemon and Pesto; Pan-Seared Scallops with Dill Citronette; Maine Summer Salsa Fresca; and such delectable desserts as Rustic Summer Berry Croustade, Julia's Apple Cream Tart, and Gratin of Berries with Sweet Cheese Topping.

Another important part of this book is the collection of recipes from 24 of the best restaurants in the state. For instance, the book includes Cleonice's wonderful Paella, a Pan Roast of Fish and Shellfish from Fore Street, Venison with Cranberry-Chipotle Pan Sauce from Moose Point Tavern, and Moody's Walnut Pie, as well as recipes from 20 other establishments around the state — from clam shacks to top-flight white-tablecloth places and everything in between.

And the next time you're heading Down East, consult the Hidden Treasures sections in the pages that follow, where you'll find listings of Maine's best clam shacks, lobster pounds, hot dog stands, and the state's famous food festivals, many off the beaten path and still well-kept secrets.

So let's dig in!

1 Starters, Snacks, Sandwiches, and So On

Jalapeño Johnnycakes Topped with Smoked Fish

Henry & Marty, a wonderful restaurant in Brunswick (see page 75), serves these savory little cakes as an accompaniment to their luxurious lobster salad (page 74). The Johnnycakes have so much intrinsic flavor that I love them as an hors d'oeuvre, topped with a small piece of almost any smoked fish — salmon, arctic char, smoked Maine shrimp, or scallops.

³/₄	cup cornmeal
¹/₂	cup all-purpose flour
2	teaspoons baking powder
¹/₂	teaspoon ground cumin
¹/₂	teaspoon dried oregano
¹/₂	teaspoon salt
1	egg
1	cup low-fat or whole milk
2	tablespoons finely chopped seeded jalapeño chiles
4	tablespoons finely chopped scallions (about 4 scallions)
1	tablespoon olive oil
1	teaspoon liquid hot pepper sauce (see Note)
1	cup corn kernels (thawed frozen corn is fine)
1	tablespoon butter

Approximately 60 small pieces (the size of a quarter) smoked salmon, arctic char, smoked shrimp, or scallops

MAKES ABOUT 60 PANCAKES (ABOUT 10 SERVINGS)

1. Whisk together the cornmeal, flour, baking powder, cumin, oregano, and salt in a bowl.

2. In another bowl, whisk the egg with the milk. Whisk in the jalapeños, 2 tablespoons of the scallions, oil, and hot pepper sauce. Gently whisk the egg mixture into the cornmeal mixture. Stir in the corn.

3. Heat the butter in a large skillet or griddle over medium-high heat. Spoon out the batter by half-tablespoons to make pancakes about the size of silver dollars. Cook, turning once, until golden brown and cooked through, about 1 to 2 minutes. Remove to baking sheets and repeat until batter is used.

4. Serve immediately, or reheat in a 375°F oven until just warm. Top each pancake with a piece of seafood, sprinkle with the remaining 2 tablespoons scallions, and serve.

Note: *At Henry & Marty in Brunswick, they prefer Frank's hot sauce. Tabasco is fine, but be aware that it is a little hotter, so adjust to your taste.*

Smoked Salmon and Scallion Triangles

I'm always looking for ways to showcase Maine's gorgeous smoked salmon. This is my version of the rather classic hors d'oeuvre, and it's one of my favorites. The dense, chewy pumpernickel makes an ideal hand-held base, the richness of the scallion butter counterpoints the salty fish, and the piquant, vinegary capers are the perfect little burst-in-the-mouth garnish.

½ cup (1 stick) butter, softened

¼ cup finely minced scallions (about 2 scallions), plus scallion brushes as garnish (optional; see Note)

2 teaspoons coarse-grain mustard

8 pieces thin-sliced sandwich-size pumpernickel bread

¼ pound thinly sliced smoked salmon

1½ tablespoons small capers, drained

Freshly ground black pepper, coarse grind

MAKES 32 TRIANGLES

1. Combine the butter, scallions, and mustard in a small bowl and mix well. (This can be made up to 3 days ahead and refrigerated. Return to room temperature before using.)

2. Place the bread on a work surface and spread evenly with the scallion butter. Arrange the salmon evenly over the butter, coming to within ¼ inch or so of the edge of the bread. With a large knife, cut off the crusts; then cut each piece of bread diagonally into four triangles. Arrange on a platter and scatter with the capers, pressing them into the salmon. Grind the pepper to taste over the top. (These can be made up to 3 hours ahead. Cover with damp paper towels, then wrap with plastic wrap and refrigerate.)

3. If desired, garnish with the scallion brushes before serving.

   Note: *To make the scallion brushes, trim 4 or 5 scallions into 4-inch lengths and cut off the root ends. Make 4 or 5 cuts (1 inch long) in the white ends of the scallions. Drop into a bowl of water and ice cubes and let stand for about 30 minutes. The ends of the scallions will open up into a feathery brush.*

— Seafood Smokes!

Chef Rich Hanson of Ellsworth's Cleonice says, "The seafood-smoking scene here in Maine is incredible right now, early in the 21st century. It's an industry that has just taken off, and there are so many good companies, large and small, that they all keep upping the ante in terms of quality. None of them can rest on their laurels, so all of us — restaurateurs and consumers in general — get to reap the rewards." More than a dozen seafood-smoking businesses are flourishing in Maine, including Stonington Sea Products, whose smoked salmon was cited by the *Rosengarten Report* as one of its top 25 favorite foods.

Salt Cod Resurgence

Before the days of refrigeration and food processing, salt cod was one of the world's most available and affordable fish. Caught in huge quantities in the North Atlantic, the cod was heavily salted, dried on open-air racks in towns all over coastal New England, then shipped to Europe and South America. It was also a staple of New England cooks, who made it into codfish cakes and codfish "balls."

The Portuguese incorporated salt cod (bacalhau) into all manner of savory dishes, the Caribbeans turned it into fritters, and the French whipped it into a lovely, light mousse called *brandade de morue*. Although the popularity of salt cod declined in this country in the 20th century, its intense flavor has caught the attention of young chefs, who are giving it a new life. The desiccated product must be rehydrated by soaking for several hours to soften it and remove the excess salt.

Salt Cod Mousse with Farmers' Market Dippers

Before the days of refrigeration and food processing, dried salt cod was a staple ingredient, an essential part of the New England diet. For about a hundred years, salt cod was packaged in cute little wooden boxes, and Mainers loved to combine it with mashed potatoes and shape it into delicate cakes (see Salt Codfish Cakes with Bacon, page 170). It was beginning to fade from the scene, but recently, because of its deliciously intense flavor, salt cod experienced something of a resurgence. This mousse, called *brandade de morue*, is a classic French treatment for the salted fish, and since Maine does have ties with French Canada, I think it can very legitimately be included here.

1 pound salt cod

2 garlic cloves, peeled

1⅓ cups heavy cream

⅔ cup olive oil

3 tablespoons snipped fresh chives, plus longer chive spears for garnish

2 tablespoons lemon juice (juice of medium lemon)

⅛ teaspoon ground nutmeg

Salt and freshly ground black pepper

Assorted firm vegetables for dipping, such as bell pepper strips, broccoli florets, carrots, grape tomatoes, asparagus, and small steamed new potatoes (about 2½ pounds total)

10—12 SERVINGS

1. Soak the cod in a large dish in cold water to cover overnight, changing the water twice.

2. Drain, place the cod in a saucepan or large skillet, add water to cover, and bring to a boil. Simmer over medium-low heat until the fish is soft and flakes easily with a fork, 15 to 20 minutes. Drain and, when cool enough to handle, strip off and discard any skin and remove any bones.

3. Place half the cod in a food processor with the garlic and ¼ cup of the cream and process, scraping down the sides once or twice, until smooth. Add the remaining cod and ¼ cup more cream, and repeat. With the motor running, drizzle the remaining cream and the olive oil through the feed tube, processing until smooth, creamy, and light.

4. Transfer to a bowl and stir in the chives, lemon juice, and nutmeg. Season with the salt and pepper to taste. It may not need salt; the salt cod may provide enough. (The mousse can be prepared a day ahead and refrigerated.)

5. Bring to room temperature (if prepared ahead), garnish with the chive spears, surround with the vegetables, and serve.

Carter Point Lemon-Tarragon Crab Spread

Coast-of-Mainers are lucky enough to be able to buy sweet, freshly picked crabmeat from local vendors during much of the year. This spread, bound with mayonnaise and some cream cheese to give it a bit of body and spiked with lemon and tarragon, is my favorite treatment of the delicate meat. It's got just enough seasoning to enhance, while allowing the incredible flavor of the fresh crabmeat to still shine through.

¼ cup mayonnaise

1 package (3 ounces) cream cheese, softened (see Note)

⅓ cup finely chopped scallions (about 2 scallions)

1 tablespoon chopped fresh tarragon (or 1 teaspoon dried), plus sprigs for garnish (optional)

1½ teaspoons grated lemon zest (from ½ medium lemon)

¼ teaspoon cayenne pepper

1 pound fresh crabmeat, picked over to remove any shell or cartilage

Salt

2 European cucumbers

MAKES ABOUT 50 HORS D'OEUVRES (ABOUT 8 SERVINGS)

1. Whisk together the mayonnaise, cream cheese, scallions, tarragon, lemon zest, and cayenne in a large bowl until smooth.

2. Add the crab and stir with a large fork until well mixed. Season with the salt to taste. (You can make this up to 6 hours ahead and refrigerate.)

3. Score the cucumbers horizontally with a fork and slice about ¼-inch thick. Spoon the crab mixture atop the cucumber slices, garnish with a tarragon sprig, if desired, and serve. (Alternatively, place the crab mixture in a bowl, surround with the cucumber slices, and let guests serve themselves.)

Note: *If you forget to leave the cream cheese out at room temperature for an hour or so to soften, simply remove from its foil wrapper and zap it in the microwave for a few seconds.*

—— Maine's Other Beautiful Swimmers ——

Maine crabmeat is now considered one of the state's most prized local delicacies, but such was not always the case. For years, the crabs (smallish sand and rock crabs) that crept into lobster traps were tossed back into the sea because most people considered the meat too troublesome to pick out. But the crabmeat is much too tasty to ignore, so now a well-regulated cottage industry thrives along the coast, and, in fact, chefs from all over the country prize meat from Maine "peekytoe" crabs (also called sand crabs). The silly-sounding name probably evolved from the local slang term "picked-toe," meaning crooked or pointed toe.

Tiny Crab Cakes with Curry-Orange Mayo

These crab cakes, made with Maine's sweet lump crabmeat, are a fabulous hors d'oeuvre, passed on a platter with a piquant curry-orange dipping sauce. Of course, you can make them with any good-quality fresh or pasteurized crabmeat. To serve the cakes as a knife-and-fork first course, shape them larger and present two or three on a plate, topped with dollops of the sauce.

CURRY-ORANGE MAYO

- 1/2 cup mayonnaise
- 1 tablespoon curry powder
- 1/2 teaspoon grated orange zest
- 1 tablespoon orange juice (juice of about 1/4 orange)
- 1/2 teaspoon Tabasco sauce
- 1 tablespoon finely chopped scallions or chives

TINY CRAB CAKES

- 1 egg
- 1 1/2 cups fresh breadcrumbs (see Note)
- 1/4 cup finely chopped scallions (2–3 scallions)
- 1 tablespoon mayonnaise
- 1 teaspoon lemon juice (juice of about 1/6 medium lemon)
- 1/2 teaspoon Worcestershire sauce
- 1/4 teaspoon seafood seasoning mix, such as Old Bay
- 8 ounces fresh lump-style crabmeat, picked over
- 2–3 tablespoons vegetable oil

Scallion brushes for garnish (optional; see page 19)

MAKES ABOUT 24 MINI CAKES (4–6 SERVINGS)

1. To make the Curry-Orange Mayo, whisk together the mayonnaise, curry powder, orange zest, orange juice, and Tabasco in a small bowl. Refrigerate for at least 2 hours or up to 3 days. When ready to serve, transfer to a pretty bowl and sprinkle with the scallions.

2. To make the crab cakes, lightly beat the egg in a large bowl. Add 3/4 cup of the breadcrumbs, the scallions, mayonnaise, lemon juice, Worcestershire sauce, and seasoning mix. Stir well to blend. Add the crabmeat and mix gently, being careful not to shred the crabmeat entirely.

3. Spread the remaining 3/4 cup of breadcrumbs onto a plate. Form the crab mixture into 24 cakes, using a scant tablespoon for each one, and dredge lightly in the crumbs. Arrange on a wax paper-lined baking sheet.

4. Heat 2 tablespoons of the oil in one or two large skillets over medium heat. Cook the cakes until golden brown and crisp on one side, about 2 to 2 1/2 minutes. Flip and repeat. The cakes should be hot inside. Repeat with any remaining cakes, adding more oil as necessary. Serve immediately, or place on a foil-lined baking sheet, wrap well, and refrigerate for up to 24 hours, or freeze for up to 2 weeks.

5. If you make the cakes ahead, remove from the refrigerator or freezer 30 minutes prior to reheating. Preheat the oven to 375°F. Bake the cakes until hot and crisp, 10 to 15 minutes.

6. Arrange on a platter with the sauce for dipping, and garnish with the scallion brushes, if desired.

   Note: *Tear 3 slices of good-quality bread into pieces and whir in a food processor to make breadcrumbs.*

Portland Public Market

The Portland Public Market, which opened in 1998, continues Maine's long tradition of downtown public markets, dating back to the 19th century. Housed in an award-winning brick, glass, and wood structure, the market, which was the brainchild of Maine philanthropist Elizabeth Noyce, is a food-lover's heaven. Vendors include organic produce farms; butchers selling locally raised meat; purveyors of Maine-made cheeses, sausages, and smoked seafood; artisan bakers; and flower sellers. Prepared take-away food includes Mexican delicacies, pizza, soups, smoothies, and sandwiches, and such well-known Portland culinary stars as Sam Hayward (see page 127) and Dana Street (see page 129) have opened casual dining concessions.

Limed Lobster and Melon Skewers

Let's be honest: even in Maine, serving lobster to a group of more than a few people can get prohibitively costly. But if you use the lobster meat as part of a single-bite hors d'oeuvre, then it becomes ever so much more affordable. The inspiration for these very pretty and absolutely delicious little skewers comes from my friend Holly Williams, who lives in Georgia. Sometimes it takes the insight of a person "from away" to illuminate what should have been obvious all along.

¼ cup olive oil

2 tablespoons chopped fresh cilantro, plus sprigs for garnish

1 teaspoon grated lime zest

1½ tablespoons lime juice (juice of medium lime)

1 garlic clove, minced

½ teaspoon salt

¼ teaspoon cayenne pepper

2 cups cooked lobster meat, cut into ¾-inch chunks

About 40 cubes (¾-inch each) honeydew melon or cantaloupe

About 40 tiny triangles of thinly sliced lime (see Note)

About 40 bamboo skewers (5 inches each) or long toothpicks

MAKES ABOUT 40 SMALL SKEWERS (ABOUT 6 SERVINGS)

1. Whisk together the oil, cilantro, lime zest and juice, garlic, salt, and cayenne in a medium-sized bowl. Add the lobster meat and stir to combine. Marinate in the refrigerator for at least 1 hour, or for up to 4 hours.

2. When ready to assemble, thread the skewers with one cube of melon, one slice of lime, and a chunk of lobster. (If using the longer skewers, stack the food near the end of the pick so that guests can eat it easily.)

3. Arrange the skewers on a platter. (The skewers can be assembled up to about an hour ahead and refrigerated, covered.) Garnish with the cilantro sprigs before serving.

Note: *To make the lime triangles, cut a lime in half lengthwise and cut several very thin slices. Cut each sliced half into triangles less than ½-inch wide.*

A Peek at Portland

Once the capital of Maine, and currently the largest city in the state, Portland (which used to be called Arundel) has exhibited an indomitable will to survive. Following three disastrous events — an Indian attack, the British invasion, and then, in 1866, a horrendous fire — Portland was rebuilt in the classic Victorian architectural style that is still represented today, particularly in the several-block area on the waterfront known as "Old Port." Today, the thriving city has many attractions, not the least of which is its lively and varied restaurant scene. In fact, Portland claims more restaurants per capita than any other city in the nation.

Citrus-Glazed Mussels

I originally developed this recipe for my *New England Cookbook* (Harvard Common Press, 1999), but out of necessity have since adapted and streamlined it because I now make these citrusy mussels in large quantities every summer for our annual Mussel Mania party. I put out large bowls of the mussels, along with baskets of cubed peasant bread. Guests serve themselves a bowl full, eat them mostly with their fingers, and mop up the sauce with the bread. The sauce gets its delightfully salty intensity from a little hit of anchovies.

3 tablespoons extra-virgin olive oil

1 cup finely chopped onion (1 medium onion)

3 garlic cloves, minced

4 anchovy fillets (from a 2-ounce can), coarsely chopped

1 teaspoon grated lemon zest

1/2 teaspoon grated lime zest

1 tablespoon lemon juice (juice of 1/2 medium lemon)

1 tablespoon lime juice (juice of medium lime)

1/4 teaspoon dried red pepper flakes

2 pounds mussels, rinsed and debearded (see Note) if necessary

1/2 cup dry white wine

1/4 cup chopped fresh flat-leaf parsley

Thin slices of lemon and lime for garnish

8–10 APPETIZER SERVINGS

1. Heat the oil in a medium-sized skillet. Cook the onion in the oil over medium heat until softened, about 5 minutes. Add the garlic and anchovies and cook, mashing the anchovies until they dissolve, for 2 minutes. Stir in the lemon and lime zest and juice and the pepper flakes. (This base can be made a day or so ahead and refrigerated, or frozen for up to 3 weeks.)

2. Combine the mussels and wine in a large pot. Cover, bring to a boil, reduce the heat to medium, and cook until the mussels open, 4 to 10 minutes, depending on size. Remove the mussels from the pot with a slotted spoon and transfer to a serving bowl.

3. Meanwhile, if the citrus sauce base has been refrigerated or frozen, reheat in a saucepan. Carefully pour the mussel broth into the citrus mixture, leaving behind the last third or so of the liquid, lest it contain any grit.

4. Pour this sauce over the mussels, sprinkle with parsley, garnish with the lemon and lime slices, and serve.

Note: *To debeard mussels, pull out the dark threads that protrude from the shell. Do this just before cooking; mussels die when debearded.*

— The Very Cultured Mussel —

It's now a huge industry, but mussel farming had to come a long way from its early days in the 1970s. Until then, mussels were considered poverty food: unloved, overlooked, and disdained by all but savvy Portuguese and Italians cooks. They were there for the taking, lying in huge blue-black clusters when the tide went out, but even when they became a more fashionable edible, wild mussels proved pesky to clean, laden as they were with mud, barnacles, pearls, and tough, wiry beards.

Enter the likes of Paul Brayton, founder of Tightrope Sea Farms in Brooklin, Maine; and Chip Davison and partners of Great Eastern Mussel Farms in Tenants Harbor. Practicing rope culture, a farming method that suspends the mussels on ropes from buoys or rafts so that they never come closer than 30 feet to the seabed, these operations produce sweet, meaty, uniformly-sized, and — most important — clean mussels, that usually require only a swish through cold water before being steamed.

J'S OYSTER BAR

J's Oyster Bar, now run by the original J's two daughters, is right smack on Portland's busy harbor. This saloon-cum-restaurant is a bustling year-round hangout, very popular with locals of all stripes — from local fishermen to three-piece-suited businessmen — but remains, mysteriously, something of a well-kept secret from tourists crowding the better-advertised eateries around the corner on Commercial Street. J's is not necessarily just about oysters, although their "nude and raw" oysters and other raw bar bivalves are certainly a specialty. Although there is no deep-fried food on J's menu, it otherwise covers the full range of New England seafood favorites, including a glorious seafood bouillabaisse pasta dish, all manner of skillet-fried fish, and a dazzling traditional Maine shore dinner, consisting of chowder, steamers, lobster, and corn on the cob.

"Nude" Raw Oysters with Sauces

These oysters are among the raw bivalves that are a specialty at the eponymously named J's Oyster Bar. (And what if I told you that half-shell oysters are, almost unbelievably, free during happy hour for the entire month of February?) J's other oyster treatments include baked stuffed oysters, oysters Rockefeller, and oysters Mornay. You can also order an oyster sampler of all of the above.

About 36 fresh raw oysters

Horseradish, either freshly grated or from a fresh bottle of prepared horseradish

Ketchup

Lemon wedges

Mignonette Sauce (recipes follow)

Tabasco sauce, or other liquid hot pepper sauce

4 SERVINGS

1. Either have the oysters shucked at the fish market or shuck them yourself (see Maine Oysters, page 32). Arrange on a large platter on crushed ice.

2. Place the horseradish, ketchup, lemon wedges, and Mignonette Sauce in separate small bowls, but leave the hot pepper sauce in the bottle. Suggest that guests dress their oysters as they desire. Slurp and eat.

Mignonette Sauce Sampler

Classic Mignonette. One tablespoon minced shallots stirred into ⅓ cup white wine or champagne vinegar, with cracked black pepper added to taste.
Variations:
Mango Mignonette. Add about 1 tablespoon finely chopped fresh mango or papaya.
Cranberry Mignonette. Add 1 tablespoon finely chopped fresh cranberries and a pinch of sugar.
Herb Mignonette. Add 1 tablespoon chopped cilantro, parsley, or tarragon.
Jalapeño Mignonette. Add about 2 teaspoons chopped jalapeño or other fresh hot chile.
Ginger Mignonette. Add about 2 teaspoons minced or grated fresh gingerroot.

Maine Oysters

In the world of oyster connoisseurship, Maine oysters enjoy a reputation for being particularly delicious, and the bivalves fetch a pretty price in white tablecloth restaurants along the East Coast and points west. "I tell my customers that Maine oysters are the Burgundy of oysters," enthuses the owner of Jack's Luxury Oyster Bar in Manhattan. Indeed, an entire oyster-descriptive vocabulary has evolved, with terms like "clean," "crisp," "briny," "creamy," "buttery," "flinty," and "sweet" bandied about to delineate differences in flavor.

With more than 25 growers licensed in the state, Maine's boutique oyster farming business is thriving. Each farmer coddles and cares for his "crop," moving the oysters about during their life cycles to produce the best results. "It's like polishing the vintage," says a spokesperson for the Maine Aquaculture Association.

Oysters are named for the bay or other body of water in which they're raised, and every cove location imparts its own particular flavor, depending on the salinity and nutrients in the water. Some of Maine's best oysters are Pemaquids, Winter Points, Long Coves, Spinney Creeks, Bagaduce, and Flying Points.

To Shuck Oysters

Note: Some people recommend freezing the oysters for about 15 minutes to relax them.

1. Wear gloves or pad your hand with a folded kitchen towel.
2. Hold the oyster with its hinge toward you, rounded side down.
3. Use a specially designed oyster knife with a strong blade, sometimes bent at the end. Insert the point into the hinge and turn the knife to pry open the shell.
4. Use the point of a knife to scrape the meat attached to the top shell into the bottom shell. Take care to keep as much of the liquid as possible in the shell.
5. Scrape the oyster meat from the bottom shell.
6. Pick out any bits of shell that have fallen into the flesh.
7. Nestle the half-shells in a bed of crushed ice or rock salt to keep them from tipping over.

Shrimpy Shrimp

Tiny Maine shrimp (a.k.a. northern pink shrimp) are the only shrimp caught fresh in Maine waters, and the season for these sweet little popcorn-size morsels is brief, from about January to March. They're sold both in the shell, often with heads still on, and shelled. Even though it's somewhat labor-intensive to peel off their papery shells, it can be a fun communal sort of task, and I'm convinced that their flavor is superior to the pre-shelled shrimp. (Just be sure to chill the shrimp before shelling.) Maine shrimp should be cooked ever so briefly — usually about 2 minutes in salty boiling water is sufficient — because overcooked Maine shrimp are tasteless and mealy and not worth eating.

Peel 'n' Eat Maine Shrimp Boil with East-West Sauces

During the brief winter season when Maine shrimp are available fresh, I like to serve and eat them as often as possible. The tiny shrimp can now be bought peeled, but I think the flavor is better when they're cooked in their shells. In this preparation, guests are invited to peel off the shrimp's papery skins themselves and dunk in a choice of two sauces. It's a delightfully messy proposition, so serve the shrimp this way at a less-than-formal occasion — and provide plenty of napkins!

2   pounds fresh Maine shrimps in shells (see Note)

About 8 thin lemon slices for garnish

FAR EASTERN DIPPING SAUCE

⅓   cup packed dark brown sugar

⅓   cup water

2   tablespoons soy sauce

2   tablespoons white wine vinegar

2   teaspoons grated or minced fresh ginger (about 1-inch piece)

2   teaspoons toasted sesame oil

½   teaspoon white pepper

1   tablespoon snipped chives or finely chopped scallion tops

ALL-AMERICAN COCKTAIL SAUCE

¼   cup chili sauce (see Note)

¼   cup ketchup

2   heaping tablespoons fresh or prepared horseradish (see Note)

1   tablespoon finely chopped red or sweet white onion

2   teaspoons lemon juice (juice of about ⅓ lemon)

8–10 SERVINGS

1. Bring a large pot of salted water to a boil. Add the shrimp and cook until pink, 2 to 3 minutes. Have a large bowl of ice water at the ready. Drain the shrimp into a colander and then transfer to the ice water. Drain again and refrigerate until ready to serve.

2. To make the Far Eastern Dipping Sauce, combine the brown sugar and water in a small saucepan. Bring to a boil, stirring to dissolve the sugar, and cook over medium heat until lightly thickened, about 2 minutes. Remove from the heat and stir in the soy sauce, vinegar, ginger, sesame oil, and pepper. Cool to room temperature and refrigerate for up to 3 days. Sprinkle with the chives before serving.

3. To make the All-American Cocktail Sauce, whisk together the chili sauce, ketchup, and horseradish. Stir in the onion and lemon juice. Serve immediately or refrigerate for up to 3 days.

4. To serve, present the shrimp on a platter garnished with the lemon slices, and surround with small bowls of the sauces. Invite guests to peel their own shrimp and dunk.

Note: *If you prefer, serve the shrimp shelled, with toothpicks for dipping. If you don't have chili sauce, use a total of ½ cup ketchup. Fresh horseradish is often available in supermarkets these days. If you can find it, it makes for a fresher-tasting sauce, but bottled horseradish is fine, too.*

Sun-Dried Tomato and Fromage Blanc Toasts

A compound butter of garlic scapes, scallions, or other fresh herbs flavors the toasts that are the base of this simple and savory goat cheese canapé. Use any fresh, tangy, spreadable goat cheese or *fromage blanc*. For a summertime party, you might also add some edible blossoms or petals (see Edible Blooms, page 69) as a garnish.

⅓ cup coarsely chopped garlic scapes (see Note), scallions, or fresh herbs, alone or in combination

½ cup (1 stick) butter, softened

1 pound baguette, 1½–2 inches in diameter

6 ounces soft fresh goat cheese or fromage blanc

⅓ cup julienned sun-dried tomatoes

MAKES ABOUT 48 TOASTS (ABOUT 8 SERVINGS)

1. Pulse the garlic scapes in a food processor until chopped. (You should have about 3 tablespoons.) In a small bowl, combine the scapes with the butter. Set aside for at least 1 hour to blend the flavors. (You may refrigerate for up to 5 days, or freeze.)

2. Preheat the broiler. Cut bread into ½-inch slices and spread with the flavored butter. Arrange the buttered slices in a single layer on a baking sheet and broil, about 5 inches from the element, until lightly browned. Cool, store at room temperature for a day, or freeze.

3. Spread the toasts with the cheese. Crisscross two or three sun-dried tomato strips on top, arrange the toasts on a platter, and serve.

   Note: *Garlic scapes are the pruned shoots of the garlic plant and are available at Maine farmers' markets in June and July (they're a bit earlier in other markets). Mildly garlicky in flavor, they look something like scallions and can be used in much the same way.*

Microbreweries and Brew Pubs

Microbrewing is a growth industry Down East, with more than two dozen craft breweries (and affiliated pubs) now operating in the state, including such well-known names as Sea Dog Brewing in Bangor, Atlantic Brewing in Bar Harbor, and Shipyard in Portland, as well as smaller breweries in such towns as Farmington, The Forks, and Skowhegan. The brewers' trade association, the Maine Brewer's Guild, has proclaimed November Drink Maine Beer Month, encouraging people to drink exclusively Maine beer for the entire month.

The Maine Cheese Scene

We must give those cute goats full credit. Of the dozen or more cheese makers in the state, the majority produce goat's-milk cheeses, and many of them say that they started raising goats because they liked them or because they wanted the milk (and because Maine produces superior hay) . . . and then they had a superabundance of milk . . . and then . . . what to do with it? Why, make cheese, of course! That was mostly in the early days, which in Maine cheese-making time was only about 25 years ago.

More recently, however, cheese making has become a deliberately chosen calling. There are commercial cheese-making operations in such Maine communities as Turner, Auburn, Brooksville, Lamoine, New Sharon, Waldoboro, Washington, Hope, Rockport, Phippsburg, and Appleton, and the cheese makers from these far-flung towns have joined together to form the State of Maine Cheese Guild. They sell their products in farmers' markets, local specialty food stores, and even in Maine-based supermarkets. Their success has much to do with Mainers' commitment to support Maine-made products and local businesses, but owes even more to the fact that these mostly hand-crafted cheeses — from young, fresh, tangy spreadable chèvres; to runny, bloomy rind, brie-types; to aged, concentrated, crumbly Cheddar-styles; and rustic blues — taste absolutely wonderful.

It's not surprising that the *New York Times* recently declared, "New England has become the most important center of American cheese craft east of California."

Pastry-Wrapped Brie with Sage and Blueberry Vinegar

Elegant and impressive, this pastry-wrapped cheese hors d'oeuvre is actually a breeze to put together with purchased frozen puff pastry. You can make it using any 6-inch cheese with a rind, such as the lovely Maine-made Eleanor Buttercup (love that name!), a cow's milk cheese from Hahn's End in Phippsburg.

1 Brie cheese (15 to 16 ounces, about 6 inches in diameter), chilled

¼ cup fresh sage leaves, plus sprigs for garnish

1 sheet frozen puff pastry (half a 17.3-ounce package), thawed

1 large egg, beaten with 2 teaspoons water

⅓ cup blueberry vinegar (see Note)

MAKES ABOUT 35 SLICES (ABOUT 8 SERVINGS)

1. Using a large knife, cut the rind off the top of the cheese and discard. Arrange the sage leaves over the rindless top.

2. On a lightly floured board, roll the pastry out to a 12-inch square. Place the cheese in the center of pastry, rindless side up. Fold two opposite corners of the pastry diagonally over the cheese. Brush the remaining two sides of the pastry all over with the beaten egg mixture, reserving some for the next step, and fold over the cheese, pressing the seams to seal and forming a rough rosette with the excess pastry on top.

3. Brush the top with the remaining egg mixture, place on a baking sheet seam-side up, and freeze for at least 30 minutes. (This can be made up to 2 days ahead, wrapped, and frozen.)

4. Preheat the oven to 400°F.

5. Bake until the pastry is deep golden brown, about 30 minutes. The seam on the top may split open somewhat, but that's fine. Cool for at least 20 minutes.

6. Pour the vinegar into a small serving ramekin for dipping. Garnish with sage sprigs, cut into small wedges, and serve hot, warm, or at room temperature.

   Note: *If blueberry vinegar is unavailable, use white wine vinegar and add a few small sage leaves and/or blueberries to the ramekin.*

Lamb Sausage Hors d'Oeuvres with Cranberry Chutney

There are a lot of lamb breeders in Maine, and lamb products can be found in farmers' markets all over the state. I especially love ground lamb, either plain or made into seasoned sausage and packed into casings. For this recipe, if you can't get lamb sausage, use any type of fresh sausage, such as Italian sausage. The tart-sweet thyme-flavored cranberry chutney is a sprightly counterpoint to the rich meat.

1	cup cranberries
1/4	seedless orange, cut into chunks
1/2	cup sugar
1/4	cup orange juice (juice of 1 medium orange)
1	tablespoon balsamic vinegar
1	tablespoon chopped fresh thyme, plus sprigs for garnish (optional)
1/2	teaspoon dried hot pepper flakes
1	pound garlic-flavored lamb sausages or other flavorful fresh sausages
1/2	cup red wine
1	tablespoon olive oil

ABOUT 8 SERVINGS

1. Pulse the cranberries and orange chunks in a food processor until coarsely chopped.

2. Combine the cranberry mixture with the sugar and orange juice in a medium-size saucepan. Bring to a boil, stirring, and cook over medium heat until the mixture is thickened, about 10 minutes.

3. Remove from the heat and stir in the vinegar, thyme, and pepper flakes. Transfer to a covered container and refrigerate for at least 1 hour to blend flavors, or for up to 4 days. Bring to room temperature before serving.

4. Prick the sausages with a fork in a couple of places and put them, along with the wine and olive oil, in a large skillet. Cover, bring to a boil, and simmer over medium-low heat, turning once, for 5 minutes. Uncover and cook briskly over high heat until the liquid evaporates. Reduce the heat to medium and cook, turning several times, until the sausages are browned on the outside and cooked within, about 8 minutes. (Alternatively, you can simmer the sausages in the liquid and then finish them on a grill.)

5. Cut the sausages into 1/2-inch slices, impale each slice on a toothpick, and pass with the cranberry chutney. Garnish with thyme sprigs, if desired.

Rosemary-Mustard Pork Canapés

One of the vendors at my farmers' market sometimes has pork — all sorts of cuts, beautifully butchered and sealed in heavy plastic pouches — and I always buy it and stock my freezer. This dish is a wonderful big-party hors d'oeuvre, and one of the best ways to treat pork tenderloins (which can be dry) that I know: first immersing the long, thin, boneless meat in a brining solution, which plumps and further tenderizes it, then roasting it at high heat. The intense flavors of garlic, mustard, and rosemary are the perfect complement to this sweet meat.

1	tablespoon kosher salt
1½	cups water
1	pound thin pork tenderloin
2	tablespoons olive oil
2	tablespoons fresh rosemary leaves, plus sprigs for garnish
2	garlic cloves, peeled
	Salt and freshly ground black pepper
6	tablespoons butter, softened
1	tablespoon grainy mustard
1	skinny baguette (12 ounces)

MAKES ABOUT 40 CANAPÉS (ABOUT 8 SERVINGS)

1. Use a large bowl or nonreactive (see Note) pot to dissolve the salt in the water. Place the pork in this brining solution and refrigerate for at least 6 hours, or overnight (up to 12 hours). Rinse well and pat dry.

2. Preheat the oven to 400°F.

3. Make a rosemary rub by pulsing the oil, rosemary leaves, and garlic in a food processor. Alternatively, finely chop the rosemary and garlic by hand, then blend with the oil. Sprinkle the pork with the salt and pepper to taste, and rub on all sides with the rosemary rub.

4. Place the pork on a shallow roasting pan. Roast until an instant-read thermometer inserted in the thickest part reads 150°F, about 35 minutes. Remove from the oven, let rest at room temperature for at least 30 minutes, then wrap in plastic wrap and refrigerate. (Pork can be roasted up to 2 days before serving.)

5. Stir together the butter and mustard in a small bowl, until well blended. (This mixture can be made up to 3 days ahead and refrigerated. Return to room temperature before using.)

6. Slice the bread ¼- to ½-inch thick. Spread with the mustard-butter. Slice the pork ⅛- to ¼-inch thick, place on the buttered bread, and arrange on a platter. (Can be prepared up to 4 hours ahead, covered, and refrigerated.) Season with more black pepper, coarsely ground, to taste, garnish with the rosemary sprigs, and serve.

Note: *Stainless steel and enameled cast iron are nonreactive; avoid aluminum and uncoated iron.*

Sweet and Salty Nuts 'n' Cranberries

I think that dried sweetened cranberries, which weren't readily available until about 10 years ago, are a brilliant invention. I use them in all kinds of ways, but this peppery sweet combination of roasted almonds and cranberries is particularly delicious and is one of my party mainstays. I always have it at my Christmas bash (where it looks especially festive served in a silver bowl), but it makes an appearance at other times of year as well. The mixture can be made well ahead and stores beautifully.

2	packages (10 ounces each) whole almonds
3	tablespoons butter, melted
2	teaspoons sugar
1	teaspoon mixed pepper seasoning, such as a Cajun blend (see Note)
1	teaspoon coarse salt
8	ounces dried sweetened cranberries

MAKES ABOUT 4 CUPS (ABOUT 16 SERVINGS)

1. Preheat the oven to 350°F.

2. On a large, rimmed baking sheet, toss together the almonds, butter, sugar, and pepper seasoning and spread in an even layer. Roast in the oven, stirring several times, until the nuts are one shade darker, about 25 minutes. Remove from the oven and sprinkle with the salt.

3. When the nuts are cool, toss them in a large bowl with the cranberries.

4. Store in airtight containers for about a week at room temperature, or freeze for up to 3 weeks.

Note: *If you don't have a Cajun pepper blend, use ½ teaspoon black pepper and ¼ teaspoon each cayenne and white pepper.*

— Wrinkles?

"Wrinkles in Vinegar." "We have Wrinkles." They're advertised proudly on the marquees of variety stores and markets up and down the Maine coast. Peer into the plastic containers and you see what look like plain boiled periwinkles or small whelks. When I first checked them out, I assumed it was a misprint. They must mean winkles, I decided, because sure enough, they are periwinkles, pickled in white vinegar. But no, in the Maine vernacular, "wrinkles" it is. And they happen to be downright delicious, especially when sliced thin and served chilled on crackers or lettuce leaves, sprinkled with a few chopped fresh herbs à la Italian conch salad.

Chipotle-Roasted Winter Squash Tacos

Among the daily vegetarian menu offerings — inspired by world cuisines — at Chase's Daily are these winter squash tacos. Probably the best tacos I've ever tasted.

CHIPOTLE-ROASTED WINTER SQUASH

4 SERVINGS

2 tablespoons canned chipotles in adobo sauce

2 tablespoons vegetable oil

1 pound winter squash, such as kabocha (buttercup) or butternut, peeled and cut into $3/8$-inch dice (3–4 cups)

Salt

SPICED BLACK BEANS

2 tablespoons vegetable oil

2 teaspoons minced canned chipotles in adobo (see Note)

1 large garlic clove, finely chopped

1 teaspoon ground cumin

3 cups cooked black beans (1$1/2$ cans [15 $1/2$ ounces each] rinsed and drained)

Salt

1. Preheat the oven to 425°F.

2. To make the Chipotle-Roasted Winter Squash, purée the chipotles with the oil in a food processor.

3. On a large, rimmed baking sheet, toss the squash with the chipotle oil to coat evenly. Spread out in a single layer; try not to have the squash cubes touch each other too much.

4. Roast until nicely browned and crusty, 30 to 40 minutes. Season with the salt to taste. Set aside at room temperature.

5. To make the Spiced Black Beans, heat the oil in a medium-large skillet over medium heat. Add the chipotles, garlic, and cumin and cook, stirring, for 1 minute. Add the beans and cook, stirring frequently, until slightly softened and heated through, about 6 minutes. Season with the salt to taste. Reheat gently before serving.

6. Toss the pepitas with the tamari and toast in a small skillet over medium heat, watching carefully so they don't burn, until the pepitas are one shade darker, about 4 minutes. Remove to a plate.

7. Toss the cabbage with the lime juice and season with the salt and pepper to taste.

TACOS AND ASSEMBLY

½ cup pepitas (pumpkin seeds)

2 teaspoons Japanese tamari

1 cup finely shredded green or red cabbage (about ¼ small head)

1 tablespoon freshly squeezed lime juice

Salt and freshly ground black pepper

8 corn tortillas (6 inches)

1 cup grated white Cheddar

About ¾ cup good-quality salsa (see Note)

4 tablespoons fresh cilantro leaves

4 lime wedges

8. When ready to assemble, warm the tortillas in a microwave, separated by paper towels, for about 30 seconds, or heat briefly in a hot skillet. Layer with the squash, warm beans, a scattering of the cheese, a spoonful of salsa, some shredded cabbage, and a bit more salsa. Top with the toasted pepitas. Garnish with cilantro leaves and a lime wedge.

Note: *Small cans of chipotles (smoked jalapeño chiles) in adobo sauce can be found in the Mexican section of many supermarkets. Chase's Daily uses crumbled dried chipotles in the black beans, but the canned product works fine, too. They also make their own fresh tomato salsa, adding a finely minced habanero (scotch bonnet) chile, and lots of chopped cilantro.*

CHASE'S DAILY

Chase's Daily is a sort of accidental restaurant. The extended family owners of Chase Farm in Freedom took their fabulous produce and baked goods to farmers' markets all over mid-coast Maine for years, until they began to wish for an enterprise that would showcase their efforts through the off-season as well. Why not a little café, they thought? Except . . . the large brick-walled, tin-ceilinged space they fell in love with on Belfast's Main Street five years ago simply cried out to be a more ambitious restaurant, plus it offered room for a bakery, coffee bar, and produce market.

But it all harkens back to the farm, where Megan Chase, one of the prime movers, grows (among other things) more than a dozen varieties of heirloom tomatoes, potatoes, and wonderful, peppery Asian greens, which give rise to the Daily's eclectic vegetarian menu offerings. Chase's draws ideas from Mediterranean, South American, Indian and Southeast Asian cuisines. One special feature is "greens of the day," sautéed with garlic, olive oil, and lemon. Soups and pastas change daily, green curry fried rice is perennially popular, and pizzas are super-thin–crusted and chewy.

Harraseeket Market Pie

Specialty pizzas at the Broad Arrow Tavern in the Harraseeket Inn include such topping combinations as fresh lobster and artichoke, woodsy; roasted wild mushroom and sage; and this one, topped with chicken strips and colorful, bright fresh vegetables.

PIZZA DOUGH

1   cup warm (105°F–115°F) water

1   package active dry yeast

2 ¾–3 cups of bread flour (see Note)

2   teaspoons salt

2   teaspoons sugar

2   tablespoons extra-virgin olive oil

1   tablespoon cornmeal

MARKET TOPPINGS

⅓   cup shredded Parmesan cheese (about 2 ounces)

¼   cup extra-virgin olive oil

3   garlic cloves, chopped

3   cups grated mozzarella cheese (12 ounces)

1½ cups cooked chicken (1 large whole breast or 2 thighs), cut into thin strips

1½ cups thinly sliced yellow summer squash (about ½ pound)

1½ cups thinly sliced zucchini (about ½ pound)

1   cup thinly sliced red onion (1 medium onion)

1   cup roasted red pepper strips or 1 jar (12 ounces), drained

Salt and freshly ground black pepper

1. To make the dough, combine the water and yeast in a small bowl and let stand until it begins to look frothy, about 5 minutes.

2. Combine 2¾ cups of the flour, the salt, and sugar in the work bowl of a food processor and pulse to sift. With the motor running, pour the yeast mixture and the olive oil through the feed tube. Process until a soft balls forms, then process for 45 seconds longer. If the dough does not form a ball, add the remaining flour, one tablespoon at a time. (The dough can also be mixed by hand and kneaded for 10 minutes; or mix in the bowl of a heavy-duty mixer and knead with a dough hook for 5 minutes.)

3. Grease a bowl with oil. Place the dough in the bowl, turn to coat, and set aside in a warm place, covered, until the dough doubles in bulk, 1 to 2 hours. Punch it down, divide into two balls, and let rest for 10 minutes before shaping.

4. Preheat the oven to 425°F. Sprinkle two baking sheets or pizza pans with the cornmeal. Using a rolling pan or your hands, roll or stretch the dough to fit the pans.

5. Combine the Parmesan, olive oil, and garlic and spread evenly over the dough. Sprinkle with 1 cup of the mozzarella. Arrange the chicken, summer squash, zucchini, onion, and red peppers over the cheese, and sprinkle with the remaining 2 cups of cheese. Season with the salt and pepper to taste.

6. Bake, rotating the baking sheets, until the crusts are crisp and speckled with brown and the cheese is melted, about 15 minutes. Cut into wedges or rectangles to serve.

Note: *At Harraseeket, they use Vermont-made King Arthur Organic Baker's Classic unbleached flour.*

BROAD ARROW TAVERN AT HARRASEEKET INN

Freeport's Harraseeket Inn is a large and elegant establishment with a beautiful, old-fashioned, formal dining room fit for a special occasion. Also on the premises is the Broad Arrow Tavern, which is a more casual, family-friendly space, fitted out in clublike fashion with dark green walls, tavern tables, and camp memorabilia (moose heads, decoys, and canoes).

The menu voices the tavern's mission statement: "We strive to procure the freshest locally grown and harvested ingredients for our menu offerings. We believe that supporting Maine's farmers, fishermen, and growers will help preserve open space and keep Maine unique and special." Considering that the Harraseeket is a good-sized commercial establishment, they fulfill their mission admirably.

In the tavern, you can choose lunch from a bounteous buffet that includes salads and chowders and all manner of hot dishes, or you can order a burger, steak, or delectable ribs from the menu. A wood-fired brick pizza oven holds a prominent place in the room, and a team of young chefs deploy the pizza peels pretty much constantly.

Pan-Fried Haddock Sandwich with Jalapeño Mayo

Haddock sandwiches could well be the most popular year-round lunchtime sandwich in Maine. The fresh fish is usually dredged in a breading mix (lightly, preferably), deep-fried, and served on a bun with a lettuce leaf and sliced tomato — tartar sauce, chips, and a dill pickle on the side. What could be better? For the home version, I've called for pan-frying the fish (less messy, less greasy) and spreading the sandwich with a jalapeño-spiked mayonnaise — non-traditional but darn good! So set yourself up with a bottle of one of Maine's microbrew beers and have an all-Maine lunch!

JALAPEÑO MAYO

3/4 cup mayonnaise

2–3 tablespoons finely chopped pickled jalapeño chiles

1 tablespoon minced scallions (1 scallion)

PAN-FRIED HADDOCK SANDWICH

1¼ pounds haddock not more than ½-inch thick

½ cup all-purpose flour

½ teaspoon salt

¼ teaspoon freshly ground black pepper

¼ teaspoon paprika

4 tablespoons vegetable oil

4 sandwich buns, split

Green leaf lettuce leaves

Sliced tomato

4 SERVINGS

1. To make the Jalapeño Mayo, whisk together the mayonnaise, jalapeños, and scallions in a small bowl. Refrigerate for at least 30 minutes to allow flavors to blend.

2. To make the sandwich, cut the fish into pieces a bit larger than the buns. Combine the flour, salt, pepper, and paprika on a plate. Dredge the haddock in the seasoned flour, shaking off the excess.

3. Divide the oil between two medium-large skillets over medium-high heat. When the oil is hot but not smoking, add the fish to the pans and cook, turning once, until golden brown and crisp on both sides and just cooked within (the fish will flake easily when tested with a fork), about 2 minutes per side.

4. Spread the buns with the Jalapeño Mayo, layer on the fish, lettuce, and sliced tomato, and serve.

Deer Isle Crabmeat Salad Roll

Deer Isle, Maine, has a long and proud fishing heritage, so it should be no surprise that fresh-picked local crabmeat is still a common commodity on the island today. You can buy a great crab roll and eat it at one of the several open-air eateries on Deer Isle (or at one of the dozens of casual clam shacks that dot the Down East coastline; see Hidden Treasures, page 54). Or just pick up a container of fresh-picked crabmeat and make your own sandwich at home. After all, most of the painstaking work of hand-picking has already been done by the experts.

3/4 pound fresh lump-style crabmeat, picked over to remove cartilage

1 tablespoon lemon juice (juice of 1/2 medium lemon)

About 1/2 cup mayonnaise

Salt and freshly ground black pepper

4 top-split hot dog buns

3 tablespoons unsalted butter, melted

4 soft lettuce leaves (optional)

4 SERVINGS

1. Toss the crabmeat with the lemon juice in a bowl. Add just enough of the mayonnaise to bind the salad, stirring gently but thoroughly to combine. Season with the salt and pepper (cautiously) to taste. Refrigerate if not using immediately.

2. Heat a cast-iron griddle or large skillet over medium heat. Brush the crustless sides of the hot dog buns with the melted butter and place on the griddle. Toast, turning once, until golden brown on both sides, about 2 minutes per side.

3. Open the rolls, spoon on the salad, add a lettuce leaf, if desired, and serve.

   Note: *If top-split hot dog buns aren't available, use conventional hot dog rolls, grilling the crusty top and bottom, not the interior.*

— Red Dogs

If you haven't grown up eating "red hots," the first time you see red hot dogs you might think they're some kind of scary joke food. In fact, these unusual-looking (but fine-tasting) franks, which are a familiar fixture all over Maine, are just ordinary hot dogs tinted a bright magenta-red hue with harmless vegetable dye. The move to tint the frankfurters was originally a nineteenth-century marketing ploy, done in a bid to differentiate one Portland company's hot dogs from the competition. Mainers developed a fondness for them, and the red dogs soon became the standard in the state.

Fried Clam Rolls

At The Clam Shack, they pile some of the freshest clams, lovingly transformed into about the best fried clams in the state of Maine, into a top-split hot dog bun for a clam roll that is definitely worth waiting in line for.

2	pints shucked medium-sized soft-shell clams
1/2	cup whole milk
1/2	cup cold water
2	teaspoons clam liquor or bottled clam juice
1	cup all-purpose flour
1	cup yellow corn flour (see Note)
2	teaspoons salt
1/2	teaspoon black pepper

Vegetable shortening for frying

4	top-split hot dog buns (see Note)
3	tablespoons melted butter

Quick Homemade Tartar Sauce (page 51) or bottled tartar sauce

Lemon wedges

4 GENEROUS SERVINGS

1. Cut off the necks (siphons) from the clams and rinse the clams gently if they are muddy.

2. Combine the milk, water, and clam liquor in one bowl. Stir or whisk together the all-purpose flour, corn flour, salt, and pepper in another bowl.

3. Using your hands, dip about a third of the clams into the milk wash, letting the excess liquid drain off. Dredge the clams in the breading mix, using your hands to make sure each clam is evenly coated. Transfer to a colander or large strainer and shake gently to remove excess breading.

4. Heat the shortening over medium heat in a deep fryer or heavy, deep pot until it melts and reaches 375°F. (Test by tossing a small bread cube into the oil. It should brown in about 1 minute.)

Yarmouth Clam Festival

The Yarmouth Clam Festival is a weeklong, mid-July celebration of all things clammy. One of the biggest and best of Maine's summer food festivals, this annual event has been happening for more than 40 years. There's a carnival and a midway and rides — and clams. Whole-belly fried clams (battered or breaded), clam strips, clam rolls, clam chowder, clam cakes . . . There's other food, too, but we go for the clams.

5. Slide the breaded clams into the hot shortening and deep fry until golden brown, about 1 to 2 minutes. Drain on paper towels. Repeat with the remaining clams. (The cooked clams can be kept warm in a slow oven at 200°F for 10 to 15 minutes.)

6. Meanwhile, heat a griddle or cast-iron skillet over medium heat. Brush the outsides of the buns with the melted butter and grill, buttered sides down, until golden, about 2 to 3 minutes.

7. Heap the fried clams into the grilled buns and serve with the tartar sauce and lemon wedges.

Note: *Corn flour is finely milled cornmeal. It is available at health food stores or can be mail ordered (see Mail-Order Sources, page 277). Or, if you don't want to go to the trouble of making this breading, use a seafood breading mix, which is usually shelved with Shake 'n Bake and other coating mixes. Typical ingredients in a good mix are corn flour, all-purpose flour, whey, salt, and sometimes baking powder. If top-split buns aren't available, use conventional hot dog rolls, grilling the crusty top and bottom, not the interior.*

THE CLAM SHACK

The little white Clam Shack in Kennebunkport is perched on a bridge right in the middle of town. The place is tiny indeed — about as big as a lobster boat, strictly walk-away, with no inside seating — but no matter. People patiently stand in line to place their orders, and it's worth the wait, for owner Steve Kingston's fried clams — sweet, tender, lightly breaded whole-belly clams — are about the best in the state.

"The key," says Steve, "is to start with the best clams — and I mean nothing but the best. I'm a stickler for quality, and my suppliers know it."

The Clam Shack is also famous for its lobster rolls done two ways (with the classic mayonnaise-bound lobster filling or with plain lobster meat and optional melted butter); a succulent fried fresh haddock sandwich, coleslaw, chowder, steamers, sweet onion rings, and about a dozen other menu items.

"I love it when it's really busy," says Steve. "I get totally energized when everything's humming and we're all working as a team, and we can hear customers' comments and compliments, stick our heads out of the windows and thank them, tease them . . . it's a great feeling."

The Classic Maine Lobster Roll

The lobster roll is one of the true glories of Maine shoreline dining. There are still plenty of places to get a great lobster roll in the state (see Hidden Treasures, page 196), but if you want to make one at home, here is the classic formula. Note the absence of additional seasonings, allowing for the pure, sea-fresh taste of lobster meat to shine through.

4 SERVINGS

2 cups cooked lobster meat, cut into chunks no smaller than ¾ inch (see Note)

2 teaspoons lemon juice (juice of about ¼ lemon)

½ cup mayonnaise, plus more if necessary

Salt and freshly ground black pepper

4 top-split hot dog buns (see Note)

3 tablespoons unsalted butter, melted

Snipped chives or chopped parsley (optional)

1. Toss the lobster with the lemon juice in a bowl. Add the mayonnaise and stir to combine, adding more if necessary to moisten the salad sufficiently. Season with the salt and pepper to taste (be cautious about how much pepper you use). Refrigerate for up to 4 hours if not using the salad right away.

2. Heat a cast-iron griddle or large heavy skillet over medium heat. Brush the crustless sides of the rolls with the melted butter and place on the griddle. Cook, turning once, until both sides are golden brown, about 2 minutes per side.

3. Open the rolls and spoon in the lobster salad, heaping it high. Sprinkle lightly with snipped chives or chopped parsley for color. Serve immediately.

Note: *Buy cooked lobster meat or steam three 1¼-pound lobsters and pick out the meat. If top-split hot dog buns aren't available, use conventional hot dog rolls, grilling the crusty top and bottom, not the interior.*

A Writer's Lunch

One LARGE slice of thick cut bread, Sliced fruit (apples, peaches, avocadoes, if you're not worried about the calories), Walnut pieces or halves, Raisins (optional), Sliced or shredded cheese (NOT tofu-type imitation cheese). Cover the bread with ¼ inch thick slices of fruit. Spot nuts over the fruit. If raisins are added sprinkle a few between the nut pieces. Cover with cheese and broil until the cheese browns . . . now eat it and get back to work!

— Robert Chute, Maine writer, as quoted in *Eating Between the Lines*

—— Why Top-Load? ——

There are two types of hot dog buns in the United States: the conventional hot dog roll, crust on top, split at the side, which is the roll of choice for most of the country; and the New England top-split roll, with the cut right down through the top crust so that both sides of the roll are crustless.

Why do New Englanders prefer the top-split (also called "soft-sided" or "top-loaded") bun? I researched and asked around. Just tradition, is what I kept hearing. My personal theory is that not

only is this a great roll for hot dogs, but it makes a superior receptacle for the lobster, crab, clam, and scallop fillings so beloved by coastal Yankees. The crustless sides get brushed with butter and griddle-toasted, and the filling nestles into the soft center, which absorbs all the wonderful juices and flavors (and tartar sauce).

If top-split rolls aren't available, use conventional hot dog rolls, grilling the crusty top and bottom, not the interior.

So...What Exactly IS a Lobster Roll?

"What's a lobster roll?" Jesse said as they looked at the menus. "A lobster roll?" "Yes. Is it a kind of sushi or what," Abby smiled. "God, you California kids," she said. "A lobster roll is lobster salad on a hot dog roll." [The food arrives.] "The lobster's in a damn hot dog roll," Jesse said. "I told you." "I didn't think you meant an actual hot dog roll."

— Robert B. Parker, *Night Passage*

A Perfect Scallop Roll with Quick Homemade Tartar Sauce

Both types of scallops — small, bay scallops and large, sea scallops — are harvested in Maine during the fall and winter months. Since they freeze very well (especially when the freezer container is topped off with salt water), these sweet, succulent beauties can be enjoyed year-round. This is a simple and classic way to shallow-fry the bay scallops. You can then heap them into a buttery toasted bun or serve them without a roll, just with French fries and coleslaw. Either way, tartar sauce is a requirement.

QUICK HOMEMADE TARTAR SAUCE

3/4 cup mayonnaise

3 tablespoons drained sweet pickle relish

1 tablespoon finely chopped or grated sweet onion, such as Vidalia

Salt and freshly ground black pepper

SCALLOP ROLL

Vegetable oil for deep-frying

1 cup milk

3/4 cup all-purpose flour

1/2 teaspoon salt

1/8 teaspoon freshly ground black pepper

1 1/4 pounds bay scallops

4 top-split hot dog buns (see Note)

3 tablespoons butter, melted

Quick Homemade Tartar Sauce (recipe above)

Lemon wedges

4 SERVINGS

1. To make the Quick Homemade Tarter Sauce, whisk together the mayonnaise, pickle relish, and onion in a small bowl. Season with the salt and pepper to taste. Refrigerate for at least 1 hour to blend the flavors. Makes 1 cup.

2. Heat about 2 inches of oil in a deep, heavy pot or deep fryer to 365°F. (Test by tossing a small bread cube into the oil. It should brown in about 1 minute.)

3. Place the milk in a bowl. In another bowl, whisk together the flour, salt, and pepper.

4. Dip the scallops in the milk, drain thoroughly in a colander or sieve, then dredge in the seasoned flour, shaking off the excess. Slide a few pieces at a time into the hot oil (do not crowd the pan) and cook until golden brown, about 1 minute. Remove with a slotted spoon and drain on paper towels. Repeat with the remaining scallops.

5. Meanwhile, heat a cast-iron griddle or large heavy skillet over medium heat. Brush the crustless sides of the rolls with the melted butter and place on the griddle. Cook, turning once, until both sides are golden brown, about 2 minutes per side.

6. Open the rolls, heap with the scallops, and serve with the Quick Homemade Tartar Sauce and the lemon wedges on the side.

   Note: *If top-split buns aren't available, use conventional hot dog rolls, grilling the crusty top and bottom, not the interior.*

HIDDEN TREASURES: HOT DOG STANDS AND CARTS

It's almost impossible to find a Main Street or local park in Maine that doesn't feature one or more umbrella-topped hot dog vending carts. Here, in order from south to north, are a few top dog stops:

Flo's Steamed Dogs, Route 1, York. Dogs with secret hot sauce, soft drinks, and chips only.

Rapid Ray's, Main Street, Saco. In addition to dogs, Ray's turns out burgers and fries.

Mark's Hot Dogs, Exchange Street and Middle Street, Portland. Franks, sausages, sauerkraut, and condiments.

Brunswick Mall, Maine Street, Brunswick. Several carts up and down the town's grassy median sell hot dogs, wraps, and other good noontime fare.

Bolley's Famous Franks, Water Street, Hallowell. A stand-turned-restaurant with dogs, smoked sausages, and their famous sautéed-all-day onions.

Simone's, Chestnut Street, Lewiston. Lunch counter specializing in steamed "red hots" with all the fixings.

Wasses, Route 1, Thomaston and Rockland, and Reny's Plaza, Belfast. Distinctive wagons selling peanut-oil-fried hog dogs, Wasses are famous statewide.

Scott's Place, Elm Street, Camden. Hot dogs, burgers, veggie burgers, and salads.

The Hot Italian

A hero (or a grinder or sub) in any other state, is, in Maine, an "Italian" (sandwich implied). It's the usual oversize crusty roll or Italian loaf split and mounded with everything from meatballs to sausage to cold cuts, cheese, and vegetables, with a sprinkle of oil and vinegar. Several companies in Maine produce really excellent smoked sausages (see Mail-Order Sources, page 277), and this is my homemade version of what in Maine is called The Hot Italian.

4 SERVINGS

4 smoked garlic sausages, about 4 ounces each

2 tablespoons extra-virgin olive oil

1 large onion, thinly sliced

1 green or yellow bell pepper, thinly sliced

1 red bell pepper, thinly sliced

½ teaspoon dried oregano

2 tablespoons red wine vinegar

4 Portuguese or grinder rolls, sliced horizontally, warmed if you like

1. Prepare a charcoal fire with medium coals or preheat a gas grill for medium heat.

2. Split the sausages in half lengthwise. When the grill is hot, cook the sausages on the grill, turning once or twice, until charred and heated through, about 6 minutes. (Alternatively, you can cook the sausages under the stove broiler or sauté them in a little oil in a large skillet.)

3. Heat the oil in a large skillet over medium to medium-high heat. Add the onions and peppers and cook, stirring occasionally, until they begin to brown and soften, about 6 to 8 minutes. Stir in the oregano, cook for 1 minute, and stir in the vinegar.

4. Layer the sausages and peppers on the rolls, slice in half diagonally, and serve.

— Show Your Moxie! —

Moxie, a dark brown, bittersweet carbonated drink, was first bottled in 1884 in Union, Maine, by a Dr. Augustus Thompson. Originally sold as "Moxie Nerve Food," the drink was a tonic to remedy whatever ailed you, including "paralysis, softening of the brain, and mental imbecility," among other maladies. Moxie evolved into a popular beverage in the early twentieth century, even contributing its name to a slang word meaning vigor, pep, or verve. Sales declined over time, but Maine lawmakers recently introduced a bill to make the odd-tasting soft drink the official state beverage.

HIDDEN TREASURES: MAINE'S QUINTESSENTIAL CLAM SHACKS

Maine's coastline is dotted with summertime outdoor eateries affectionately known as "clam shacks." Clam shacks are usually walk-away venues, with one window for ordering and another for picking up. Sometimes you can sit at communal picnic tables, sometimes you munch your clam roll perched on the hood of your car. Freshly fried seafood, especially fried whole-belly clams, reign supreme, but other options, such as lobster and crabmeat salad rolls and burgers, hot dogs, fries, and coleslaw, are menu standards. Mainers set the bar high for these rustic summer eateries.

These hidden treasures are listed west to east.

Bob's Clam Hut, Route 1, Kittery. Right on the busy Route 1 roadside (hence light on charm), but Bob's delicate touch with fried seafood makes this a favorite stop.

The Clam Shack, Route 9, Kennebunkport. Some of the very best fried clams and lobster rolls (with mayo or with butter) in the state of Maine.

Two Lights Lobster Shack, Two Lights Road, Cape Elizabeth. Just minutes from Portland, this charming spot on a headland between two lighthouses feels remote from any city. The food is all excellent, but you might try the Maine shrimp basket here.

Scales Seafood, The Portland Public Market, Preble Street, Portland. Noted chef Sam Hayward has opened a city clam shack in the market, serving up delicious, impeccably fresh seafood, fried and otherwise.

Harraseeket Lunch and Lobster, Main Street, South Freeport. It's a lobster pound *and* a fried seafood take-out window, with great batter-fried clams, coleslaw, and onion rings.

Red's Eats, Route 1, Wiscasset. Meat from a whole lobster goes into Red's famous lobster rolls. They are not cheap, and the picnic tables are smack on Route 1, but the seafood rolls and other menu items — fried and otherwise — make Red's a must-stop on the mid-coast.

Cod End Cookhouse, Commercial Street, Tenants Harbor. Impeccably fried seafood and other Down East fare served up on a wharf on one of Maine's beautiful harbors.

The Fish Net, Main Street, Blue Hill. Chatting in the line is part of the fun at this local take-out seafood joint in downtown Blue Hill.

Bagaduce Lunch, Route 176, Penobscot. Well off the beaten path, tiny Bagaduce Lunch stands alone on a lovely tidal estuary. Fried clams are a specialty, but be sure not to miss their sweet crabmeat rolls.

Jordan's Snack Bar, Route 1, Ellsworth. The lines are a given at this Route 1 clam shack and dairy bar. If you're getting seafooded out, try one of their burgers with the works.

Slivered Raw Asparagus Salad

Seasonality and fresh ingredients dictate the menu at Francine Bistro in Camden, so in springtime this wonderful slivered raw asparagus salad might be on the menu — but if not, you can re-create it at home.

LEMON VINAIGRETTE

1	teaspoon grated lemon zest
2	tablespoons lemon juice (juice of medium lemon)
2	tablespoons Dijon mustard
1	teaspoon honey
1	teaspoon red wine vinegar
1	small garlic clove, crushed
½	cup extra-virgin olive oil
½	teaspoon sea salt
¼	teaspoon freshly ground black pepper

ASPARAGUS SALAD

3	large eggs (see Note)
4	slices prosciutto
2	spring bunching onions (see Note) or 1 small Vidalia onion, thickly sliced
2	teaspoons olive oil
	Salt and freshly ground black pepper
1½	pounds fresh thick-stemmed asparagus, tough ends trimmed
1	tablespoon flat-leaf parsley leaves
4	ounces Parmesan or pecorino Romano cheese, slivered with a vegetable peeler

4 SERVINGS

1. To make the Lemon Vinaigrette, whisk together the lemon zest and juice, mustard, honey, and vinegar in a small bowl. Add the garlic, whisk in the olive oil, then season with the sea salt and black pepper.

2. Place the eggs in a small saucepan and cover with cold water. Bring to a boil, cover, remove from the heat, and let sit for 8 minutes, and then plunge the eggs into a bowl of cold water and ice cubes. When cold, peel the eggs and quarter them.

3. Preheat the oven to 375°F. Place the prosciutto on a nonstick baking sheet. Place the sliced onion on a separate, rimmed baking sheet, toss with the oil, and season with the salt and pepper to taste. Roast the prosciutto until crisp, about 8 minutes. Roast the onions until wilted and beginning to brown, about 20 minutes.

4. Holding the asparagus spears at an angle, cut into very thin slices using a mandoline, a sharp box grater, a Swiss-style vegetable peeler, or very sharp knife. In a bowl, toss the asparagus with the roasted onions, the parsley, and 2 to 3 tablespoons of the dressing. Transfer the asparagus mixture to a platter or individual plates. Coarsely crumble the crisped prosciutto over the top, scatter with the cheese parings, and surround with the quartered eggs. Adjust the seasonings to taste, and serve.

Note: *At Francine, they use local duck eggs in this salad. If you can find them, use them! (Just add about 4 minutes to the cooking time.) They're rich and delicious. Bunching onions are fresh spring onions with a large bulb and their greens still attached.*

FRANCINE BISTRO

"I think we have a very happy little bistro here," says Brian Hill, chef and owner of Francine Bistro in Camden. He's being modest. Francine is indeed a happy little place — but it's also a great deal more.

The room is sophisticated country French, with chocolate brown walls, glowing candles, and a charming collection of slightly mismatched china and linens gracing the tables. The service is professional but not stuffy. And the food in this two-year-old establishment is superb.

The mission at Francine is simple: Taking the freshest ingredients possible, they create a new menu each day, with four starters, four entrées, and four desserts. Seasonality dictates each day's bill of fare and "local" is the watchword. Hill has about 20 suppliers from the midcoast area — fishermen, cheese makers, farmers, and foragers. So a typical early spring dinner, for instance, might start with Pemaquid oysters gratinéed with spinach and Roquefort, or grilled octopus with fried capers and lovage. Then move to roast chicken with morels and baby beet greens, or seared black sea bass with garlicky fiddleheads and saffron cream, or their signature pan roast of bistro steak with provençal herb frites.

Mixed Greens with Simple Shallot Vinaigrette

A jar of this basic vinaigrette is always there in my refrigerator, ready to dress greens or all manner of other salads, or even to dribble over steamed vegetables or grilled meats and fish. It can be varied in numerous ways. For lighter salads, for instance, use lemon juice instead of vinegars, and light olive oil only, or for an Asian slant, add a touch of toasted sesame oil.

SIMPLE SHALLOT VINAIGRETTE

3 tablespoons minced shallots (2 shallots)

2 tablespoons balsamic vinegar

2 tablespoons white wine vinegar

2 teaspoons whole-grain Dijon mustard

1 teaspoon salt

3/4 cup extra-virgin olive oil or a combination of olive and vegetable oils

GREENS

6 cups mixed mesclun greens (about 12 ounces)

4–6 SERVINGS

1. To make the Simple Shallot Vinaigrette, whisk together the shallots, balsamic vinegar, white wine vinegar, mustard, and salt in a small bowl. Whisk in the oil. Use immediately or store in a covered container in the refrigerator for up to a week. Shake or whisk again before using.

2. Place the greens in a large salad bowl. Drizzle with just enough dressing to coat the leaves, toss gently, and serve.

Wild Things

Wild greens thrive in the long, cool, damp Maine spring. Some of the most common Maine wild greens are dandelions, fiddleheads, dock, chicory, watercress, peppergrass, wild mustard, lamb's quarters, and purslane. As with any plant, younger greens are more tender and less bitter than mature leaves. Before foraging for wild greens, consult a good field guide to help you identify what to pick. The youngest and most tender can be tossed into a salad, but if they are a bit older, the greens need to be cooked as follows: Rinse and trim the leaves or shoots and simmer in a little salted water for just a few minutes until tender. Top with a knob of sweet butter and pass lemon wedges or a cruet of vinegar, and/or chopped hard-cooked eggs for sprinkling on top, or make Dandelion Greens with Bacon and Vinegar (opposite).

Dandelion Greens with Bacon and Vinegar

This is one of the classics: tender young bitter greens, bacon, and vinegar. If you've not tasted it, do try this "wilted" (from the warm dressing) salad. And if you can't get dandelions, the other greens mentioned will do just fine.

4 SERVINGS

2 tablespoons olive oil

¼ pound slab or thick-sliced bacon, cut into ½-inch cubes

¼ cup chopped sweet onion, such as Vidalia or Walla Walla (¼ medium onion)

3 tablespoons white wine vinegar

1 tablespoon sugar

About 7 cups torn dandelion leaves or other bitter greens, such as chicory or frisée, washed and trimmed

Freshly ground black pepper

1. Film the bottom of a large skillet with the oil and place over medium-low heat. Add the bacon and cook until crisp, about 10 minutes.

2. Add the onion and cook until it softens, about 4 minutes.

3. Add the vinegar and sugar and bring to a boil, stirring.

4. Put the greens in a bowl, pour the hot dressing over them, and toss to coat. Season with pepper to taste, and serve.

Dandy-lions

In early May, when you begin to see Mainers — often the older generation — out in their yards or in fields or at roadsides, still swathed in winter coasts, bending over and rooting in the ground with sturdy old Case knives, clutching plastic bags snapping in the chill breeze, you know that spring really might arrive.

It's dandelion-digging time.

Something of an acquired taste, to be sure, dandelions were prized in earlier times for their medicinal qualities as well as for their culinary versatility. Whether you forage for the dandelions or buy from a market, look for the youngest, most tender leaves and toss them into salads or make Dandelion Greens with Bacon and Vinegar.

Oven-Roasted Asparagus

A Dutch farmer has been credited with bringing asparagus to Massachusetts in the 18th century, and, once here, it proved to grow well in most parts of New England. Asparagus beds also seem congenial with the cultural climate of the region. The beds take years of watchful waiting until they begin to produce a good crop, a situation that is not incompatible with the patient, low-key Yankee temperament. During the spring asparagus orgy, when you'd like a change from simple steamed asparagus, try roasting the spears. They emerge from the oven slightly caramelized, and their flavor is intensified.

4 SERVINGS

1½   pounds asparagus, preferably medium-thick

2   tablespoons extra-virgin olive oil

Salt and freshly ground black pepper

Juice from half a lemon

1. Preheat the oven to 475°F.

2. Snap the tough ends off the asparagus and spread out onto a rimmed baking sheet. Drizzle with the olive oil, season with the salt and pepper to taste, and toss or roll to coat with the oil.

3. Roast until tender crisp and the tips are tinged with dark brown, 6 to 10 minutes, depending on size.

4. Squeeze lemon juice over the asparagus and serve.

Fiddledeedee

Fiddlehead ferns are the tightly coiled heads of the ostrich fern. They resemble a violin — hence, their name. Vase-shaped clumps of the ostrich fern can be found growing in damp, shady woods and on floodplains during April and May. When foraging, pick the heads off near the base of the clump (no more than one or two fiddleheads per clump). When you get them home, trim and wash or rub off the papery brown membrane.

The mild flavor of fiddleheads has been likened to that of asparagus, artichokes, or broccoli, but I think they taste just like themselves: of the damp, just-awakening bracken from which they spring. Cook fiddleheads by blanching, steaming, or sautéing for just a few minutes. Season them simply, with butter, salt and pepper, and a spritz of lemon juice or vinegar. Or chill the blanched fiddleheads and serve as a finger food with lemon mayonnaise or other dipping sauce.

Sauté of Fiddleheads, Sugar Snaps, and Baby Carrots

Fiddleheads are one of the most significant culinary harbingers of spring in Maine, and in this recipe they're combined with two other seasonal vegetables to create a gorgeous, colorful mélange. If you can't get fiddleheads, asparagus cut into 2-inch lengths is a fine substitute.

½ pound fiddlehead ferns

½ pound baby carrots (see Note)

½ pound sugar snap peas, stems and strings removed

2 tablespoons butter

½ teaspoon sugar

Salt and freshly ground black pepper

6 SERVINGS

1. If the fiddleheads have papery brown membrane clinging to them, immerse them in a sink full of cold water and rub it off. Trim the ends.

2. Fill a large bowl with ice water. Bring a large pot of salted water to a boil. Add the carrots and cook until they are almost tender, about 5 minutes. Add the fiddleheads and continue to cook until they are almost tender, about 4 minutes longer. Finally, add the snap peas and cook for about a minute, until they turn bright green.

3. Drain the vegetables into a colander, then transfer to the ice water to stop the cooking and set the color. (The recipe can be prepared up to 4 hours ahead to this point. Drain on paper towels, cover, and refrigerate.)

4. Melt the butter in a large skillet. Add the vegetables, sprinkle with the sugar, and cook over medium-high heat, stirring frequently, until heated through, 2 to 3 minutes. Season with the salt and pepper to taste, and serve.

Note: *Peeled baby carrots in bags are just fine, but if you should come across local young carrots, so much the better. If the pretty green stems are still attached, leave them on, but trim them down to about ½-inch.*

Homesick for Fiddleheads

When my friend Sally Rooney's son moved to Australia, one of the Maine foods he missed most was fiddleheads. "So," says Sal, who then lived in Aroostook County, where the ostrich fern is plentiful, "we'd go fiddleheadin' in the spring, pick about a bushel full, eat lots ourselves, and then I'd blanch and freeze the rest so that our homesick son could eat his fill when he came to visit."

Garden Club Salad Composition

I made this beautiful composed salad for a summertime garden club luncheon. It's a very free-form affair and its vegetables can vary according to whim or according to whatever you couldn't resist buying at the farmers' market. To turn it into supper, just add some oil-packed tuna, anchovies, and a scattering of niçoise olives.

About ¾ pound each of 2 or 3 fresh vegetables (see Note)

2 tablespoons olive oil

Salt and freshly ground black pepper

1 pound small red- or white-skinned new potatoes (cut potatoes in half if larger than about 1-inch diameter)

2 tablespoons vermouth or dry white wine

About ⅔ cup Simple Shallot Vinaigrette (page 58)

1 pound ripe tomatoes, sliced

½ cup chopped fresh herbs (such as parsley, chives, basil, tarragon, or dill, or a combination)

Nasturtium blossoms or other edible blossoms (see Edible Blooms, page 69) (optional)

4 MAIN-COURSE SERVINGS

1. Preheat the oven to 450°F.

2. On two rimmed baking sheets, toss the vegetables with the olive oil and sprinkle with the salt and pepper to taste. Roast uncovered, stirring once or twice, until the vegetables are tender and tinged with dark brown on the edges, 15 to 20 minutes. Cool to room temperature. (Or, grill the vegetables on a moderately hot grill, brushing with oil and turning until tender and lightly charred.)

3. In a large pot of boiling salted water, cook the potatoes until tender, 15 to 20 minutes. Drain and cut into ½-inch dice. Transfer to a bowl, sprinkle with the vermouth, and let stand for 10 minutes. Toss with about ¼ cup of the vinaigrette.

4. Select a serving platter large enough to display all the elements of the salad. Spoon the potato mixture into the center of the platter and arrange the roasted vegetables around one side and the sliced tomatoes around the other. (Or make up your own design.) Cover and refrigerate for at least 1 hour or for up to 4 hours.

5. When ready to serve, drizzle with more vinaigrette, sprinkle with the herbs, and garnish with the blossoms, if desired.

Note: *Some good vegetable choices include: asparagus (cut into 2-inch lengths), bell peppers (seeded and cut into ¾-inch-wide strips), broccoli florets, eggplant (sliced ½-inch thick), green or yellow summer squash (cut diagonally ½-inch thick), green or wax beans (trimmed; cut into 3-inch lengths if large), sweet onions (cut into chunks).*

My Best Creamy Coleslaw

After years of tinkering, I have settled on this as the ideal coleslaw formula. I used to think it was virtuous to make the dressing with less sugar, but have come to believe that coleslaw needs sweetness to balance the natural bitterness of the cabbage. And I freely admit to sometimes buying the pre-shredded bags of cabbage and carrots — as long as it looks fresh and green, that is.

6—8 SERVINGS

7 cups shredded green cabbage (about half of a medium-sized head) or a 1-pound package of coleslaw blend

1 carrot, peeled and grated

3 tablespoons minced sweet onion

1/2 cup mayonnaise

1/4 cup sugar

1/4 cup cider or distilled white vinegar

1/2 teaspoon dry mustard

1/2 teaspoon salt

1. Toss together the cabbage, carrot, and onion in a large bowl.

2. Whisk together the mayonnaise, sugar, vinegar, mustard, and salt in a large bowl.

3. Pour the dressing over the cabbage mixture and stir well to combine. Refrigerate for at least 2 hours, or for up to 8 hours.

4. Before serving, pour off any excess liquid that has accumulated around the edges of the coleslaw and stir well.

A Sleuth's Food Musings

Simple food. The best food? A perfectly ripe, juicy tomato, corn picked fresh and rushed into the waiting pot, steamed lobster so succulent it didn't even need melted butter.

— Katherine Hall Page, *The Body in the Lighthouse*

Maine Potato Salad with Egg and Pickles

Almost all summertime potluck suppers or buffets in Maine boast at least one potato salad. Every version is slightly different, and comparing recipes is a perennial pastime. This deliciously eggy, slightly sweet (from the pickle juice) potato salad is my rendition of a good, old-fashioned New England potato salad.

6—8 SERVINGS

2 eggs

2 pounds waxy potatoes (such as red-skinned or Yukon gold) cut into 2-inch chunks

3 tablespoons sweet-pickle juice

Salt and freshly ground black pepper

2/3 cup mayonnaise, plus more if necessary

2 tablespoons Dijon mustard

2 tablespoons milk or cream

3/4 cup finely chopped celery (about 1 large rib)

1/2 cup finely chopped red or sweet white onion (about 1 medium onion)

2 tablespoons chopped gherkins or sweet pickles

2 tablespoons minced fresh parsley or dill, or a combination

1. Place the eggs in a small saucepan and cover with cold water. Bring to a boil, cover, remove from the heat, and let stand for 10 minutes. Drain and, when cool, peel and coarsely chop.

2. Cook the potatoes in a covered pot of boiling salted water over medium heat until just fork-tender, about 15 minutes. Drain well. When cool enough to handle, peel and cut into ½-inch cubes. (You should have about 8 cups.) Toss in a large bowl with the pickle juice and salt and pepper to taste. Set aside to cool for about 15 minutes.

3. Whisk together the mayonnaise, mustard, and milk in a small bowl. Stir in the celery, onion, pickles, and hard-cooked eggs. Pour the dressing over the potatoes, stir gently to combine, and refrigerate, covered, for at least 1 hour, or for up to 24 hours.

4. Before serving, stir again to redistribute the dressing, adding more mayonnaise if it seems dry. Adjust the seasonings to taste. Sprinkle with the fresh herbs, and serve.

Green Bean, Walnut, and Feta Salad

I especially love this salad when I can get tender young beans from the garden or farmers' market, but it's actually wonderful at any time of year. It makes a lovely first course for a dinner party or quite a spectacular offering on a buffet table.

6 SERVINGS

½   cup chopped walnuts

1   pound young green or wax beans, or a combination, trimmed

⅓   cup Simple Shallot Vinaigrette (page 58)

¾   cup crumbled feta

Nasturtium or other edible blossoms (optional)

1. Spread the walnuts in a dry skillet and toast over medium heat, stirring frequently, until one shade darker, about 4 minutes.

2. Blanch the beans in a large pot of boiling salted water until just tender crisp, 3 to 6 minutes. Do not overcook! Remove with a slotted spoon to a large bowl of ice water to stop the cooking and set the color. Lift out of cold water and drain thoroughly on paper towels. Wrap in plastic and refrigerate for up to 6 hours if not using immediately.

3. When ready to serve, toss the beans with about half the dressing and arrange on individual plates or on a large platter. Scatter with the feta and walnuts, drizzle with the remaining dressing, garnish with the blossoms, if desired, and serve.

Belle of Maine

For four generations, the Wells family of Wilton, Maine, has been canning dandelions, fiddleheads, dilly beans, and baked beans and selling them under the Belle of Maine label. While others struggle to chop, spray, or uproot their dandelions, Butch Wells and his crew cultivate a field full and harvest them several times a summer. Fiddleheads cannot be cultivated, but since their season is short and intense, the family has built up a network of fiddlehead pickers who fan out across the state to pluck the furled fern heads from their damp, shady hiding places. "It's a small forgotten part of the canning market, but it's all mine," says Wells.

Down East Cobb Salad

Just because cobb salad was invented in California doesn't mean it can't happily travel Down East for a visit. I make this with as many farm-fresh ingredients as I can get, including locally smoked bacon, organic turkey and eggs from a nearby farm, and fresh mesclun from a local specialty grower (like Eliot Coleman, pictured opposite).

10	slices bacon, preferably double-smoked
6	cups mixed mesclun greens
2	tablespoons olive oil
1	tablespoon sherry vinegar
	Salt and freshly ground black pepper
2	cups diced cooked turkey (about 1 pound)
1	large ripe avocado, peeled and sliced
2	cups diced seeded tomatoes (about 3 large tomatoes)
3	hard-cooked eggs, peeled and chopped
1	cup crumbled blue cheese (4 ounces)
½	cup Simple Shallot Vinaigrette (page 58)
2	teaspoons Dijon mustard
2	tablespoons snipped fresh chives

4 MAIN-COURSE SERVINGS

1. Cook the bacon in a large skillet over medium-low heat until crisp, about 12 minutes. Drain on paper towels and crumble coarsely.

2. Spread the greens out on a large platter to make a bed. Drizzle with the oil and vinegar and season with salt and pepper to taste.

3. Make rows or a spokelike design with the bacon, turkey, avocado, tomatoes, and eggs. Scatter the cheese over the top.

4. Whisk together the vinaigrette and mustard in a small bowl and pour the dressing over the salad in a spiral pattern. Sprinkle with the chives and serve.

A Dilly of a Pickled Beet Salad

Pickled beets are one of those simple old-fashioned mainstays that are always a welcome addition to any meal, summer or winter. Here, they are dressed up with a drizzle of vinaigrette and shower of chopped fresh dill.

1½ pounds beets of uniform size, trimmed

¾ cup cider vinegar

¼ cup water

⅓ cup sugar

½ teaspoon dill seeds

½ teaspoon salt

3 tablespoons Simple Shallot Vinaigrette (page 58)

1 tablespoon chopped fresh dill

4 SERVINGS

1. Cook the beets in a pot of salted water until they are tender when pierced with a sharp knife, 30 to 45 minutes, depending on size. Drain and, when cool enough to handle, peel and slice into a bowl.

2. Bring the vinegar, water, sugar, dill seeds, and salt to a boil in a medium-sized saucepan. Cook, stirring, until the sugar dissolves, about 1 minute. Pour the hot liquid over the beets and stir gently to combine. Cool to room temperature, then cover and refrigerate for at least 1 hour, or for up to 1 week.

3. To serve, spoon the beets out of the pickling liquid and place in a shallow bowl. Drizzle with the vinaigrette and sprinkle with the dill.

Edible Blooms

A pretty blossom adds a kind of magical grace note and sense of surprise to a salad. Some of the edible flowers that have lately reentered the culinary realm include the flowers from most herbs (chives, basil, mint, marjoram, parsley, sage, tarragon), as well as the blossoms of dwarf marigolds, Johnny-jump-ups, borage, clove pinks, and, of course, nasturtiums.

Nasturtiums are easily seeded and grow well all summer in Maine, as well as in most of the rest of the country. They come in a rainbow of hues and their almost addictive flavor is at once pungently peppery and flowery sweet. The small, scalloped leaves of the plant are also deliciously edible.

Market Salad with Berries and Local Chèvre

The flavors, textures, and colors in this lovely combination salad play off each other so well. You've got the crunch of greens and snap peas, the sweetness of berries and maple, the salty smokiness of nuts, and the tang of cheese. It makes a wonderful first course.

4 SERVINGS

4 cups mixed mesclun greens

24 small sugar snap peas, strings removed (see Note)

²/₃ cup fresh blueberries, or ¹/₃ cup dried blueberries

¹/₂ cup dried cranberries

¹/₂ cup crumbled local goat cheese (2 ounces)

¹/₄ cup smoked salted almonds, coarsely chopped

About ¹/₄ cup Simple Shallot Vinaigrette (page 58)

1 teaspoon pure maple syrup

1. Spread out the greens on either a large platter or individual plates, to make a bed. Arrange the snap peas over the greens and scatter with the blueberries, cranberries, cheese, and almonds.

2. Whisk together the vinaigrette and maple syrup in a small bowl. Drizzle over the salad and serve.

Note: *If the sugar snap peas are large, cut them in half on the diagonal.*

A Festival for Cheese

At The Maine Cheese Festival in Rockport every October, a dozen or more of the state's cheese makers get together to showcase their handmade cheeses. They offer tastes of these wonderful artisan cheeses — these days everything from manchego-style sheep's-milk cheese to Cheddar-style cow's-milk cheese to runny brie-like goat's-milk cheese.

Pole- and Shell-Bean Salad with Mint Vinaigrette

Shell beans are the fresh version of dried beans — that is, the mature seeds of the bean plant. In Maine, most fresh shell beans I've encountered in farmers' markets in the summertime are one relative or another of the cranberry bean, which is a cream-colored bean with red streaks housed in a long, knobby, brown- or red-speckled pale yellow pod. Fresh shell beans have a more herbaceous, nutlike flavor and a somewhat more delicate texture than their dried counterparts. As they cook, they lose their mottling and take on a uniform pink-tan color. In this appealing salad, the shell beans are combined with their relatives — pole beans and peas — and dressed with a minty vinaigrette.

1   cup fresh shell beans, such as cranberry beans (about 1 pound beans in their pods; see Note)

1   cup trimmed wax beans, cut into 1½-inch lengths (about ¼ pound)

1   cup trimmed green beans, cut into 1½-inch lengths (about ¼ pound)

½   cup fresh peas (½ pound)

About ⅓ cup Simple Shallot Vinaigrette (page 58)

Salt and freshly ground black pepper

3   tablespoons slivered fresh mint, plus sprigs for garnish

4—6 SERVINGS

1. Cook the shell beans in salted water in a covered saucepan over medium-low heat until just tender, 20 to 45 minutes, depending on their size and age. Remove with a slotted spoon to a bowl of ice water.

2. Add the wax beans to the simmering water and cook for 1 minute. Add the green beans and peas and simmer until crisp-tender, about 3 minutes longer. Drain in a colander and transfer to the bowl of ice water. Drain well and pat dry with paper towels.

3. Shell the peas and toss them in with the beans with about ¼ cup of the dressing in a large bowl. Refrigerate for at least 1 hour, or for up to 3 hours. Toss again, add salt and pepper to taste, and add more dressing, if desired.

4. Sprinkle with the mint, toss again, garnish with mint sprigs, and serve chilled or at room temperature.

Note: *If shell beans are not available, you could use frozen baby lima beans. Cook in boiling salted water for about 5 minutes.*

Special Occasion Lobster Salad

The lobster salad for The Classic Maine Lobster Roll (page 49) must be utterly pristine and simple. This composed version of lobster salad, however, is flavored a bit more assertively and is decorated brightly with snow peas and radishes. Add a basket of warm Maine Johnnycake (page 211) or Grange Supper Baking Powder Biscuits (page 212) for an absolutely splendid lunch or supper.

CREAMY DIJON-TARRAGON DRESSING

2/3 cup mayonnaise

3 tablespoons chopped fresh tarragon, plus sprigs for garnish

1 tablespoon grainy Dijon mustard

1 teaspoon grated lemon zest

1 tablespoon lemon juice (juice of 1/2 medium lemon)

1/4 teaspoon cayenne pepper

SALAD

3 1/2 cups diced cooked lobster meat (about 1 pound)

2/3 cup minced celery (about 1 medium rib)

4 thinly sliced scallions

Salt and freshly ground black pepper

Bibb lettuce leaves

1 cup trimmed and blanched snow peas (2 ounces)

4 radishes, thinly sliced

4 SERVINGS

1. To make the dressing, whisk together the mayonnaise, tarragon, mustard, lemon zest, lemon juice, and cayenne in a small bowl.

2. To make the salad, toss together the lobster, celery, and scallions. Add most of the dressing and stir gently but thoroughly to mix. The salad can be made up to 4 hours ahead and refrigerated, covered.

3. To serve, stir the salad, adding more dressing if necessary, and season with the salt and pepper to taste. Line a large platter with the lettuce leaves, spoon the lobster over the lettuce, and arrange the snow peas and radishes around the edge. Garnish with the tarragon sprigs, and serve.

Lobster Salad with Roasted Corn Salsa

Leave it to Henry D'Alessandris and Marty Perry to come up with this fabulous lobster salad, one of their most popular dishes. It is a new and creative take on Maine's prized crustacean. At the restaurant, little Jalapeño Johnnycakes (page 18) accompany the salad.

4 SERVINGS

ROASTED CORN SALSA

3 tablespoons olive oil

2 cups fresh (4 medium ears) or frozen corn kernels

2 medium-sized plum tomatoes, diced

Half of a large red bell pepper, diced

Half of a small red onion, diced

1 jalapeño chile, seeded and minced

1 large lemon

Salt and freshly ground black pepper

1/4 cup chopped fresh cilantro

LOBSTER AND GREENS

Meat from four 1½-pound cooked lobsters (about 4 cups; claw meat intact, if possible, tail meat split; see Note)

3 tablespoons olive oil

1 cup dry white wine

5 cups mixed mesclun greens

About 2 tablespoons Simple Shallot Vinaigrette (see Note)

2 tablespoons snipped fresh chives

1. To make the Roasted Corn Salsa, heat 1 tablespoon of the olive oil in a large skillet set over high heat. Add the corn and cook, shaking or stirring frequently, until lightly colored, 3 to 4 minutes. Transfer to a bowl.

2. When the corn is cool, add the tomatoes, red pepper, onion, and jalapeño and toss to combine. Grate 2 teaspoons of zest from the lemon, squeeze 2 tablespoons of juice, and add to the corn mixture. Stir in the remaining 2 tablespoons of olive oil and season with the salt and pepper to taste. (The salsa can be made up to 3 hours ahead and held at cool room temperature.) When ready to serve, stir in the cilantro.

3. In a large skillet over medium-high heat, toss the lobster meat with the olive oil and wine until just warm (not hot), 2 to 3 minutes.

4. Divide the greens among four dinner plates and drizzle with the vinaigrette. Heap the salsa in the center of the plates. Remove the lobster from the skillet with tongs and arrange around the salsa. Pour any remaining cooking liquid into four small ramekins and place on the side of the plates for dipping the lobster, if desired. Sprinkle with chives, and serve.

Note: *You can buy cooked lobster from the fish market or steam your own (see page 192) and pick out the meat. At Henry & Marty, they serve the meat in intact pieces, but you can choose to cut it into smaller bite-size chunks. Make the Simple Shallot Vinaigrette (page 58) using 3 tablespoons lemon juice instead of the vinegars. Remaining dressing can be stored in the refrigerator for up to a week.*

HENRY & MARTY

The ambience at Henry & Marty in downtown Brunswick is wonderfully eclectic. It's sophisticated, with a highly professional wait staff, but festive and welcoming. The décor sports rich saffron-yellow glazed walls, white tablecloths, gilt-framed mirrors, and fabulous yet whimsical art, while a swath of maroon fabric drapes the ceiling like a flying carpet.

And Henry D'Alessandris' and Marty Perry's menu reflects this same eclectic sensibility. Locally produced and grown ingredients are featured, and specials reflect the best of each season's offerings. Fresh local vegetables, seafood, and meat from Wolfe's Neck Farm or Caldwell Farms are all presented in inventive ways. Rich mixed seafood chowder, pan-roasted mussels with spicy green curry sauce, salmon with a vivid sauce verte, lobster capellini, and blueberry trifle with layers of gingerbread and homemade lemon curd are a few of the offerings.

Community-Supported Agriculture

CSA, as it's commonly called, is an association of farmers who sell shares in their gardens to local people, who then make weekly trips to the farms to pick up their share of the harvest. The shareholders participate in the bounty of a good year and in the losses of a bad year. In 1990, Maine had fewer than five CSAs, but 15 years later the numbers have grown to upwards of 100 such farms. In addition to all the important philosophical and political reasons for joining a CSA, you can't simply can't get fresher — hence, better-tasting — produce anywhere.

Smoked Salmon Seashell Pasta Salad

This wonderful summer supper salad is a perfect vehicle for "hot smoked" salmon or other smoked seafood. (See Seafood Smokes! page 19). Or you can also use just about any non-smoked canned or leftover fish — tuna, salmon, and so on. The seashell-shaped pasta echoes the ocean theme, but of course any pasta shape will work fine.

LEMON-DILL MAYO

3/4 cup mayonnaise

2 tablespoons lemon juice (juice of medium lemon)

2 tablespoons white wine vinegar

1½ tablespoons chopped dill, plus sprigs for garnish (optional)

1 tablespoon whole-grain Dijon mustard

1 teaspoon grated lemon zest (from ⅓ of medium lemon)

PASTA SALAD

8 ounces small or medium seashell-shaped pasta or other similar pasta shape

1 yellow bell pepper, chopped

1 cup thinly sliced celery (about 1 large rib)

Half of a small red onion, chopped

6 ounces hot smoked (or "roasted") salmon, broken into bite-size chunks, or other smoked fish

Romaine lettuce leaves

Salt and freshly ground black pepper

2 medium-sized ripe tomatoes, cut into wedges

1. To make the Lemon-Dill Mayo, whisk together the mayonnaise, lemon juice, vinegar, dill, mustard, and lemon zest in a small bowl.

2. To make the pasta salad, cook the pasta in a large pot of boiling salted water until al dente, about 10 minutes. Drain into a colander, run under cold water to stop the cooking, and transfer to a large bowl.

3. Add the bell pepper, celery, and red onion, pour most of the dressing over, and stir to combine. Add the salmon and stir gently but thoroughly, taking care not to mash the fish too much. Refrigerate for at least 30 minutes, or for up to 4 hours.

4. To serve, line a platter with the lettuce leaves. Stir the pasta salad again, adding the remaining dressing if it seems dry. Season with the salt and pepper to taste, and spoon over the lettuce. Arrange the tomatoes around the edges, sprinkle them with more salt and pepper to taste, garnish with dill sprigs, if desired, and serve.

Seafood Primavera Salad for a Crowd

This stellar recipe is adapted from a community cookbook put out by the Emerson Hospital Auxiliary in Concord, Massachusetts. It traveled to Maine for a summer vacation by way of my good friend Barbara, and it is now firmly ensconced as a favorite dish to serve to a crowd at a summer party. Don't be daunted by the length of the recipe. It's broken down into easily accomplished steps, all of which can be done a day or so ahead, so all you need to do on the day of the party is assemble and serve. (And even that can be done a couple of hours beforehand.) The result is a singularly beautiful and absolutely delicious dish.

PASTA

1   pound fettuccine, broken into 2-inch lengths (see Note)

1/3   cup olive oil

1/4   cup white wine vinegar

2   tablespoons dry sherry

1/2   teaspoon salt, or to taste

1/4   teaspoon freshly ground black pepper, or to taste

VEGETABLES

16   thin asparagus, trimmed and cut into 1 1/2-inch lengths

3   cups small broccoli florets (about 3/4 pound)

2 1/2 cups fresh (from 2 pounds in the shell) or frozen peas

2   cups halved grape tomatoes (about 1 pound)

6   scallions, thinly sliced

10 SERVINGS (MORE IF PART OF A BUFFET)

1. Cook the pasta in a large pot of boiling salted water until al dente, about 8 minutes. Drain into a colander, rinse with cold water, and drain again. Transfer to a large bowl and toss with the oil, vinegar, sherry, and salt and pepper. (The pasta can be prepared a day ahead. Cover and refrigerate.)

2. Bring a large pot of salted water to a boil. Fill a large bowl with ice water. Blanch the asparagus until crisp tender, about 2 minutes. Remove with a slotted spoon and place in the bowl of cold water to stop the cooking, then drain on paper towels. Add the broccoli to the pot, cook for 2 minutes and cool in the same manner. If using fresh peas, blanch for 2 minutes and cool in the same manner. If using frozen peas, thaw them. Place the vegetables in resealable plastic bags. Toss the tomatoes with the scallions in a small bowl. (The vegetables can be prepared a day ahead and refrigerated.)

3. To make the dressing, combine the vinegar, mustard, salt, pepper, and garlic in a food processor and pulse to chop the garlic. Add the basil and pulse to make a textured paste. With the motor running, slowly pour the oil through the feed tube. Add the sour cream, cream, and parsley and pulse until smooth. (The dressing can be made a day ahead. Cover and refrigerate. Whisk to blend before serving.)

4. Fill a large pot about half-full with water. Bring to a boil and add salt. If using large sea scallops, cut them in half. Add the scallops to the pot, return to a boil, immediately reduce the heat to medium, and cook until barely firm, 1 to 2 minutes. Remove the scallops with a slotted spoon,

CREAMY HERB DRESSING

- 1/3 cup white wine vinegar
- 2 tablespoons grainy mustard
- 1 teaspoon salt
- 1/4 teaspoon freshly ground black pepper
- 2 garlic cloves
- 3/4 cup loosely packed fresh basil leaves
- 1/3 cup olive oil
- 1 cup sour cream
- 1/2 cup heavy or whipping cream
- 1/4 cup fresh flat-leaf parsley

SEAFOOD

- 2 pounds bay or sea scallops (tough muscle removed from side of each sea scallop, if necessary)
- 2 pounds large shrimp, shelled and deveined
- 1/3 cup olive oil
- 3 tablespoons dry sherry
- 3 tablespoons white wine vinegar
- 2 scallions, finely chopped
- 1 large garlic clove, minced
- 1 teaspoon salt
- 1/2 teaspoon freshly ground black pepper
- 4 cups baby spinach leaves for platter (9 ounces)

drain in a colander, and rinse with cold water to stop the cooking. Add the shrimp to the same pot and cook just until pink, about 2 minutes. Drain and rinse with cold water.

5. Cut the shrimp in half crosswise, or, for a slightly fancier presentation, longitudinally. Toss the scallops and shrimp in a large bowl with the oil, sherry, vinegar, scallions, garlic, salt, and pepper. (This can be prepared a day ahead. Cover and refrigerate.)

6. To serve, choose a large round or oval platter. Arrange the spinach leaves around the edge to make a border. Toss the pasta with the vegetables and mound in the center of the platter. Make a well in the center of the pasta and spoon the seafood into the middle.

7. Transfer the dressing to a bowl and pass separately to spoon over the salad.

Note: *You can use other pasta, such as small penne or seashell-shaped pasta, but the fettuccine somehow makes a more elegant presentation. Break it into 2-inch lengths about 1/4 pound at a time.*

Summer Squash Custard

This delicate custard casserole is the perfect way to showcase the prodigal flood of tender summer squash that inundate us every August. You can make it with any of the squashes listed in the recipe, but somehow it always seems to taste best with a mix of yellow and green.

1½ pounds summer squash, such as zucchini (green or yellow), yellow crookneck, or pattypan, alone or in combination, sliced about ¼-inch thick (6–8 cups)

1¼ cups shredded medium-sharp Cheddar (6 ounces)

½ cup crumbled feta cheese (2 ounces)

3 eggs

2 cups whole or low-fat milk

½ teaspoon dry mustard

½ teaspoon salt

¼ teaspoon freshly ground black pepper

Scant ⅛ teaspoon cayenne pepper

1. Preheat the oven to 325°F. Grease a shallow 2- to 2½-quart baking dish with butter.

2. Blanch the squash in a large pot of boiling salted water until it is tender crisp, about 2 minutes. Drain in a colander.

3. Pour the squash into the baking dish. Sprinkle with the Cheddar and feta and toss gently to mix.

4. Whisk together the eggs, milk, mustard, salt, and black pepper in a bowl. (This recipe can be prepared up to 6 hours ahead up to this point; refrigerate the squash and the egg mixture separately.)

5. Pour the egg mixture evenly over the squash and sprinkle with the cayenne. Place the baking dish in a larger pan and pour hot water into the pan, halfway up the sides of the baking dish.

6. Bake, uncovered, until a small knife inserted three-quarters of the way to the center comes out clean, 35 to 45 minutes. Serve hot or warm.

Eat Local

The Eat Local Foods Coalition is comprised of both individuals and organizations committed to promoting and increasing in-state consumption of Maine farm products. In addition to keeping money circulating within the local economy, buying local also helps keep Maine farmers farming and their farms as part of the natural landscape. Plus, fresh, locally grown food is more nutritious — and tastes better!

Terroir Defined

The French word *terroir* is used to describe all the ecological factors that make a particular produce item special to its region of origin. Originally applied only to wine and viticulture, *terroir* has come to be used to describe the combination of soil, climate, plants and their evolution, and the role that humans play to produce crops with a flavor unique to that place. Portland's renowned chef, Sam Hayward (see page 127), credits the wonderful produce of a farmer, Frank Gross, with helping to define his cooking.

"Talk about *terroir*!" says Hayward of Gross' midcoast Maine farm. "Midcoast Maine is the site of a giant glacial land dump, which turned it into rich farmland that can support important agriculture. Even though our growing season is short, smart gardeners have managed to produce wonderful crops — and for more months a year than you might imagine."

TOMATOES
OLIVIA'S GARDEN
NEW GLOUSTER, MAINE
PESTICIDE FREE 2.99/lb.
ROSEMONT market & BAKERY

MAINE GROWN
HYDROPONIC
GREENHOUSE
TOMATOES
No PESTICIDES
ROSEMONT market & BAKERY 2.99/lb.

The Common Ground

The Common Ground Country Fair, held on a 230-acre site in Unity, Maine, has been called Maine's annual party. Sponsored by the Maine Organic Farmers and Gardeners Association (MOFGA), and eschewing the carnival rides and honky-tonk trappings that many country fairs have acquired over the years, the three-day event celebrates rural living. Not only is the Common Ground festive and fun, but the site also serves as a venue for showcasing MOFGA's teachings about the importance of ecologically sound farming and gardening.

The September fair is a kaleidoscope of sights, sounds, and tastes. There are sheep-shearing competitions, fiddling contests, and cider-pressing demonstrations to watch. In the exhibition hall, gorgeous displays of Maine-grown organic vegetables, fruits, flowers, and herbs vie with delicious-looking home-canned and home-baked goods. And the food stalls are astonishing. All ingredients must pass the organic and pesticide-free test, and include such offerings as bean-hole baked beans, pulled-pork sandwiches, fajitas, Italian sausages, clam chowder, home-smoked beef jerky, hot-off-the-grill lamb kebabs, chicken curry, farmstead goat cheeses, and barbecued free-range chicken. Finish your walkabout meal with a "pie cone" of Indian pudding, a fruit smoothie, or a chewy ginger cookie.

Carding Brook Farm Scalloped Tomatoes with Garlic Crumbs

Carding Brook Farm in Brooklin, Maine, brings all kinds of wonderful things to local farmers' markets, including its famous mesclun, herbs, baby potatoes — and most recently, tomatoes. Like many farmers, Jon Ellsworth and Jen Schroth have been doing more and more experimenting with tomato varieties that do well in Maine, and they've come up with some winners, with names like Ida Gold, Aunt Ruby's German Green, and Black Prince. Mostly we simply turn these beauties into fabulous tomato salads, but this delicious "scallop" is a lovely way to serve the tomatoes in a lightly cooked state.

4   cups fresh breadcrumbs (see Note)

2   tablespoons chopped fresh oregano or marjoram

2   tablespoons chopped fresh parsley

1   large garlic clove, minced

½   teaspoon salt

½   teaspoon freshly ground black pepper

4   tablespoons butter, melted

6   large ripe tomatoes, cored and sliced about ½-inch thick

6—8 SERVINGS

1. Preheat the oven to 375°F.

2. Combine the breadcrumbs, oregano, parsley, garlic, salt, and pepper in a bowl. Drizzle with the melted butter and toss to combine.

3. Spread half the breadcrumbs evenly in the bottom of a shallow 2-quart baking dish (such as an 11-by-9-inch dish) and press down firmly to make an even layer. Bake until golden, about 10 minutes. (The crust can be prepared up to 3 hours ahead, covered loosely, and held at cool room temperature.)

4. Arrange a layer of sliced tomatoes over the crust and sprinkle with some of the remaining breadcrumbs. Repeat until all the tomatoes are used, ending with a layer of breadcrumbs.

5. Bake, uncovered, until the tomatoes just begin to soften, the juices begin to run, and the breadcrumbs are golden, about 20 minutes.

Note: *Tear 4 to 5 slices of good-quality bread into pieces and whir in a food processor to make the breadcrumbs.*

Eggplant Baked with Tomatoes and Chèvre

Eggplant, which one generally associates with Mediterranean cuisine, actually grows quite well in Maine — especially some newer types, like the slender Italian (or baby eggplant) and Japanese varieties. Peak season is midsummer to mid-autumn, coinciding with prime tomato season, so combining these two is our natural inclination. If the eggplants are young and very fresh, they don't really need preliminary salting to draw out bitterness, but I like to give them just a sprinkle of salt because it helps keep them from absorbing quite so much oil. This eggplant dish works as a side dish and also makes an excellent vegetarian entrée.

2 pounds young eggplants (either small Italian eggplant or the skinny, straight Japanese variety)

1 teaspoon salt

½ cup lightly packed fresh basil sprigs

½ cup flat-leaf parsley sprigs

2 garlic cloves, peeled and chunked

6 tablespoons extra-virgin olive oil

Freshly ground black pepper

3 cups (2 pounds) diced seeded tomatoes

1 cup goat cheese (4 ounces)

6—8 SIDE-DISH SERVINGS

1. Preheat the oven to 350°F. Lightly grease a large baking dish, such as a 13-by-9-inch dish, or two smaller dishes, with oil.

2. Cut the unpeeled eggplants into ½-inch slices and arrange in the baking dish, overlapping slightly. Sprinkle with the salt and set aside for about 15 minutes.

3. Combine the basil, parsley, and garlic in a food processor and pulse to coarsely chop. With the motor running, pour the oil through the feed tube to make a coarse paste.

4. Blot the eggplant with several paper towels to thoroughly remove the excess salt. Season generously with the pepper. Spoon the parsley mixture over the eggplant. Scatter the tomatoes over all, and cover with foil. (This recipe can be prepared up to 3 hours ahead and held at cool room temperature.)

5. Bake the casserole for 35 to 45 minutes, until the eggplant is tender.

6. Uncover and spoon dollops of cheese over the top.

7. Bake, uncovered, until the eggplant is very soft and the cheese is slightly melted, 5 to 15 minutes longer. Serve warm or at room temperature, directly from the dish.

Steamed Fingerlings with South Paris Mint-Walnut Pesto

More and more Maine farmers' market vendors are recognizing their customers' infatuation with baby vegetables of all types, but particularly potatoes. Fingerlings (skinny, a couple of inches long, and sweet-tasting) and tiny, earthy, round potatoes in various hues (white, pink, crimson, and blue) start showing up all over the state in late summer. And what better topping for simply steamed baby potatoes than pesto? This minted variation is from a fascinating pesto workshop I attended in South Paris, Maine. The teacher demonstrated half a dozen or so variations on the pesto theme, including, in addition to the classic basil and pine nut pesto, an arugula pesto, a parsley and almond pesto, and this delectable mint pesto.

4 SERVINGS

½ cup lightly packed fresh basil sprigs

½ cup lightly packed fresh mint sprigs

½ cup lightly packed fresh flat-leaf parsley sprigs

¼ cup grated Parmesan cheese (1 ounce)

¼ cup walnuts

1 garlic clove, peeled

1 tablespoon lemon juice (juice of ½ medium lemon)

½ teaspoon salt, or to taste

⅓ cup extra-virgin olive oil

1 pound fingerling or other new potatoes, cut into 1½-inch chunks if necessary

1. To make the Mint-Walnut Pesto, combine the basil, mint, parsley, cheese, walnuts, garlic, lemon juice, and salt in a food processor. Pulse 3 or 4 times to make a very rough paste.

2. With the motor running, pour the oil through the feed tube and process just until the sauce is puréed. Do not overprocess, or the pesto will lose some of its bright color and full flavor. (The pesto can be stored, covered, for a day or two in the refrigerator, but it will darken. To help prevent this, pour a skim of oil on the surface. Bring to room temperature before putting it on the hot potatoes.)

3. Scrub the potatoes and boil in a saucepan of well-salted water until tender when pierced with a small knife, 15 to 20 minutes. Drain into a colander, transfer to a bowl, toss with the pesto, and serve.

Classic Scalloped Potatoes

This is an old-fashioned scalloped potato recipe — not terribly rich, lightly flour-thickened, and not fancied up with anything more than a sprinkling of herbs. These potatoes go with absolutely everything, including Cranberry-Glazed Mixed Meat Loaf (page 136), Maple-Mustard Venison Medallions (page 151), or a plain grilled steak or burger.

2   pounds all-purpose potatoes, such as Maine potatoes or Yukon golds

1   small onion, thinly sliced

2   tablespoons all-purpose flour

1   teaspoon salt

½   teaspoon freshly ground black pepper

3   cups whole or low-fat milk

3   tablespoons butter

2   tablespoons chopped fresh herbs, such as parsley, thyme, or sage, or a combination

6 SERVINGS

1. Grease a shallow 2½- to 3-quart baking dish with butter.

2. Peel the potatoes and cut into thin slices. (You should have about 5 cups.)

3. Preheat the oven to 350°F.

4. Combine the potatoes, onion, flour, salt, and pepper in a large bowl, and use your hands to mix thoroughly. Spread the potato mixture out in the prepared dish. (The recipe can be prepared up to 2 hours ahead to this point. Set aside, covered, at room temperature.)

5. Combine the milk and butter in a medium-sized saucepan. Warm over medium heat until the butter melts and steam rises, about 2 minutes. Pour over the potatoes and cover the dish with foil.

6. Bake for 30 minutes. Uncover, sprinkle with the chopped herbs, and continue to bake, uncovered, until the potatoes are tender, about 30 minutes. Serve hot or warm.

Potato Blossom Festival Blooms

The town of Fort Fairfield in Maine's Aroostook County has celebrated the potato harvest with an annual week-long summer festival since 1937. Held in mid-July, when potato plants are in full bloom with their beautiful white, pink, or lavender impatiens-like blossoms, the festival attracts thousands of attendees, even in this rather remote locale. Food concessions emphasize — what else? — potatoes, with the longest line by far stretching from the homemade, freshly fried potato chip booth. Festival events include a parade, the Little Miss Potato Blossom Pageant, the Maine Potato Queen Contest, a Potato Picking Contest, a Potato Recipe Contest, and (no lie) Mashed Potato Wrestling.

Sabbathday Lake Shaker Herbs

The history of Maine's Sabbathday Lake Shakers has been intertwined with herb growing for more than 160 years. After a few decades of relative inaction, the Shakers, a small, well-respected religious group, revived their herb business in the 1960s.

The Shakers grow or forage nearly all their herbs on the 1,700 acres of land they own in Poland Spring, in the southwest part of Maine, and the quality and freshness of their products is far superior to most. Their exhaustive line of herbal teas and culinary herbs is available at the community's store or can be mail-ordered. The store, which is at Sabbathday Lake near New Gloucester, Maine, is open from May through early December, and you can also visit their museum depicting Shaker life. Visit their Web site at www.shaker.lib.me.us.

Maine Potato History

Scottish-Irish settlers brought potatoes to Maine around 1750. A pioneer named Joseph Houlton is credited with planting the first potato crop — a variety called Early Blue or Blue Nose — in Aroostook County in 1807, where the mineral-rich soil and climate combined to create ideal potato-growing conditions. At first, potatoes were just a garden and livestock crop, but as rail lines extended into Aroostook, more were grown and exported, and Maine quickly became the nation's biggest potato grower. Interestingly, much of the crop in the nineteenth century went not for eating but for starch to stiffen men's shirts and ladies' petticoats.

Although Maine now ranks behind several other states in total production, potatoes are still the state's number one agricultural crop, and most of that crop is still grown in Aroostook County. Located in the northernmost part of Maine, Aroostook, often referred to simply as "The County," is larger than all the rest of the counties in the state combined. Much of the production these days goes directly to the French fry plant, but many tons of all-purpose "Superiors" or "Kennebecs" are sold in five-pound bags in supermarkets all over the northeast.

"Big E" Maine Baked Stuffed Potato

At the enormous annual summer exposition in Springfield, Massachusetts, known fondly as the "Big E," each New England state has a large hall where they showcase their best products, culinary and otherwise. In the Maine hall, it's seafood, of course, and blueberries, naturally — but the real attraction is the concession stand run by the Maine Potato Board. At lunchtime, the lines snake out the door and down the street. They're all waiting for the best lunch deal in "town" — the "Big E" Maine Baked Stuffed Potato. Upwards of 5,000 potatoes per day are freshly baked, split, and topped with butter, cheese sauce (they use a commercial variety, and you can, too, but this homemade version is easy to prepare and tastes delicious), sour cream, bacon bits, and chives.

4 SERVINGS

4	large baking potatoes, such as Maine Superiors, or any Russet potato
4	tablespoons butter
2	tablespoons flour
1/4	teaspoon dry mustard
1 1/4	cups whole or low-fat milk
1/2	cup shredded orange Cheddar (2 ounces)
	Salt and freshly ground black pepper
1/2	cup cooked crumbled bacon (4 slices)
1/2	cup or more sour cream
1/4	cup snipped fresh chives

1. Preheat the oven to 400°F.

2. Scrub the potatoes and prick in a couple of places with a fork. Bake the potatoes directly on the oven rack until soft, 45 minutes to 1 hour.

3. Meanwhile, set out 2 tablespoons of the butter and the bacon, sour cream, and chives for topping the potatoes.

4. To make the cheese sauce, melt the remaining 2 tablespoons butter in a medium-sized saucepan. Add the flour and mustard and cook over medium-high heat, whisking, for 1 minute. Add the milk and bring to a boil over high heat, whisking almost constantly. Cook for 1 minute. Remove from the heat and add the cheese, stirring until it melts. Season with the salt and pepper to taste.

5. Split the baked potatoes lengthwise and press the sides to expose more of the potato flesh. Top with the cheese sauce, butter, bacon, sour cream, and chives, and serve.

Mashed Mainers and Variations

People who live in Maine are called Mainers, and Mainers love their potatoes. And, some Mainers call the potatoes grown in the state "Mainers." (Just to confuse the issue.) I think the best mashed potatoes are made with a high-starch "floury" potato such as a russet, but actually, most any all-purpose potato will also produce a fine result.

3   pounds potatoes, such as Maine, Yukon golds, or any russet potato, peeled and cut into 2-inch chunks

3   tablespoons butter

About ¾ cup whole, low-fat, or skim milk or light cream

Salt and freshly ground black pepper

6 SERVINGS

1. Cook the potatoes in a large pot of boiling, well-salted water until very tender, 15 to 20 minutes. Drain, return to the pot, and place over low heat for about 1 minute, until the potatoes are thoroughly dry. Transfer to a large bowl or leave them in the saucepan if mashing by hand or with a hand mixer.

2. Mash the potatoes with a ricer, potato masher, or electric mixer. Add the butter and most of the milk, and mash or beat until smooth, adding more milk as necessary to make a smooth, fluffy purée. Season with the salt and pepper to taste. Serve immediately or hold for up to 45 minutes and reheat in a microwave. Alternatively, keep the potatoes warm by setting the bowl, loosely covered with foil, over a pan of barely simmering water.

VARIATIONS

Mashed Mainers with Mint. Add about 2 tablespoons of shredded fresh mint and a pinch of sugar to the potatoes.

Garlic Mashed Potatoes. Cook 3 peeled and halved garlic cloves with the potatoes (or roast the garlic separately) and mash along with them.

Chive or Scallion Mashed Potatoes. Stir in 3 to 4 tablespoons of snipped fresh chives or minced scallion tops. Garnish with a purple chive blossom, if available.

Super-Rich Mashed Potatoes. The master recipe is on the lean side, allowing for the potato flavor to shine through. For richer potatoes — for Thanksgiving dinner, say — increase the amount of butter by a tablespoon or two and use cream instead of milk.

Trio of Autumn Greens

At Arrows Restaurant, the chefs' garden supplies ingredients that inspire creative cuisine as well as deliciously simple sides like these lightly sautéed and steamed greens. They celebrate the season.

4 SERVINGS

7   tablespoons butter

8   ounces kale, coarsely chopped

1   head (5 ounces) frisée, coarsely torn

1   package (9 ounces) baby spinach

Salt and freshly ground black pepper

1. Melt the butter in a very large skillet.

2. Add the kale and cook over medium heat, tossing frequently, until wilted and beginning to soften, about 5 minutes.

3. Add the frisée and cook, tossing and stirring, until it is wilted, about 2 minutes.

4. Add the spinach and cook, stirring and tossing, until it is wilted, about 2 minutes.

5. Season with the salt and pepper to taste, and serve.

ARROWS RESTAURANT

Arrows Restaurant in Ogunquit, Maine, is a destination unto itself. And even if the restaurant didn't serve world-quality food in lovely dining rooms, their gardens alone would be worth the detour. Chef/owners Clark Frasier and Mark Gaier have created a country restaurant in the finest European tradition, curing their own hams and fish, making all pastas, breads, and desserts in-house, and using Maine ingredients in new and intensely creative ways. But it's the garden's fresh herbs, edible flowers, vegetables, and fruits, employed in virtually every dish, that really inspire the chefs to sublime heights.

A summer tasting menu might start with house-cured prosciutto with local goat cheese and baby greens, sliced heirloom tomatoes, and grilled baguette. It then might move on to Maine lobster in three preparations (cannelloni with a tomato and lobster filling, lobster chunks with fresh mozzarella and parsley oil, and lobster and brioche bread pudding with saffron oil and pea shoots). An autumn specialty is sautéed Bay of Fundy halibut with a creamy corn custard and this trio of greens.

The duo has recently opened a casual, moderately priced restaurant in Ogunquit called MC Perkins Cove. It's sure to join Arrows on the destination list for discriminating food lovers.

Maple-Painted Baked Winter Squash

All kinds of winter squash grow beautifully in the northern climes. They start showing up in farmers' markets and supermarkets in the fall: scalloped dark green butternuts, oblong orange acorns, striped delicatas, and big chunks of meaty Hubbard. They all take well to this kind of simple glaze of butter, maple syrup, and ginger.

4 SERVINGS

2   whole winter squash or 4 serving-size chunks of larger squash, such as Hubbard (2–3 pounds total weight; see Note)

2   tablespoons butter

2   tablespoons pure maple syrup

½   teaspoon ground ginger

Salt and freshly ground black pepper

1. Preheat the oven to 375°F.

2. Cut the whole squashes in half lengthwise and scoop out the seeds. Place the squash, cut-sides up, in a large baking dish. Divide the butter and maple syrup among the cavities and season with the ginger and salt and pepper to taste. Pour about ½ inch of hot water into the bottom of the pan and lay a sheet of foil over the squash.

3. Bake for 30 minutes. Uncover and brush the squash with the melted filling. Return to the oven and bake, uncovered, until the squash is easily pierced with a small knife and the tops are lightly glazed, 15 to 30 minutes, depending on thickness.

Note: *The easiest way to cut squash in half is to begin with a heavy cleaver, then use a hammer to help the cleaver cut through the squash.*

From the Farmers' Point of View

It's a community experience. People come [to the farmer's market] for the fresh food, but they also just like getting together. It's almost like church. And it's entertaining.

— Chris Hurley, Lazy C Farm, Penobscot, Maine

Farmers' Markets in Full Bloom

The U.S. Department of Agriculture reports that the number of farmers' markets increased 79 percent nationwide between 1994 and 2002. In Maine, that number has jumped from a single market in Portland in 1970 to more than 70 across the state. Their success is driven by consumers' demands for produce that is both fresh and has origins easily traced, as well as the ability of small growers to reap significant savings by cutting out the expense of the middleman.

Nutmeg-Scented Parsnip and Carrot Purée

This beautiful pale orange purée of parsnips and carrots is a harmonious marriage of the two vegetables. They're cooked in two separate pots to preserve the integrity of each; otherwise, the stronger parsnip would overwhelm the sweeter carrot in the cooking process. Parsnips have always been esteemed in Maine, but in recent years, they have begun to be shipped around the country, so now this versatile root vegetable is better known everywhere. Parsnips are harvested both in late fall and early spring, but the "spring-dug" crop stays underground all winter, allowing the natural starches to convert to sugar, resulting in sweeter and somewhat more herbaceous vegetables.

1 pound carrots, peeled and cut into 1-inch slices

1 pound parsnips, peeled and cut into 1-inch slices

½ cup half-and-half

4 tablespoons butter, cut into 4 pieces

1 teaspoon sugar

¼ teaspoon ground nutmeg

Salt and freshly ground black pepper

6 SERVINGS

1. Cook the carrots and parsnips in two separate saucepans of salted water until each is very tender, 15 to 20 minutes. Drain in one colander, return to one pot, and place over very low heat until the vegetables are quite dry, about 1 minute.

2. Transfer to a food processor or leave in the pot to mash. Add the half-and-half, butter, sugar, and nutmeg, and process or mash with a potato masher or beat with an electric mixer to make a fairly smooth purée. Season with the salt and pepper to taste. (The purée can be made up to 6 hours ahead and reheated in a microwave.)

— MOFGA's Mission

"The mission of the association [Maine Organic Farmers and Gardeners Association] is to help farmers and gardeners grow organic food, to protect the environment, and to recycle natural resources; to increase local food production, to support rural communities, and to encourage sustainable farm economies; and to illuminate for consumers the connections between healthful food, environmentally sound farming practices, and vital local economies."

Winter Salad of Oranges, Radishes, and Basil

In the dead of Maine (or any) winter, when color and life seem drained from the world, I crave vibrancy in my food — vivacious, spicy flavors and bold, bright colors. I created this gorgeous salad to be just such an antidote to the winter doldrums. For full visual effect, spread it out on a large platter in all its glory.

5 seedless navel oranges

1 bunch (preferably large) radishes

Half of a medium red onion

1 cup basil leaves, cut crosswise about ¼-inch wide, plus sprigs for garnish

3–4 tablespoons extra-virgin olive oil

2 tablespoons balsamic vinegar

Salt and cracked or coarse-ground black pepper

4 SERVINGS

1. Remove the orange peels and most of the white pith with a large knife and cut the oranges crosswise into thin slices. Spread them out onto a large platter.

2. Thinly slice the radishes and arrange them over the oranges. Cut the red onion into thin half-moons and scatter over the radishes. Scatter the basil artfully over the top. (The salad can be prepared several hours ahead to this point and refrigerated.)

3. Drizzle the salad with the oil and vinegar, and season with salt and pepper to taste. Garnish with the basil sprigs and serve.

Miss Rumphius and Her Lupine

All that summer Miss Rumphius, her pockets full of seeds, wandered over [Maine] fields and headlands, sowing lupines. She scattered seeds along the highways and down the country lanes. She flung handfuls of them around the schoolhouse and back of the church. She tossed them into hollows and along stone walls.

— Barbara Cooney, *Miss Rumphius*

Classic Down East Haddock Chowder

The virtue of Maine-style fish chowder is its simplicity. It's a milky, brothy chowder, unembellished with wine or heavy cream, tasting mostly of the good, fresh, locally caught haddock from which it is made. This recipe is classic, with the main concession to modernity being the addition of fresh thyme, which you can omit or reduce if you so prefer. The secret to chowder's depth of flavor lies in the aging process (see Soup and Chowder Ageism, page 113) during which all the chowder's elements have a chance to meld and blend, resulting in a most successful and happy marriage.

3	ounces bacon or salt pork, cut into small pieces (about 3/4 cup)
1	large onion, sliced
1	celery rib, sliced (optional)
2	cups bottled clam juice
1	cup water, plus more, if necessary
3	cups diced russet or all-purpose potatoes, such as Yukon gold (about 1 pound)
1	teaspoon salt, plus more to taste
1/2	teaspoon freshly ground black pepper
2	cups half-and-half
2	tablespoons chopped fresh thyme, or 2 teaspoons dried
2	pounds haddock or other similar mild white fish, such as cod or pollock, cut into 2- to 3-inch chunks
2	tablespoons butter

ABOUT 2 QUARTS (4–6 MAIN COURSE SERVINGS)

1. Cook the bacon in a large soup pot over medium heat until the bacon is crisp and the fat is rendered, 10 to 15 minutes. Remove the bacon bits with a slotted spoon and drain on paper towels (refrigerate until ready to serve). You should have 1 to 2 tablespoons of fat.

2. Add the onion and celery, if desired, to the drippings and cook over medium heat until the vegetables begin to soften, about 5 minutes. Add the clam juice, water, potatoes, salt, and pepper, and bring to a boil. Reduce the heat to medium-low, and cook, covered, until the potatoes are tender, about 15 minutes.

3. Add the half-and-half and thyme. Add the fish, bring to a simmer over medium heat, and cook until the fish is opaque, about 5 minutes. Cool, uncovered, and refrigerate for at least 4 hours, or overnight.

4. When ready to serve, add the butter and reheat gently (do not boil), adjusting the seasonings and adding more water if necessary, and ladle into bowls. Pass a bowl of the reserved bacon bits for sprinkling on top, if desired.

Creamy Smoked Fish and Corn Chowder

My writing partner, Melanie Barnard, and I developed this chowder recipe when we were doing a regular monthly column for *Bon Appétit* magazine called "30-Minute Main Courses." Every dish had to come in at under half an hour, plus ingredients lists needed to be short. This chowder is based on one of those recipes, and it's a real keeper. The salty-smoky fish not only replaces the traditional bacon or salt pork, but also provides plenty of great fish flavor. As one happy magazine reader reported, "This recipe had a lot of bang for the buck, time-wise and flavor-wise." Just add a dark leafy green salad and a basket of country bread, and you've got a truly terrific meal.

2 tablespoons butter

1 medium-large onion, chopped

1 cup bottled clam juice

1 cup water

1 pound red-skinned potatoes, diced

4 cups half-and-half

1½ cups fresh (2 large ears) or thawed frozen corn kernels

8 ounces smoked peppered mackerel, smoked trout, or other smoked fish, skin and bones removed, broken into rough ¾-inch chunks

2 tablespoons chopped fresh tarragon

Coarse-ground black pepper (if not using peppered fish)

ABOUT 2 QUARTS (4 MAIN-COURSE SERVINGS)

1. Melt the butter in a medium to large soup pot. Add the onions and cook over medium heat, stirring occasionally, until softened, about 6 minutes.

2. Add the clam juice, water, and potatoes. Bring to a boil, reduce the heat to medium-low, and cook, covered, until the potatoes are almost tender, about 10 minutes.

3. Add the half-and-half and corn and continue to simmer gently over medium to medium-low heat until the corn and potatoes are both tender, about 10 minutes. (Do not boil vigorously or the chowder could curdle.)

4. Stir in the fish, tarragon, and pepper, if desired. Let stand for at least an hour before serving to allow flavors to blend, or refrigerate for up to a day. Reheat gently, being careful not to boil.

One Morning in Maine

**He dug in the mud with his clam rake, and then
they looked carefully and felt around in the muddy
hole for clams . . . "When we get home we're going
to have CLAM CHOWDER FOR LUNCH!"**
Robert McCloskey, *One Morning in Maine*

Portland Quahog Chowder

Mainers traditionally preferred chowders made with soft-shell steamer clams. In fact, if they built a chowder made with hard-shell clams, they would specifically call it quahog (say *ko-hog*) chowder as a differentiation. However, the further south you got — especially from Portland on down to the state line — the more likely you'd be to encounter the Boston-style brew: lightly flour-thickened and made with chopped hard-shell clams. These days, steamers are in somewhat short supply and hard-shells are still widely available (and in particularly convenient form, given that you can now buy containers of pasteurized chopped quahogs in their liquor in most fish markets), and this chowder is now popular all around the state.

ABOUT 3 QUARTS (6–8 MAIN-COURSE SERVINGS)

4 ounces salt pork, chopped (about 1 cup)

1 large onion, chopped

¼ cup all-purpose flour

4 cups clam liquor, clam broth, bottled clam juice, or a combination (see Note)

3 cups whole or low-fat milk

4–5 cups diced all-purpose potatoes, such as Maine Superiors or Yukon golds (about 1½ pounds)

2 tablespoons chopped fresh thyme, or 2 teaspoons dried

3 cups coarsely chopped hard-shell clams (see Note)

2 cups half-and-half

Salt and freshly ground black pepper

2 tablespoons butter

1. Cook the salt pork in a large soup pot over medium heat until the fat is rendered and the pork bits are crispy, about 10 minutes. Remove the pork bits with a slotted spoon and drain on paper towels (refrigerate until ready to serve), leaving the drippings in the pan.

2. Add the onion and cook, stirring frequently, until it begins to soften, about 5 minutes. Sprinkle on the flour and cook, stirring, for 2 minutes.

3. Add the clam liquor and milk, whisking until smooth. Add the potatoes and dried thyme, if using. (If using fresh thyme, add at step 4.) Simmer, uncovered, over medium to medium-low heat for 10 minutes.

4. Add the clams and fresh thyme, if using, and stir in the half-and-half. Continue to simmer until the potatoes are very tender, 5 to 10 minutes longer. Season with the salt and pepper to taste. Remove from the heat and let the chowder sit at cool room temperature for at least an hour or refrigerate for up to 2 days.

5. Before serving, add the butter and reheat gently. Ladle into bowls and pass the reserved pork bits, if desired.

   Note: *You can buy chopped fresh clams in their juice from a fish market or seafood section of the supermarket, and use the juice ("liquor") for part of the chowder liquid. Or use 5 quarts scrubbed hard-shell clams (see About Clams, page 187) and steam them in a small amount of water just until they open, about 5 minutes. Then scrape out the clam meat and chop or cut it with scissors into cranberry-size pieces. Pour the cooking liquid into a glass measuring cup, let any sediment settle, and pour off the clean broth.*

Milky Maine Steamer Chowder

This is the archetypal Maine clam chowder, made with briny steamer clams, with nary a trace of flour thickener. "Flour in chowder," says noted chef Sam Hayward, "is anathema in Maine." Instead, the chowder derives a bit of body from the starch released by the floury potatoes and creaminess from evaporated milk, which, in the old days, was used for its convenience but has now become fairly standard in many traditional recipes. This chowder most definitely benefits from a longer (at least a day) aging time, which allows that incomparable clam flavor to deepen and intensify. The classic accompaniment is Pilot biscuit (see Pilot Biscuit Survival, opposite).

2 ½–3 pounds (about 50) soft-shell clams (see Note)

4 ounces salt pork, chopped (about 1 cup)

1 large onion, chopped

5 cups clam broth, clam liquor, bottled clam juice, or a combination

4–5 cups diced russet or all-purpose potatoes (about 1 ½ pounds)

3 cups whole milk

1 can (12 ounces) evaporated milk

Salt and freshly ground black pepper

2 tablespoons butter

ABOUT 3 QUARTS (6–8 MAIN-COURSE SERVINGS)

1. Scrub the clams well and steam them in a large pot with about 1 cup water just until they open, about 5 minutes. Remove the clams from their shells over the cooking pot to catch the juices. Pull off the black skin and, if the clams are large, separate the soft bellies from the firm parts; chop the firm parts. (If small, leave whole.) Pour the broth into a bowl, leaving any sediment in the pot. Let the broth stand, allowing any remaining sediment to settle. When ready to use for the chowder, pour into a glass measure, and supplement with bottled clam juice to make the 5 cups.

2. Cook the salt pork in a large soup pot over medium heat until the fat is rendered and the pork bits are crispy, about 10 minutes. Remove with a slotted spoon and drain on paper towels (refrigerate until ready to serve), leaving drippings in the pot.

3. Add the onion to the drippings and cook until it begins to soften, about 5 minutes.

4. Add the 5 cups clam broth, leaving behind any additional sediment, and the diced potatoes, bring to a boil, reduce the heat to medium-low, and simmer, partially covered, until the potatoes are almost tender, about 10 minutes.

5. Add the clams and simmer until the potatoes are very tender, 5 to 10 minutes.

6. Stir in the milk and evaporated milk and heat through. (Do not boil.) Season with the salt and pepper to taste. Remove from the heat and let sit for at least an hour, or refrigerate for up to 2 days.

7. Add the butter and reheat over very low heat, stirring frequently, until the chowder steams and is heated through. This chowder should not boil or it could curdle. Adjust the seasonings to taste, and add more liquid, if necessary.

8. Ladle into bowls and pass the reserved pork bits for sprinkling, if desired.

    Note: *If you can buy shucked raw steamer clams, they are a good option. Drain and use the liquor as part of the cooking liquid.*

— "Salt Pork Was Everywhere" —————————————

In early New England, salt pork was the Yankee cook's basic cooking fat. It also served as seasoning (sometimes the only seasoning, apart from pepper) and it accented chowders, baked beans, gravies, and stews with its incomparable rich, salty flavor. French-Americans, too, used salt pork, as described by Maine author Rhea Cote Robbins in *Eating Between the Lines* (Maine Writers and Publishers Alliance, 1998).

"Salt pork was everywhere. Salt pork in the soup. *Soupe aux pois.* Fresh string beans in the pressure cooker cooked with salt pork thrown in *pour donner d'bon goût.* Salt pork as a staple. No French-Canadian, later called Franco-American, cook would be caught without the salt pork in her kitchen."

Pilot Biscuit Survival

"Losing the Pilot." "Crown Pilotless." "Nabisco May Crack Down on Crown Pilots." "No More Hardtack, Matey?" These were some of the headlines in the late 1990s, when Nabisco decided to cease production of the cracker  that most Yankees consider a necessary accompaniment to chowders. The Crown Pilot, which is a large, rectangular, unsalted biscuit, is a direct descendent of hardtack, or ship's biscuit. Eventually, in a textbook example of Down East determination, a grass roots "cracker crusade" convinced the company to reconsider its decision, and, after a several-month hiatus, headlines cheered the fact that "Crown Pilots are Back by Popular Demand."

THURSTON'S LOBSTER POUND

Thurston's Lobster Pound, in the village of Bernard on the so-called "quietside" of Maine's Mount Desert Island, sits on a wharf overlooking beautiful Bass Harbor, one of the few remaining working fishing harbors on the island. The Thurston family started a lobster wholesaling business on this wharf back in the 1940s, and when Mike and Libby Radcliffe took over the family business a few years ago, they understood that this prize location would be an ideal site for an eat-in-the-rough restaurant featuring some of the freshest lobsters to ever hit the plate.

So, after placing your order at the window, you sit on an awning-shaded deck and watch the fascinating and colorful doings of a working fishing dock. Lobsters, mussels, clams, and corn are cooked in seawater in string bags in a huge propane-fired cooker. Homemade chowders, all aged at least a day, rotate from scallop to haddock to mussel, and the menu is rounded out with seafood rolls, burgers, and dogs. Desserts are three kinds of homemade pie, shortcakes, and Ben and Jerry's ice cream.

Mussel Chowder with Colorful Vegetables

While many Maine chowders look alike, this gorgeous brew has eye appeal to add to its gustatory delight. Thurston's Lobster Pound ages all its chowders, including this mussel specialty, for at least a day. You can get away with 4 hours of aging, but overnight is best.

2	cups water
1	cup bottled clam juice
4	pounds mussels, scrubbed (debearded, if necessary; see Note)
6	tablespoons butter
3	tablespoons olive oil
4	cups peeled diced all-purpose potatoes (about 1¼ pounds)
1	teaspoon salt
½	teaspoon freshly ground black pepper
2	carrots, peeled and finely diced
2	leeks, cleaned and thinly sliced (white and pale green parts only)
1	yellow bell pepper, seeded and finely diced
1	large shallot, chopped
1	tablespoon minced garlic
¾	cup dry white wine
2	cups heavy cream

ABOUT 2 QUARTS (6 MAIN-COURSE SERVINGS)

1. Bring the water and clam juice to a boil in a large pot. Add the mussels, return to a boil, reduce the heat to medium-low, and cook, covered, until the shells open, 4 to 6 minutes, depending on size. Using a slotted spoon, transfer the mussels to a bowl, discarding any that do not open. Set aside 16 mussels in their shells and shuck the rest. Pour the mussel broth into a large glass measure and set aside to allow any sediment to settle.

2. Heat the butter and oil in a large soup pot. Add the potatoes, salt, and pepper, and cook over medium heat, stirring occasionally, for 5 minutes. Add the carrots, leeks, bell pepper, and shallot, and cook, covered, over low heat until all the vegetables are tender, about 10 minutes. Add the garlic and cook, stirring, for 1 minute.

3. Add the wine, raise the heat to high, and cook briskly until reduced by about one-third, about 3 minutes.

4. Add the reserved mussel broth, leaving any sediment behind, and add the cream and the shucked mussels. Simmer, uncovered, for 5 minutes to blend flavors.

5. Add the reserved mussels in their shells. Season with additional salt and pepper to taste. (The chowder is best when allowed to age for at least 4 hours, or overnight.)

6. Reheat gently. Ladle into bowls, making sure that each serving contains at least 2 mussels in their shells, and serve.

    Note: *To debeard mussels, pull out the dark threads that protrude from the shell. Do this just before cooking; mussels die when debearded.*

Best Bar Harbor Lobster Stew

If you've never eaten lobster stew in a classic, straightforward Down East eatery of the type that abound in Bar Harbor on Mount Desert Island . . . well, then, not only do you have a treat in store, but you may be somewhat surprised by the simplicity of this brew.

Traditionally, nothing more than lobster, butter, milk and/or cream, and a dash of paprika, lobster stew is something of a cherished heirloom. A kind of alchemy happens when this stew is allowed to ripen for the requisite several hours, so that each mouthful is fully infused with the essence of lobster. It makes an elegant lunch, or can star as the centerpiece of a summer seafood spectacular, perhaps preceded by Cundys Harbor Crab Cakes on Local Greens Vinaigrette (page 191) and accompanied by Maine Johnnycake (page 211).

3	live 1¼-pound lobsters
6	tablespoons butter
¾	cup dry white wine
2	teaspoons paprika
3	cups whole milk
2	cups heavy cream

Salt (optional)

Sprinkling of snipped fresh chives (heretical, but nice)

4 MAIN-COURSE SERVINGS

1. Place the lobsters in the freezer for 10 minutes to numb them, if desired. Steam the lobsters in a large pot in 1½ inches of salted water just until red, 8 to 10 minutes. Drain and, when cool enough to handle, crack the shells over a bowl, catching and saving as much juice as you can. Pull out the meat, chop into 1-inch chunks, and add to the reserved juices. Scoop the green tomalley (or liver) out of the bodies and reserve. (Although the tomalley looks unappetizing at this point, the color will not affect the finished stew. Reserve two of the lobster bodies.

2. Melt the butter in a large, heavy soup or stew pot. Add the tomalley and simmer for 5 minutes. Add the wine, bring to a boil, and cook over medium-high heat until reduced by about half, about 5 minutes. Add the lobster meat and saved juices, sprinkle on the paprika, and cook, stirring, for 2 minutes.

3. Slowly add the milk and cream, stirring constantly. Add the reserved lobster bodies, pushing them down so they're submerged in the liquid. (They will contribute flavor.) Cool to room temperature and then refrigerate for at least 6 hours, or up to 24 hours.

4. Remove and discard the lobster shells. Reheat the stew over very low heat, stirring often so it does not curdle. Add salt, if desired. Ladle into bowls, sprinkle with the chives, if desired, and serve.

Coffin on Tomalley

It is the green stuff in the central core of the lobster which is the quintessence of the creature and the nearest we mortals can come to the ambrosia of the Greek gods. It is the tomalley. People have been known to shy away from this substance and put it gingerly to one side . . . Multiply all the taste in the lobster by ten, by twenty, and you have this emerald delicacy which tops all flavors of the world.

— Robert P. Tristram Coffin, *Maine Cooking*

COD END COOKHOUSE

After three days of "researching" (in other words, eating) up and down the Maine coast, I landed at Cod End in tiny Tenants Harbor as the last stop before home (and salad for three days).

I was full.

But the aromas wafting out of the cookhouse were so enticing that I mustered an appetite and forged ahead. Cod End, housed in a charming old wooden building on a working fishing wharf, is both a retail seafood market with some of the finest looking fresh fish I've ever seen, and a summer-only, eat-in-the-rough restaurant. You order at a window, pick up your tray, and head for a wooden picnic table overlooking the harbor or, in bad weather, duck indoors.

Anne Miller, who has been the prime mover for more than 30 years now, is a fabulous cook and a great manager, with unwaveringly high standards. All the seafood dishes, of course, are impeccably fresh and taste wonderful — whole steamed lobster dinners, steamed mussels, seafood rolls of all types on butter-grilled buns, fresh fish cakes seasoned with dill, and this Mediterranean-style seafood stew.

Some people make their way to the Cod End Cookhouse just to sample Anne's pies (blueberry and mixed berry are particular favorites) and her scrumptious blueberry cake.

Some Mussel Facts

Mussels can live out of water, refrigerated, for up to 7 days in summer and 12 days in winter. In the proper cool, moist environment, their shells will be slightly agape in order to breathe. Mussels cannot stand in melted ice water; they must be given proper drainage. Store mussels in mesh bags or plastic bags with holes and place ice on top of the bags. If stored in airtight containers, they will suffocate. Scrub off any barnacles or beards, but do not soak mussels before cooking.

Mediterranean Seafood Stew

To be served at Cod End Cookhouse, a seafood dish has to live up to the lofty expectations of longtime owner Anne Miller. Locally caught fish help this dazzling Mediterranean-style stew make the grade.

8 MAIN-COURSE SERVINGS

½ cup olive oil

4 leeks, white and pale green parts only, chopped

2 medium-sized yellow or green bell peppers, seeded and chopped

2 celery ribs, thinly sliced

3 garlic cloves, finely chopped

1 tablespoon fennel seed

1-2 teaspoons dried red pepper flakes (see Note)

2 teaspoons ground turmeric

1½ teaspoons dried thyme

5 cups water

2 cups dry white wine

1 can (28 ounces) diced tomatoes with juice

⅓ cup chopped fresh flat-leaf parsley, plus more for sprinkling

24 clams, scrubbed (see About Clams, page 187)

24 mussels, scrubbed (debearded if necessary; see Note)

2½ pounds lean white fish, cut into large chunks (haddock, cod, pollock, or a combination)

Salt and freshly ground black pepper

1. Heat the oil in a very large soup pot. Add the leeks, bell peppers, celery, and garlic and cook over medium heat until the vegetables soften, about 10 minutes.

2. Add the fennel seed, red pepper flakes, turmeric, and thyme and cook, stirring, for 2 minutes.

3. Add the water, wine, tomatoes, and parsley. Bring to a boil, reduce the heat to medium-low, and simmer, uncovered, for about 15 minutes to blend flavors. (The base can be made up to a day ahead and refrigerated. Reheat before proceeding.)

4. Add the clams and mussels to the stew base and cook gently until the shells begin to open, 5 to 8 minutes. Add the fish and simmer until it is cooked through and the mollusk shells are completely open, about 5 minutes. Season with the salt and pepper to taste. Set aside for at least 2 hours.

5. Reheat if necessary. Ladle into bowls, sprinkle with the parsley, and serve.

Note: *To debeard mussels, pull out the dark threads that protrude from the shell. Do this just before cooking; mussels die when debearded. Use the larger amount of pepper flakes if you like things spicier.*

Split Pea Soup with Smoky Ham

A fogbound or snowy day in Maine seems to demand soup — especially a stick-to-the-ribs potage such as this split pea soup flavored with smoky ham. Save that wonderful Christmas ham bone (preferably with a goodly amount of meat still attached) and freeze it until pea soup-making day, or simply buy a juicy smoked ham hock and supplement with a bit of additional chopped ham. Either Maine Johnnycake (page 211) or buttered rye toast go well with this soup, along with a simple side salad of mixed greens.

1 pound dried split peas, rinsed

1 large meaty ham bone or 1 smoked ham hock, plus 1 cup diced smoked ham (optional) (see Note)

5 cups water

4 cups chicken broth

1 bay leaf

1 large onion, chopped

2 large carrots, peeled and chopped

1 large celery rib, chopped

2 garlic cloves, chopped

3 tablespoons chopped fresh flat-leaf parsley

2 tablespoons chopped fresh thyme, or 2 teaspoons dried

½ cup dry sherry

½ teaspoon freshly ground black pepper

Salt

4–5 MAIN-COURSE SERVINGS

1. Combine the peas, ham bone, water, broth, and bay leaf in a large soup pot. Bring to a boil, reduce the heat to low, and cook, covered, until the peas are almost tender, about 1 hour.

2. Add the onion, carrots, celery, garlic, parsley, and thyme. Cook, uncovered, over medium heat until the split peas and vegetables are tender, about 30 minutes.

3. Remove the ham bone and strip off the meat. Discard the bone and fat. Chop the ham and return it to the soup. (If using the additional chopped ham, add it now.) Discard the bay leaf. You can add the sherry and seasonings and serve the soup now, but I prefer to purée it as follows.

4. Process the soup in batches in a food processor, pulsing to make a textured, not completely smooth, purée.

5. Return to the pot and add the sherry, pepper, and salt to taste. Adjust the liquid as necessary, boiling down to reduce thickness, adding broth or water to thin. Let the soup sit at cool room temperature for at least an hour, refrigerate for up to 3 days, or freeze for up to 1 month.

6. Reheat over medium heat before serving.

Note: *You can get a couple of ½-inch-thick slices of smoked ham from a deli, or use a ham steak.*

Aroostook Potato, Cheese, and Broccoli Soup

When I was up in Aroostook County a few years ago researching a magazine story on Maine potatoes, I cooked for an afternoon with a charming mother-daughter team affiliated with the Maine Potato Board. After cooking all morning, we sat down to an all-potato lunch (except for a large bowl of crisp homemade pickles). We ate potato "lasagna" (sliced potatoes in lieu of the pasta), potato rolls, new potato salad, chocolate cake made with mashed potatoes, and this broccoli and cheese potato soup, which has remained one of my all-time favorites. The main ingredients are "all county," because broccoli is Aroostook's second largest cash crop.

4–6 SERVINGS

1	tablespoon butter
1	medium onion, chopped
1	teaspoon dry mustard
3	cups chicken broth
4	cups peeled diced all-purpose potatoes (about 1¼ pounds)
5	cups broccoli florets, coarsely chopped (about 1 pound)
2	cups half-and-half or light cream
1	cup grated Cheddar cheese (4 ounces)
⅛	teaspoon ground nutmeg
	Salt and freshly ground black pepper

1. Melt the butter in a large, heavy saucepan or soup pot. Add the onions and cook over medium heat until softened, about 5 minutes. Stir in the mustard and cook, stirring, for 1 minute.

2. Add the broth and potatoes, bring to a boil, reduce the heat to medium-low, and cook, covered, until the potatoes are tender, about 15 minutes.

3. Using a slotted spoon, remove about a cup of the potatoes to a plate, mash well with a fork, and return to the pot. (This will thicken the soup.)

4. Add the broccoli and half-and-half and simmer gently (do not boil vigorously) until the broccoli is tender, about 5 minutes. Remove from the heat.

5. Add the cheese and nutmeg and stir until the cheese melts. Season with the salt and pepper to taste, and serve.

For the Love of Potatoes

I cook dinner every night. And no, we don't ever get tired of potatoes. I fix them all kinds of ways, many times a week. But I know I'm probably spoiled, because I get all my potatoes directly from the farmers.

— Carol Adams, from a potato-farming family, Presque Isle, Maine

Curried Roasted Squash Soup

My husband, Richard, grills meat; he smokes fish and game; he makes a mean tuna sandwich for lunch. But he rarely cooks. Except that every now and then he does get a yen to make soup (it is quite frequently soup weather in Maine), and recently he perfected (occasionally consulting me) this really wonderful puréed curried roasted squash soup. Be sure to allow enough time (upwards of 2 hours) for the vegetables to get very soft and to caramelize.

5   pounds winter squash, such as Hubbard, butternut, or kabocha

6   tablespoons butter

¼   cup packed brown sugar

1   large onion, cut into chunks

3   large carrots, peeled and cut into 2-inch lengths

4   large garlic cloves, unpeeled

1   tart apple, such as Granny Smith, peeled, cored, and cut into quarters

Salt and freshly ground black pepper

About 7 cups chicken or vegetable broth

2   tablespoons curry powder

2   cups apple cider or apple juice

1   teaspoon ground ginger

½   teaspoon ground mace

½   cup plain yogurt or sour cream

4 MAIN-COURSE SERVINGS

1. Preheat the oven to 400°F.

2. Cut the squash into large chunks and scoop out the seeds. Place cut sides up in a large roasting pan and divide the butter and brown sugar among the cavities.

3. Arrange the onion, carrots, garlic, and apple around the squash, sprinkle with the salt and pepper to taste, and pour 2 cups of the broth in the bottom of the pan. (You may need to use two roasters.) Cover with foil and roast, stirring once or twice, until the vegetables are all very soft and caramelized, 1½ to 2 hours.

4. Scoop the squash pulp out of the skins. Squeeze the garlic out of its skins. Process the squash and other vegetables in a food processor in batches, adding a bit of the broth through the feed tube, to make a smooth purèe.

5. Toast the curry powder in a small skillet over medium heat, stirring once or twice, until it is one shade darker, about 2 minutes.

6. Combine the squash purée, toasted curry powder, remaining broth, apple cider, ginger, and mace in a large soup pot, whisking together until smooth. Bring to a simmer and cook for a few minutes to blend the flavors. Season with more salt and pepper to taste. (The soup can be stored in the refrigerator for up to 3 days or frozen for up to 1 month.)

7. Reheat before serving. Ladle into bowls and top with a dollop of yogurt.

Soup and Chowder Ageism

Aging. Aging brings out flavor no spices or sudden terrific heat can reach. Pea soup is three times better three days old. A lobster stew, made and set aside for two days tastes like something the mermaids might think up after they have sat out in the white Maine surf for three hours of a sun-drenched day and sung all their shrillest and most silvery songs. If that is lyricism, so is old pea soup.

— Robert P. Tristram Coffin, *Maine Cooking*

State of Maine Beans

Housed in a former woolen mill, the Kennebec Bean Company specializes in Maine-grown beans: yellow-eye, soldier, Jacob's cattle, and red kidney. Since they are grown mostly on nearby farms, these dried beans are generally fresher-tasting and quicker-cooking than beans packaged by larger companies and shipped from far away. The yellow-eyes get their name from the dark spots on their light flesh; soldier beans are a large plump reddish-brown bean with brown markings; Jacob's cattle beans resemble the spotted and speckled cattle raised by the biblical figure Jacob; and red kidneys are large and showy, with glossy dark skins. All lose most of their distinctive markings when cooked — especially when simmered for hours with molasses and brown sugar.

Molasses-Baked Maine Yellow-Eyes

Yellow-eye beans are my favorite Maine baking bean. They have a mellow, earthy flavor that persists through the long simmering, and their texture is smooth and creamy while still holding its shape. Of course, you can use any number of other beans in this recipe, including soldier or Jacob's cattle beans or Great Northern, or even smaller pea beans (although they would mark you as a Boston type). This recipe is my tried-and-true formula, and the beans come out perfect every time. Although both molasses and maple syrup are used as sweeteners, the dark flavor of molasses predominates. Saturday-Night Supper Steamed Brown Bread (page 215) is a traditional accompaniment.

6—8 SERVINGS

1	pound dried yellow-eye or other similar medium-sized beans, such as Great Northern, rinsed and picked over
8	cups water
1½	teaspoons salt
¼	pound salt pork
1	large onion, peeled
⅓	cup molasses
¼	cup pure maple syrup
¼	cup cider vinegar
2	teaspoons dry mustard
1	teaspoon ground ginger

Boiling water, if necessary

1. If you like, soak the beans in water to cover for 4 hours, or overnight (see To Soak or Not to Soak? page 119). Drain.

2. Bring the water to a boil in a large soup pot. Add the soaked or unsoaked beans and 1 teaspoon of the salt and return to a boil. Reduce the heat to low and cook, covered, until the beans are just tender, 1½ to 2 hours. Drain in a colander, discarding the water.

3. Preheat the oven to 325°F. Bring to a boil a medium saucepan of water.

4. Score the salt pork and onion. For the salt pork, make shallow cuts in a diamond pattern up to but not through the rind. Cut the onion with a criss-cross through the root end.

5. Stir together the molasses, maple syrup, vinegar, mustard, ginger, and remaining ½ teaspoon of salt in a 2½- to 3-quart casserole dish or bean pot. Add the beans and enough of the boiling water to cover by about ½-inch. Push the salt pork and onion into the beans. Cover the dish with a lid or foil and bake for 3 hours. Check the water level every 45 minutes or so and, if it has cooked away, top off with more boiling water so that the beans remain soupy.

6. Uncover, stir to bring the salt pork to the top of the beans, and cook 45 minutes to 1 hour longer, or until the sauce thickens and the salt pork browns. Serve directly from the bean pot, divvying up the salt pork among those who are partial to it.

Kyra's Herbed Crabmeat Quiche

Kyra Alex, cookbook author and chef/owner of Lily's Café in Stonington, is famous for her quiches. She makes them with all manner of additions to the basic custard formula — one with tomatoes, basil, and local goat cheese, another with fresh spinach, one using flavorful Deer Isle sausage — but this one, utilizing the wonderful fresh local crabmeat, might be my favorite. Quiche is an ideal showcase for sweet lump crabmeat. The herbed custard mixture doesn't overwhelm the crab's delicacy. You need only half a pound of picked meat, making it somewhat gentler on the pocketbook than other crabmeat recipes. This makes a great luncheon dish, served with a side salad of halved grape tomatoes tossed with Simple Shallot Vinaigrette (page 58).

One 9-inch piecrust, unbaked (see My Flaky Pie Pastry, page 235 or use purchased pie pastry)

6 eggs

1 cup heavy or whipping cream

2 tablespoons snipped fresh chives

2 tablespoons chopped fresh cilantro

2 tablespoons chopped parsley

3/4 teaspoon salt

1/4 teaspoon freshly ground black pepper

1/8 teaspoon cayenne pepper

1/2 pound fresh crabmeat, picked over

1/2 cup grated Monterey Jack cheese (2 ounces)

1/2 cup grated Gruyère or Swiss cheese (2 ounces)

6–8 SERVINGS

1. Fit the crust into a 9-inch glass pie plate or quiche pan. Prick the bottom with a fork and freeze for 30 minutes.

2. Preheat the oven to 375°F.

3. Press a sheet of foil into the bottom of the pie shell. Bake in the preheated oven for 20 minutes. Remove the foil and continue to bake for 5 to 8 minutes, until pale golden. If the pastry starts to puff up, press the bottom gently with a large spatula or oven-mitted hand to flatten. Fill immediately or cool on a rack.

4. Reduce the oven temperature to 325°F.

5. Whisk the eggs in a large bowl. Whisk in the cream, chives, cilantro, parsley, salt, pepper, and cayenne. Stir in the crabmeat and two cheeses. Pour the filling into the prepared pie shell and carefully transfer to the oven.

6. Bake for 30 to 40 minutes, or until the filling is puffed and a knife inserted about two-thirds of the way to the center comes out clean. The center should still be slightly jiggly.

7. Cool on a rack, and serve the quiche warm or at room temperature.

Note: *For a delicious variation, substitute 4 ounces of chopped smoked salmon for the crabmeat, and instead of the three herbs listed, use 3 tablespoons of chopped fresh dill.*

First Lady Farmers' Market Pasta with Maine Chèvre

During her husband John's first term as governor, Maine First Lady Karen Baldacci actively sponsored initiatives near and dear to her heart, including one known as "Focus on the Farm," to encourage and support farmers and food producers in the state. This meatless pasta dish showcases not only the kind of height-of-summer produce to be found in abundance at summer and early fall farmers' markets, but also the tangy fresh goat cheese (chèvre) produced by a growing number of artisan cheese makers in Maine. The recipe is meant to be a rather free-form affair whose basic proportions can be adapted to other vegetables, other pasta shapes, and other cheeses.

4 SERVINGS

1½ pounds of a mixture of any of the following: asparagus, yellow or green summer squash, bell peppers (any color), broccoli, small eggplant, portabella mushrooms

About 3 tablespoons extra-virgin olive oil

Salt and freshly ground black pepper

12 ounces penne or other similarly-shaped pasta

¾ cup heavy cream

4 ounces fresh chèvre

2 cups (1 pint) grape tomatoes, halved; or seeded, chopped beefsteak-type tomatoes (about 1 pound)

Half of a sweet red onion, chopped

¼ cup torn basil leaves (or a mixture of other chopped herbs, such as tarragon, thyme, chervil), plus sprigs for garnish

½ cup grated pecorino Romano cheese (1½ ounces)

1. Slice or chop the vegetables into manageable sizes for grilling. Toss with the olive oil, season with the salt and pepper to taste, and enclose in a grill basket. Grill over moderately high heat until somewhat softened and blackened in spots. (Or spread out onto a rimmed baking sheet and roast at 450°F to a similar degree of doneness.)

2. Cook the pasta in a large pot of boiling salted water until al dente, about 10 minutes. Ladle out and reserve ½ cup of the cooking water. Drain the pasta into a colander.

3. Return the pasta to the still-warm cooking pot and add the cream, chèvre, and reserved cooking water. Toss until the cheese begins to melt. (The residual heat should do the job, but if not, place the pan over very low heat.) Add the tomatoes, onion, basil, and vegetables and toss gently until heated through. Season with additional salt and pepper to taste.

4. Garnish with basil sprigs and pass the pecorino Romano at the table for sprinkling over the pasta.

Pantry Bean Bake with Rum and Brown Sugar

If you don't have the time to do baked beans from scratch, I heartily endorse this version of doctored-up canned pinto beans in a spirited rum-enhanced sauce, which bakes in about an hour. (You can even leave out the rum and the beans are still utterly delicious.)

1	tablespoon olive oil
1	large onion, chopped
3	garlic cloves, minced
1	tablespoon dry mustard
2–3	teaspoons chili powder (see Note)
2	teaspoons ground cumin
1	can (8 ounces) tomato sauce
¼	cup packed brown sugar
¼	cup dark rum or bourbon
4	cans (14 ½ ounces each) pinto beans, drained
2	cups water, plus more if necessary
3	tablespoons cider vinegar
	Salt and freshly ground black pepper

6–8 SERVINGS; MORE AS A SIDE DISH

1. Preheat the oven to 350°F.

2. Heat the oil in a large skillet. Add the onions and cook over medium heat, stirring occasionally, until they begin to soften, about 4 minutes. Add the garlic, mustard, chili powder, and cumin and cook, stirring, for 1 minute. Add the tomato sauce, brown sugar, and rum and bring to a boil, stirring. Transfer to a 3-quart baking dish or ovenproof casserole dish, add the beans, and stir in the water. Cover.

3. Bake for 30 minutes. Uncover, stir, and continue to bake until the sauce is reduced and somewhat syrupy, 45 to 50 minutes. If the beans have absorbed all the liquid, thin with a bit more water. They should remain slightly soupy. Stir in the vinegar and season with the salt and pepper to taste. (The casserole can be baked several hours ahead. Reheat until bubbly.)

Note: *Use the larger amount of chili powder if you like things spicier.*

— Strict Supper Schedule —

9 a.m. Beans go into oven, 10 a.m. Prepare sauce for chop suey [that's American chop suey, a ground meat and macaroni public supper favorite], 11 a.m. Put brown bread in steamer, 12 noon Prepare coleslaw and chill, 3 p.m. Put water on to boil for macaroni, 4 p.m. Put bread, butter and milk for coffee on tables, 4:10 p.m. Put macaroni in boiling water, 4:30 p.m. Cut pies and put on tables, 4:35 p.m. Drain macaroni and add sauce, 4:40 p.m. Put coleslaw on tables, 4:45 p.m. Begin dishing up beans and chop suey, 4:50 p.m. Begin cutting brown bread, 5:00 p.m. Supper begins.

— Schedule for bean supper volunteer cooks, Greenwood Grange, Eastbrook, Maine

To Soak or Not to Soak?

You do not necessarily need to soak beans in water overnight before you cook them. After much research and testing for my book *Full of Beans* (HarperPerennial, 1996), I found that presoaking (or quick-soaking for an hour or so) shortens the cooking time by only 30 minutes or so. The other slight advantage to presoaking is that the beans rehydrate somewhat more evenly. So . . . if you have planned ahead, presoak if you like, but otherwise just follow the recipe and cook the beans for the extra half hour or so.

Coastal Seafood Lasagna
with Tomato and Béchamel

When I told a good friend (who also happens to be a very good cook) about writing this book, she said she hoped I'd be sure to include a seafood lasagna like the one in my *New England Cookbook*. So this is for Joy — a slightly modified and updated version of that recipe (including a couple of tweaks suggested by her). It is, indeed, quite a sumptuous dish with its layering of rich cream sauce, delicate herbed seafood, and piquant tomato topping. Serve it for a special, festive occasion, with Lamb Sausage Hors d'Oeuvres with Cranberry Chutney (page 37), a spinach salad, seeded Italian bread, and maybe Orange Crème Brûlée (page 271) to finish.

FRESH TOMATO SAUCE

2	tablespoons butter
2	garlic cloves, minced
2	cups seeded and diced plum tomatoes (7–8 tomatoes) (see Note)
3/4	cup dry white wine
1/4	teaspoon dried red pepper flakes
3	scallions, thinly sliced
2	tablespoons slivered fresh basil
1	tablespoon chopped fresh tarragon
1	teaspoon sugar
1/2	teaspoon salt
1/4	teaspoon freshly ground black pepper

8 SERVINGS

1. To make the fresh tomato sauce, melt the butter in a large skillet over medium heat. Add the garlic and cook, stirring, for 1 minute. Add the tomatoes, wine, and red pepper flakes. Bring to a boil, reduce the heat to medium, and simmer uncovered until the tomatoes give off their liquid and the sauce begins to reduce, about 10 minutes. Stir in the scallions, basil, tarragon, sugar, salt, and pepper and simmer for 2 minutes. If the consistency is too thick — it should be pourable — add up to ½ cup of water. (The sauce can be made a day or two ahead and refrigerated.)

2. To make the seafood filling, melt the butter in a large skillet over medium heat. Add the scallops and shrimp and cook, stirring often, until the shrimp begin to turn pink, about 1 minute. Add the wine, bring to a boil, and cook for 1 minute. Add the fish, tarragon, thyme, salt, and pepper, and continue to cook, stirring gently, just until the seafood is opaque, 3 to 5 minutes. Remove the seafood with a slotted spoon and transfer to a bowl. Reserve the liquid remaining behind in the skillet to use in the béchamel. You should have about ½ cup; add water, if necessary, to make up the difference. (The seafood can be cooked a day ahead. Cover and refrigerate.)

3. To make the béchamel sauce, melt the butter in a medium-sized saucepan over medium heat. Add the flour and cook, whisking constantly, for 2 minutes. Gradually whisk in the cream, bring to a boil, and

SEAFOOD FILLING

2	tablespoons butter
1	pound bay scallops or quartered sea scallops (tough muscle removed from side of each sea scallop, if necessary)
1/2	pound medium shrimp, shelled and deveined
1/2	cup dry white wine
3/4	pound haddock (or other lean white fish, such as cod or pollock) fillets, cut into 1-inch chunks
1	tablespoon chopped fresh tarragon
1	tablespoon chopped fresh thyme
1/2	teaspoon salt
1/2	teaspoon freshly ground black pepper

BÉCHAMEL SAUCE

4	tablespoons butter
1/4	cup all-purpose flour
2 1/2	cups heavy or whipping cream
1/2	cup reserved seafood cooking juices
1	teaspoon salt
1/2	teaspoon freshly ground black pepper
1/8	teaspoon ground nutmeg
1	pound fresh pasta sheets or 9 ounces dried "no-boil" lasagna noodles
1/2	cup grated Parmesan cheese (2 ounces)

cook, whisking, for 2 minutes. Whisk in the reserved seafood juices and season with salt, pepper, and nutmeg. (If not using within about 30 minutes, place a sheet of plastic wrap directly on the surface of the sauce to prevent a skin from forming. The béchamel can be made a day ahead and refrigerated, covered.)

4. Grease a 3- to 4-quart baking dish, such as a 14-by-10-inch lasagna pan, with butter. Preheat the oven to 375°F.

5. Spoon about one-third of the tomato sauce into the prepared dish, spreading to coat the bottom. Make a layer of one-third of the pasta sheets, then half the seafood, then one-third of the béchamel, spreading each layer out evenly. Make a second layer with another third of the tomato sauce and pasta sheets, the remaining seafood, and another third of the béchamel; then finish with the last third of the pasta and béchamel. Spread the remaining tomato sauce over the final béchamel layer and sprinkle with the Parmesan. (The lasagna can be assembled several hours ahead. Cover with foil and refrigerate.).

6. If recently assembled, bake the lasagna, uncovered, until the cheese is golden and the filling is bubbly and tender, 35 to 40 minutes. If the lasagna has been refrigerated, bake the foil-covered casserole for 25 minutes; uncover and continue to bake until heated through, 20 to 30 minutes. Let rest for about 15 minutes before cutting into squares.

Note: *You can also use drained chopped canned tomatoes.*

Paella Cleonice

True to Cleonice restaurant's Mediterranean focus, this fabulous paella, chock full of local in-season seafood and flavorful sausage, is almost always on the menu. It's colorful, festive, and tastes sublime — a fabulous dish for a party.

8—10 SERVINGS

2   cups arborio rice

1/2   teaspoon crushed saffron threads

2   cups water

1/4   cup olive oil

3/4   pound boneless chicken thighs, cut into 1 1/2-inch chunks (about 1 1/2 cups)

8   ounces spicy Spanish chorizo or Portuguese chourico or linguiça, sliced (see Note)

1   large onion, chopped

1   red bell pepper, seeded and chopped

3   garlic cloves, finely chopped

3/4   cup dry white wine

16–20 sea scallops (about 1 1/2 pounds; tough muscle removed from side of each)

12   littleneck clams, scrubbed (see About Clams, page 187)

1. To blanch the rice, heat a large skillet (with lid) over medium-high heat. Add the rice and saffron to the dry skillet and cook, shaking the pan gently and stirring with a wooden spoon, until the rice starts to change to a more opaque white color, about 1 minute. The rice should be hot, but not turning brown. Tilt the pan away from you to avoid splashing, and pour in the water. Bring to a boil, cover, and cook for 1 minute. Remove from the heat and set aside, covered, until ready to use in the paella. (This blanching process helps create the "crust" texture that is considered the best part of the rice. The blanching can be done a day ahead and the rice held at cool room temperature.)

2. Heat the oil in a very large skillet (with lid) or paella pan over medium-high heat. Add the chicken and cook until browned, about 5 minutes. Add the sausage, onion, bell pepper, and garlic and cook, stirring frequently, until the vegetables begin to soften, about 5 minutes. (The paella can be prepared to this point up to 3 hours ahead and held at cool room temperature.)

3. Add the wine to the pan and cook over high heat, stirring up any brown particles in the bottom of the pan. Add the scallops, clams, mussels, the blanched rice, and the clam juice, stirring to distribute the ingredients evenly. Bring to a boil, reduce the heat to medium-low, and cook, covered, for 15 minutes.

24 mussels, scrubbed (debearded, if necessary; see Note)

3   cups bottled clam juice, chicken broth, water, or a combination

1   pound raw shrimp (preferably Maine shrimp), shelled and deveined, or ½ pound crab meat

2   cups fresh (about 2 pounds in shell) or thawed frozen tiny green peas

1   cup coarsely chopped fresh herbs, such as Italian parsley, tarragon, oregano, and rosemary

Salt and freshly ground black pepper

4. Add the shrimp, peas, and herbs and cook until the shrimp turn pink, about 5 minutes. Discard any clams or mussels that didn't open. Season with the salt and pepper to taste. Serve directly from the pan or transfer to a serving platter.

Note: *If you can't find spicy sausage, substitute Polish kielbasa and add 1 teaspoon paprika (preferably smoked Spanish paprika), 1 teaspoon ground cumin, and ½ teaspoon cayenne pepper when you brown the sausage. To debeard mussels, pull out the dark threads that protrude from the shell. Do this just before cooking; mussels die when debearded.*

CLEONICE

"Local ingredients, international flavors" is the motto at Cleonice (pronounced cleo-niece). Chef and owner Rich Hanson and his wife, Cary, opened the bistro in 2002 after finding a wonderful 1930s-vintage space on Ellsworth's Main Street that was fitted out with original art deco fixtures, glorious mahogany paneling and booths, and a 30-foot bar. The bar, reminiscent of the tapas bars all over Spain, inspired the restaurant's Mediterranean focus.

A single item or two from the lengthy, always-changing tapas and meze menu can be your appetizer, or an order of several can turn into dinner. The list might include little meatballs in an almond pepper sauce, spicy garlic chicken wings, salt cod brandade, baba ghanouj, grilled octopus, and Spanish anchovies. Main courses also change seasonally, with different specials every night. So in winter you might see crispy duck breast with a Provençal olive sauce, an Italian dish of local pork braised with wine and pancetta, or roasted day-boat cod puttanesca.

HIDDEN TREASURES: MAINE'S FOOD FESTIVALS

Lots of people build their summer vacations around one of Maine's famous food festivals — and, of course, locals turn out in droves — to participate in the fun and the eating. Here's a partial listing. Most have Web sites to check for dates and details.

July

Seafood Festival, Bar Harbor. An outdoor event held over the Fourth of July weekend, with an Independence Day blueberry pancake breakfast, patriotic parade, lobster-eating contest, fried seafood booths, a strawberry shortcake concession, and fantastic fireworks over the harbor.

Ployes Festival, Fort Kent. Celebration of Franco-American culture with ployes (traditional French-Canadian buckwheat pancake) cooking *and* eating contests, a street bazaar selling crafts, traditional music, and dancing.

Potato Blossom Festival, Fort Fairfield. A high-summer festival to celebrate the potato fields in blossom, this event includes a huge parade, the crowning of Miss Potato Blossom Queen, a mashed potato wrestling contest, and food booths that feature potatoes in many guises — most notably, the largest heap of delicious, skin-on fries you've ever seen. (www.potatoblossom.org)

Moxie Festival, Lisbon Falls. "Moxie and Maine, The Way Life Should Be" is the slogan for this nostalgic festival celebrating Moxie, the old-time soda pop that has been declared the official state drink. Festivities include a recipe contest, trivia contest, and a pancake breakfast. (www.moxiefestival.com)

Clam Festival, Yarmouth. A Maine summertime tradition, with music, a parade, and clam stands showcasing the bivalve in a myriad of preparations. Think clam chowder, crumb-fried whole belly clams and clam strips, clam cakes, steamed clams, batter-fried clams . . . Non-clam goodies include fried calamari, fried oysters, lobster and crabmeat rolls, boiled lobster, blueberries and more. (www.clamfestival.com)

August

Blueberry Festival, Wilton. A low-key, two-day event featuring a blueberry pancake breakfast, a blueberry bazaar, and a blueberry cook-off, as well as a lobster-roll bag lunch, a chicken barbecue, and a fish chowder supper.

Lobster Festival, Rockland. An annual event for almost 60 years, this huge festival hosts thousands of visitors every year. There are lobster street sculptures, a parade featuring the crowned Maine Sea Goddess, music galore, an arts tent, a race on half-submerged lobster crates and . . . lobster. In 2005, more than 12 tons of lobster was prepared in the world's largest lobster cooker. Other seafood is, of course, available. (www.mainelobsterfestival.com)

Wild Blueberry Festival, Machias. This town, in the heart of Down East Maine's blueberry barrens, has hosted this splashy bash for more than 30 years. Festivities include a blueberry musical, a blueberry museum, a blueberry blues band, a blueberry farm tour, a blueberry race, as well as a blueberry pie eating contest, a blueberry dessert bar, and a baked bean supper and chicken barbecue. (www.machiasblueberry.com)

September

Potato Feast Days, Houlton. The usual festival features (arts and crafts, livestock exhibits) vie for the participatory potato events, which include a potato-picking contest and a potato-barrel–rolling contest.

Maine Shrimp Linguine

When Maine shrimp have their brief, few-weeks-long season in midwinter, I try to cook them as often as possible. Maine shrimp freeze pretty well, but of course there's nothing quite like seafood fresh from the cold ocean. This pasta dish is garlicky, lemony, utterly delicious — *and* it's so simple and easy to make ahead that it's perfect for entertaining. Just add a basket of seeded semolina or other Italian bread and an arugula and red pepper salad, and you're all set. Except, if it's a special occasion, you might consider Graham-Cracker Cream Pie (page 246) for dessert.

4 SERVINGS

6	tablespoons butter
6	tablespoons olive oil
4	garlic cloves, minced
3	tablespoons minced shallots (about 3 large shallots)
1	cup bottled clam juice
1	cup dry white wine
2	teaspoons angostura bitters
2	teaspoons grated lemon zest
1	tablespoon lemon juice (juice of 1/2 medium lemon)
1/4	teaspoon dried red pepper flakes
12	ounces linguine or other strand pasta
1	pound shelled Maine shrimp or other small to medium shrimp (see Note)
1/2	cup chopped fresh parsley
	Salt and freshly ground black pepper

1. Heat the butter and oil in a large skillet over medium heat. Add the garlic and shallots and cook for 1 minute. Add the clam juice and wine, raise the heat to high, and boil briskly until reduced by about one third, about 5 minutes. Add the bitters, lemon zest, lemon juice, and red pepper flakes. (The sauce base can be made ahead and held at cool room temperature for an hour or two.)

2. Cook the pasta in a large pot of boiling salted water until al dente, about 8 minutes.

3. Meanwhile, reheat the sauce. Add the shrimp and cook over medium heat, stirring often, until the shrimp just turn pink, about 2 minutes. Stir in the parsley and season with the salt and pepper to taste.

4. Drain the pasta, spoon the shrimp and sauce over it, and serve.

Note: *This recipe also works beautifully with other seafood, especially chopped or baby clams and bay scallops.*

Pan Roast of Fish and Shellfish

At Fore Street, entrée choices change daily and with the seasons, as would be expected from a chef as well-regarded as Sam Hayward. This pan roast of fish and shellfish is another example of why he's earned such praise.

6—8 SERVINGS

5   tablespoons extra-virgin olive oil

1   carrot, peeled and thinly sliced

1   leek, cleaned and thinly sliced (white and pale green parts only)

1   spring onion or medium yellow onion, thinly sliced

2   garlic cloves, thinly sliced

3/4   cup dry white wine

1   bouquet garni (see Note)

2   cups fish stock or bottled clam juice

1   Maine lobster, 1 1/2 pounds

1 1/2   pounds assorted fillets of white-fleshed fish such as monkfish, whiting, wolf fish, skate, or hake (use at least 3 varieties), cut into large chunks

1   large ripe tomato, cored, seeded, and cut into large pieces

24   smallish littleneck clams, scrubbed (see About Clams, page 187)

24   mussels, scrubbed (debearded, if necessary; see Note)

12   medium-sized sea scallops, tough muscle removed from side of each if necessary

1. Heat 2 tablespoons of the oil in a medium-sized saucepan over medium-high heat. Add the carrot, leek, onion, and garlic and cook until just softened, about 5 minutes. Add the wine, raise the heat to high, and boil for 2 minutes. Add the bouquet garni and fish stock, bring to a boil, reduce the heat to medium-low, and simmer for 10 minutes.

2. Preheat the oven to 450°F.

3. Place the lobster in the freezer for 10 minutes, if desired. Plunge a sharp knife into the top of the lobster's head just behind the eyes and split the lobster in half lengthwise, through the tail. Twist off the tail pieces and claws. Remove the digestive tract from the tails and cut the tail halves in half crosswise. Crack the large claws. Put all the lobster pieces, including the body, into a large, deep ovenproof pot. (At Fore Street they use a *cazuela* — a Spanish pottery vessel — but a large enameled cast iron or other similar ovenproof casserole dish works fine.)

4. Arrange the fish, tomato, clams, mussels, and scallops over and around the lobster, sprinkle with the parsley, chervil, and thyme, drizzle with the remaining 3 tablespoons olive oil, and season with the salt and pepper to taste. Ladle the broth and vegetables over the seafood and cover the baking dish.

5. Bake until the bivalves open, about 30 minutes. (Even if the clams are just cracked open, remove from the oven now so as not to overcook the rest of the seafood. You can wedge the clams open further if you like.)

¼ cup fresh parsley leaves, chopped

2 tablespoons coarsely chopped fresh chervil

2 tablespoons stripped fresh thyme leaves

Sea salt and freshly ground black pepper

6. Remove and discard the lobster body, the bouquet garni, and any unopened clams or mussels. Serve the pan roast directly from the cooking vessel.

Note: *For the bouquet garni, tie together 4 parsley sprigs, 4 thyme branches, and 1 bay leaf with kitchen twine. To debeard mussels, pull out the dark threads that protrude from the shell. Do this just before cooking; mussels die when debearded.*

FORE STREET

Chef Sam Hayward of Portland's Fore Street has received a lot of press. Hayward — and his food and his restaurant and his philosophy — have been extolled in the *New York Times*, *Saveur*, *Gourmet*, and other food magazines. But he's not an attention-grabbing celebrity chef.

"I'm interested," says Hayward, "in the transcendent snap of food and place; in exceptional raw materials that are strongly connected through history and ecology." He has forged powerful links with such local suppliers as produce farmer Frank Gross and Bill Mook of Mook Sea Farms, and he doesn't gussy up their exquisite raw materials.

At the restaurant, which is housed in a handsomely rehabbed brick industrial building in Portland's Old Port, all the food is cooked on a 17-foot open hearth, and the bouquet of wood smoke permeates the air. So much on the menu tempts that ordering is almost agonizing. Will it be the iced Pemaquid oysters or gratin of slacked salmon or a lobster and maitake tart or cool-weather greens and roasted walnuts to start? Among the difficult main-course choices might be a fabulous grilled hanger steak, local scallops grilled over Maine applewood, two-texture duckling, spit-roasted pork loin, or roast rabbit with wild mushrooms.

Luscious desserts include fresh fruit sorbets, warm chocolate soufflé cake, warm apple or cranberry tarte tatin, or a selection of local cheeses. Indeed, Sam and his cooking truly merit all the accolades — and then some.

Creamy Seafood Casserole with Lemon Crumbs

This recipe was inspired by a similar dish in the *Portland Symphony Cookbook* (Portland Symphony Orchestra Women's Committee, 1974), one of the many wonderful community cookbooks produced annually in Maine. It's a deliciously extravagant, special-occasion dish fit for entertaining the maestro himself — or a few friends at a gracious (yet trouble-free) dinner party. Here's what I might serve to round out the menu: Sun-Dried Tomato and Fromage Blanc Toasts (page 34) and Sweet and Salty Nuts 'n' Cranberries (page 39) to start, then, to accompany the casserole, Trio of Autumn Greens (page 91) and/or Winter Salad of Oranges, Radishes, and Basil (page 96), buttery dinner rolls, and Walnut Pie (page 262) for dessert.

6 – 8 SERVINGS

5 tablespoons butter

4 tablespoons minced shallots (about 4 large shallots)

3 tablespoons all-purpose flour

1/2 cup bottled clam juice

1 1/2 cups half-and-half

1/4 cup sherry, dry or medium-dry

3/4 teaspoon salt, or to taste

1/4 teaspoon freshly ground black pepper, or to taste

1/8 teaspoon fresh nutmeg

1/2 pound wild mushrooms, or cultivated mushrooms such as portabella or shiitake, quartered or sliced

1 pound medium shrimp, shelled and deveined

1/2 pound bay scallops (see Note)

1 cup cooked crabmeat, picked over (1/2 pound)

1 tablespoon lemon juice (juice of 1/2 medium lemon)

Salt and freshly ground black pepper

1. To make the sauce, melt 3 tablespoons of the butter in a medium-large saucepan over medium heat. Add the shallots and cook, stirring, for 1 minute. Sprinkle on the flour and cook, whisking, for 2 minutes. Gradually whisk in the clam juice, half-and-half, and sherry. Bring to a boil, whisking, and cook until the sauce is smooth and thickened, 2 to 3 minutes. Add the salt, pepper, and nutmeg.

2. Melt the remaining 2 tablespoons of butter in a large skillet. Add the mushrooms and cook over medium-high heat, stirring frequently, until they soften and begin to brown lightly, about 5 minutes. Add the shrimp and scallops and cook, stirring frequently, until the shrimp begin to turn pink, about 5 minutes. Gently stir in the crabmeat and lemon juice. Pour the sauce over the seafood, stir to combine, and season with additional salt and pepper to taste, if necessary.

3. Preheat the oven to 375°F. Grease a shallow 2½-quart baking dish or oven-to-table casserole dish with butter. Scrape the seafood mixture into the dish. (The recipe can be made up to a day ahead to this point, covered with foil and refrigerated.)

4. To make the Lemon Crumbs, melt the butter in a medium skillet over medium heat. Add the breadcrumbs and toss until barely colored, 2 to 3 minutes. Stir in the parsley and lemon zest. (The crumbs can be made up to a day ahead and stored in a sealed plastic bag.)

LEMON CRUMBS

2 tablespoons butter

1½ cups fresh breadcrumbs (see Note)

3 tablespoons chopped fresh flat-leaf parsley

1½ teaspoons grated lemon zest

---

5. Sprinkle the crumbs over the seafood mixture. Bake for 20 to 25 minutes, or until heated through and bubbly and the crumbs are golden. If the casserole has been refrigerated, bake the foil-covered casserole for 20 minutes; uncover and finish baking for 15 to 20 minutes, or until heated through and bubbly. Serve directly from the dish.

Note: *Sea scallops, halved or quartered, can be substituted for bay scallops. Tear about 3 slices of good-quality white sandwich bread into pieces and whir in a food processor to make the breadcrumbs.*

France in Maine

French-speaking Canadians (or Acadians) flocked south to Maine by the thousands in the early 20th century, and many found work at the state's numerous mills and factories turning out essentials from buttons to brass tacks, shirts to shoes. Many families stayed in Maine, enriching the melting pot with a soupçon of French language, food, and customs.

French (or Franco) Americans (or Americaines), as they are also known in Maine, stage annual festivals around the state as a way to celebrate and preserve Acadian culture and traditions. One such event is in Biddeford, in southern Maine, where I enjoyed lilting French music and dancing while eating my way through the food tents, savoring *la tourtiere* (meat pie), *cretons* (pork paté), thick yellow pea soup, chicken pie, *boudin* (blood sausage), fruit-filled crêpes, and that sticky-sweet far-north confection, maple taffy. Other towns with French festivals include Lewiston, Augusta, and Madawaska.

Down East Cassoulet with Fresh Herb Crumbs

Cassoulet, the celebrated bean and smoked and preserved meat dish that originated in southwest France, transplants in a most natural way across the ocean. After all, isn't Maine famous for beans and smoked meats and game? I have substituted some of the traditional French elements (pork rind, goose, duck confit) with readily available fresh duck and garlicky smoked sausages, and the result is a most delicious Down East rendering of the classic. Cassoulet is labor intensive, to be sure, but don't be daunted. There's nothing complicated in the recipe, and it can all be done well in advance. For a winter dinner party, start with Smoked Salmon and Scallion Triangles (page 19); accompany the cassoulet with Winter Salad of Oranges, Radishes, and Basil (page 96); and finish with Julia's Apple Cream Tart (page 260).

BEANS

1   pound dried small white beans such as pea, navy, or Great Northern, rinsed and picked over

12   cups water

1   smoked ham bone or smoked ham hock

1   large onion, coarsely chopped

2   large garlic cloves, peeled and crushed

4   branches fresh thyme

2   bay leaves

MEATS

1   duck (about 4 pounds), cut into 8 pieces (see Note)

Salt and freshly ground black pepper

1   pound lean boneless lamb (leg or sirloin), cut into 2-inch chunks

8—10 SERVINGS

1. Soak the beans, if you like, in water to cover for 4 hours, or overnight. (see To Soak or Not to Soak? page 119). Drain.

2. Bring the water to a boil in a large soup pot. Add the soaked or unsoaked beans, ham bone, onion, garlic, thyme, and bay leaves. Return to a boil, reduce the heat to low, and cook, covered, until the beans are just tender, 1½ to 2 hours. Remove and discard the ham bone, thyme, and bay leaves.

3. Sprinkle the duck with salt and pepper to taste. Heat a large deep skillet or Dutch oven over medium heat. Arrange the duck pieces, skin-side down, in the pan and cook, turning once, until deep golden brown and some of the fat is rendered, 15 to 20 minutes. Remove to a plate, leaving ¼ cup of drippings in the pan.

4. Cook the lamb and sausage in the pan drippings until nicely browned, about 10 minutes. Remove to a plate, leaving the drippings in the pan.

5. Cook the onions and garlic in the drippings, stirring occasionally, until softened, about 8 minutes. Add the wine, raise the heat to high, and boil, stirring up browned bits in the bottom of the pan, until the liquid is slightly reduced, about 3 minutes.

1	pound smoked garlicky sausage such as linguiça, chourico, or kielbasa, cut into 3/4-inch slices
2	medium onions, sliced
4	garlic cloves, chopped
2	cups dry white wine
1	tablespoon chopped fresh rosemary
1	tablespoon chopped fresh thyme
1/8	teaspoon ground nutmeg
2	cups chicken or beef broth
1	can (15 ounces) diced tomatoes with juice

FRESH HERB CRUMBS

2 1/2	cups fresh breadcrumbs (see Note)
1/3	cup chopped fresh parsley
1 1/2	tablespoons chopped fresh rosemary
1 1/2	tablespoons chopped fresh thyme
1	teaspoon freshly ground black pepper
2	tablespoons olive oil

6. Return the meats to the pan and add the rosemary, thyme, nutmeg, broth, and tomatoes. Bring to a boil, reduce the heat, and cook, covered, until the duck meat is no longer pink, about 20 minutes. Spoon off excess fat that has risen to the surface. (Or refrigerate and lift the fat off when cold.)

7. Preheat the oven to 350°F.

8. Transfer the meat mixture to a 4- to 5-quart casserole dish or two smaller dishes. Drain the beans, reserving the liquid. Add the beans to the meat mixture, stirring gently to avoid mashing them, and add enough reserved bean liquid to come to the top of the solids. Taste and add salt, if necessary. (The recipe can be prepared up to 2 days ahead to this point and refrigerated. Return to room temperature before final baking, adding more liquid if it has all been absorbed. The cassoulet should be somewhat soupy when it goes into the oven.)

9. Toss together the breadcrumbs, parsley, rosemary, thyme, and pepper in a bowl. Drizzle with the olive oil and toss until well mixed.

10. Sprinkle the crumb mixture over the cassoulet. Bake, uncovered, until most of the juices are absorbed and the crumbs are crusty and golden brown, 1 to 1½ hours. Serve directly from the baking dish.

Note: *You can request that the supermarket meat department cut up the duck with a saw. To make the fresh breadcrumbs, tear 4 to 5 slices of good-quality bread (day-old country bread works well) into pieces and whir in a food processor.*

Stephen King's Lunchtime Ghoul-ash

I make this when my wife, Tabby, isn't home. [Home is Bangor, Maine.] She won't eat it; in fact doesn't even like to look at it. Here's the recipe: Take 2 cans Franco American spaghetti (without meatballs) and 1 pound cheap, greasy hamburger. Brown hamburg in large skillet. Add spaghetti and cook 'til heated through. Do not drain hamburg, or it will not be properly greasy. Burn on pan if you want — that will only improve the flavor. Serve with buttered Wonder Bread.

— From *Eating Between the Lines: A Maine Writers' Cookbook*

Bradford Camps Bean-Hole Bean Bake

Igor and Karen Sikorsky run beautiful Bradford Camps, a sporting camp on Maine's Munsungan Lake near Ashland. (See Pan-Fried Trout, page 183). Most Saturday nights the centerpiece of dinner is their mouth-wateringly delicious beans baked in a bean-hole. Guests love watching and participating in the day-long process, even reveling in the sweet agony when the lid comes off and gusts of the rich, molassesy perfume escape into the evening air. At Bradford, they serve the beans with glazed baked ham, coleslaw (made with cabbage from their garden) tossed with homemade dressing, corn muffins, and carrot cake or chocolate pie for dessert. Here, in Igor's own words, is how it's done:

"Friday night (or the night before), rinse 2 cups of dried beans — Jacob's cattle, navy pea beans, or other bean of choice — and soak them in cold water to cover overnight. If not already dug, dig your bean hole. It should be about 30 inches in diameter and at least 2 feet deep, like a shallow old-fashioned well. Line with stones, which hold the heat.

"Saturday morning around 8 a.m., build a fire in your bean hole. The fire should be made of hardwood split to 3 inches in diameter sticks, no larger. If the logs are too fat, they won't burn down to coals well. When the fire is going well, throw all the sticks in to fill the hole and round it up. Leave lots of air spaces between the sticks. The flames may reach 3 to 4 feet in the air. Do the bean-hole dance around the fire.

"Get your pot ready. You will want a true cast-iron bean-hole pot with a raised rim on the lid. Pour the beans and soaking water into the bean pot and place on the stove indoors. Bring to a boil. Remove from the heat, drain, and add new water, about twice the amount of beans. Put back on the burner and add 2 tablespoons sugar, 2 tablespoons brown sugar,

1 teaspoon salt, dash each of black and white pepper, ½ teaspoon dry mustard, small spoonful Dijon mustard, 4 tablespoons molasses, splash of pickapeppa [Jamaican hot sauce], and a hunk of salt pork or bacon cubes. Bring to a good simmer before heading to the bean hole.

"After 1 or 2 hours, the fire should have died down to red-hot coals. Dig out most of the coals to make room for the bean pot. You will find that you want a long-sleeved shirt, long pants, oven mitts, and a long-handled shovel for this job. The heat radiates pretty well. Place the pot in and nest it level in the coals; then shovel all the coals back on. I put an old cookie sheet on top of the coals just so I won't upset the lid when it comes time to harvest. On top of all that, pile on the dirt, at least a foot of it, more is better. Make sure no heat is escaping from the sides. Recite the bean-hole prayer.

"Now you are ready to go out in the woods, fish a pond, hike a mountain, canoe a stream, and think about supper. The beans will cook all day and gradually the temp will go down so they will stay hot until whenever you dig them up.

"We make sure everyone is around the bean hole when we dig them up, and everyone gets a spoon to have a first sampling. It's a bit scary every time for the cook, who hopes he put the right amount of water in! Dig 'em up, don't knock the lid off, take a look, have a taste, head to the kitchen, and bon appétit!

"If you don't want to dig a big hole in your backyard, the recipe also works great cooked in a pottery bean pot for 8 hours or so in a 250°F oven. If you wish, check to make certain that there is enough liquid (advantage over the bean hole) but try to resist the temptation to stir!"

4 Maine-Style Meat and Poultry

Wood-Grilled Peppered Steaks with a Bouquet of Grilled Vegetables

Mainers pride themselves on being a hardy bunch, so bragging rights are claimed for chipping ice off the grill in order to pry off the lid in January. Not me. But by the month of May, when standing outside feels more like pleasure than pain, we begin to go at it with a vengeance, grilling all manner of fish, chicken, meat, and vegetables. This simple peppered steak with its bouquet of summer vegetables showcases the very best of the height-of-grilling season.

Hardwood chips for grilling (optional)

4 club steaks or shell steaks, 1–1½ inches thick

Salt

About 4 teaspoons cracked black peppercorns

16 scallions, green parts only, trimmed to about 4 inches long

8 medium-large mushrooms, such as portabella, trimmed

1 large red bell pepper, cut into 2-inch strips

1 large yellow crookneck squash, diagonally sliced ¼-inch thick

1 large zucchini, diagonally sliced ¼-inch thick

¼ cup olive oil

3 tablespoons coarsely chopped fresh tarragon

Freshly ground black pepper

4 SERVINGS

1. Build a hot barbecue fire or preheat a gas grill to high. If desired, soak hardwood chips, such as hickory, in water for 30 minutes.

2. Season the steaks with salt to taste and the cracked pepper, patting in evenly.

3. Toss the scallions, mushrooms, bell pepper, squash, and zucchini in a large, shallow dish with the olive oil and tarragon. Season with salt and pepper to taste. Thread the vegetables onto metal skewers. (Or cook in a wire grill basket or simply place directly on the grill.)

4. Toss a handful of the soaked chips onto the coals, if desired. Grill the meat, turning once, to the desired degree of doneness, 3 to 4 minutes per side for medium-rare. Place the skewers around the cooler edges of the grill and cook until the vegetables are softened and lightly charred, about 8 minutes.

5. Place the meat on a platter, surround with the vegetables, and serve.

Little Meatballs with Applesauce-Cider Gravy

These delectable little meatballs, which came originally from the recipe files of my madcap mother-in-law Mamie (a very good cook), have a really pleasant sweet-and-sour thing going for them. Some slightly sweet elements (applesauce, cornflake crumbs) are offset nicely by the sharp edge of the vinegar that gets added at the end. Spoon the little meatballs over cooked egg noodles or Mashed Mainers (page 90) and add some steamed green beans to the plate for a scrumptious supper.

4 SERVINGS

1 pound meat loaf mix (equal parts ground beef, veal, and pork)

½ cup crushed cornflake crumbs (1½ cups whole)

¾ cup applesauce

1 small onion, finely chopped

1 garlic clove, minced

1 egg

2 teaspoons dried thyme

½ teaspoon salt

½ teaspoon freshly ground black pepper

1 can (10¾ ounces) condensed tomato soup (see Note)

1 cup water

2 tablespoons apple cider vinegar

1. Combine the meat loaf mix, cornflake crumbs, ½ cup of the applesauce, onion, garlic, egg, 1 teaspoon of the thyme, salt, and pepper in a large bowl. Use your clean hands to mix gently but thoroughly. Shape the mixture into about thirty 1-inch meatballs and place them on waxed paper or a baking sheet.

2. Whisk together the tomato soup, remaining ¼ cup applesauce, remaining 1 teaspoon thyme, and water in a very large skillet with a lid, or a Dutch oven. Bring to a simmer.

3. Drop the meatballs gently into the sauce, return to a simmer, and cook, covered, over medium-low heat until the meatballs are no longer pink inside, about 30 minutes. (The meatballs can be made up to a day ahead and refrigerated. Spoon off any congealed fat and reheat gently.)

4. Skim off any excess fat that rose to the surface, stir in the vinegar, and serve.

Note: *Don't be put off by the condensed tomato soup. It's actually perfect for this dish, contributing just the right flavors and color, and it doesn't add any unpleasant processed taste.*

Cranberry-Glazed Mixed Meat Loaf

This is my favorite meat loaf recipe. It is juicy but sliceable, crusty but not dry, flavorful but not too spicy, and comforting but not boring. The mix contains rolled oats, which contribute flavor and a slightly crumbly texture, and some tangy plain yogurt to offset the richness of the meats. You choose to bake it either as a free-form loaf (giving it a bit more crustiness) or in a loaf pan (making it slightly juicier). Just add potatoes — either scalloped, baked, stuffed, or mashed (see chapter 2 for recipe suggestions) and some steamed broccoli or broccolini for the quintessentially comforting meal.

2 pounds meat loaf mix (equal parts ground beef, veal, and pork)

1 cup rolled oats (regular or quick-cooking, not instant)

1 cup tomato sauce or tomato juice

1 small onion, chopped

1/3 cup plain yogurt, regular or nonfat

1/4 cup chopped fresh parsley

2 tablespoons Dijon mustard

1 tablespoon chopped fresh thyme, or 1 1/2 teaspoons dried

1 teaspoon salt

1/2 teaspoon freshly ground black pepper

1 egg

3 tablespoons jellied cranberry sauce

1 tablespoon white wine vinegar

6—8 SERVINGS

1. Preheat the oven to 350°F.

2. Combine the meat loaf mix, rolled oats, tomato sauce, onion, yogurt, parsley, mustard, thyme, salt, pepper, and egg in a large bowl. Use your clean hands to work the mixture together gently but thoroughly until well blended.

3. Transfer the meat mixture to a shallow baking dish and shape into an oval loaf about 10 inches long and 2 1/2 inches high. (Alternatively, pack the meat mixture into a 9-by-5-inch loaf pan.) Bake for 45 minutes.

4. Whisk the cranberry sauce with the vinegar in a small bowl. (It doesn't matter that the mixture is not smooth.) Brush the meat loaf with the cranberry mixture, return to the oven, and cook for 20 to 30 minutes, or until the juices run clear and an instant-read thermometer inserted in the center registers 160°F.

5. Let stand for 10 minutes, pour off any excess fat, slice, and serve.

Wolfe's Neck Farm

In the early 1950s, Wolfe's Neck Farm pioneered organic beef farming in the eastern United States. Eleanor and Lawrence Smith, who also became great proponents of satellite farming, started raising natural beef on their 600 acres of saltwater farmland in coastal Freeport, Maine, and Wolfe's Neck now works hand-in-hand with over 50 other farms to produce humanely raised, hormone- and antibiotic-free livestock. Consumer demand keeps growing. Today, Wolfe's Neck is not only a business operation but also a conservancy, providing education programs focusing on preserving the environment and farming, nature trails, and agricultural internships.

Nezinscot Farm

Named for the river that flows past their pastures and cropland, Nezinscot Farm in beautiful Turner, Maine, is a second generation family-owned farm with close ties to the surrounding community. Nezinscot, which was started as a dairy farm by current owner Gregg Varney's grandfather, still milks cows and goats, but has diversified and now produces organic meats, vegetables, herbs, eggs, cheeses, and yarns from their own sheep, llamas, and alpacas. You can buy all these wonderful products at their farm store/café, where you can also enjoy a homemade meal and freshly made baked goods.

North Woods Molasses and Cumin Seed Chili

The map of inland Maine is pocked with dots showing the location of more than four dozen sporting camps with names like Bear Spring Camp, Eagle Lake Camp, Indian Rock Camp, and Leen's Lodge. After a day spent hiking, hunting, or fishing in the North Woods (or anywhere!), a hearty, filling meal such as chili is definitely the order of the day. Although this molasses-flavored chili is actually my own recipe, I took inspiration from the likes of Moose Chili and Venison Chili in a book called *The Maine Sporting Camp Cookbook* (Down East, 2004). I dedicate this fabulous chili to all the hard-working cooks and appreciative eaters at the sporting camps of Maine. Serve over white rice or with cornbread, if desired.

1 tablespoon vegetable oil

2 pounds ground beef

2 onions, chopped

6 garlic cloves, chopped

1 teaspoon salt

½ teaspoon freshly ground black pepper

¼ cup chili powder

2 teaspoons ground cumin

2 teaspoons whole cumin seeds

2 teaspoons dried oregano

½ teaspoon cayenne pepper

1 can (28 ounces) crushed tomatoes with juice

2 cups beef broth

3 cups drained kidney beans (about two 15½-ounce cans)

1 large bay leaf, broken in half

2 tablespoons molasses

Suggested toppings: diced red onion, cilantro leaves, sour cream, shredded Cheddar or Monterey Jack cheese, minced green chiles

6–8 SERVINGS

1. Heat the oil in a large Dutch oven or other large pot over medium-high heat. Add the beef, onions, garlic, salt, and pepper and cook, stirring to break up large clumps of ground meat, until it loses its pink color, about 10 minutes.

2. Add the chili powder, cumin, cumin seeds, oregano, and cayenne, and cook, stirring, for 2 minutes.

3. Add the tomatoes, broth, beans, bay leaf, and molasses. Bring to a boil, reduce the heat to medium-low, and simmer, uncovered, until the chili begins to reduce and thicken, about 20 minutes. Using the back of a large spoon, crush about one-third of the beans against the side of the pot to thicken the chili further. Continue to simmer, stirring occasionally, for 10 to 15 minutes. Taste and adjust for seasonings or thickness, if desired. (The chili can be made up to 2 days ahead and refrigerated, or frozen for up to 1 month.)

4. Serve with small bowls of the toppings of your choice.

Corned Beef Harvest Supper with Horseradish Cream

Along about October, signs start appearing outside church halls and community centers: "Harvest Supper Tonight. All Welcome!" Harvest suppers, which serve as fund-raisers for local organizations of all kinds, celebrate autumn in Maine and the bounty of the season. The menus vary. One might be turkey and all the trimmings, another a ham bake or a spaghetti supper, or my favorite, a New England boiled dinner. Boiled dinner Maine-style is similar to Irish corned beef and cabbage, with the addition of beets and parsnips, and it's one of those hearty and soul-satisfying meals that are also celebratory and festive — perfect for a large informal gathering. While it's not necessarily traditional, I like to serve this horseradish-spiked sour cream sauce, which is a welcome rich and sharp counterpoint to the plain boiled meat and vegetables.

HORSERADISH CREAM

- 3/4 cup sour cream, regular or low-fat
- 1/4 cup prepared horseradish
- 3 scallions, thinly sliced
- 2 teaspoons grainy mustard

BEEF AND VEGETABLES

- 1 corned beef brisket or round, 4–5 pounds
- 12 whole peppercorns
- 2 bay leaves
- 2 whole cloves
- 1 teaspoon mustard seeds
- 12 medium-sized beets (about 2 pounds), trimmed

6 GENEROUS SERVINGS, WITH SOME LEFTOVERS

1. To make the Horseradish Cream, combine the sour cream, horseradish, scallions, and mustard in a small bowl and refrigerate. Return to room temperature before serving.

2. Place the corned beef in a large pot, cover with cold water, and bring to a boil. Skim off the foam that rises to the surface for the first few minutes. Add the peppercorns, bay leaves, cloves, and mustard seeds. Reduce the heat to low and simmer, covered, until the meat is tender when tested with a fork, 2 to 3 hours.

3. Meanwhile, cook the beets in a pot of boiling salted water until tender, about 30 minutes. Drain, and when cool enough to handle, peel. Leave whole if small, and halve or quarter if larger. Set aside in a bowl and reheat in a microwave before using.

4. Cook the potatoes in another large pot in boiling salted water to cover for 10 minutes. Add the carrots and parsnips and cook until all three vegetables are tender, about 10 minutes longer. Drain; reheat in a microwave before serving, if necessary.

About 15 small red-skinned
potatoes, cut in half if larger

10 large carrots (about 2 pounds),
peeled and cut into 3- to 4-inch
lengths

6 parsnips (about 1½ pounds),
peeled and cut into 3-inch
lengths

1 medium-sized green cabbage,
cut into 16 wedges

4 tablespoons butter

Salt and freshly ground black
pepper

5. About 15 minutes before the beef is done, add the cabbage to the pot and cook until tender.

6. Cut the corned beef into thin crosswise slices and arrange on a large platter. Surround the beef with the vegetables, dot with butter, and spoon a bit of hot cooking liquid over, to heat. Season the vegetables with salt and pepper to taste. Pass the horseradish cream at the table.

— "Corned" Beef

Corned beef has nothing to do with corn. Rather, it is brisket or round of beef cured in a brine (salt) solution. The name derives from the English use of the word "corn" to mean any small particle, such as the grains of salt used for the cure. Mainers depended on preserved meats such as corned beef and salted and smoked pork products to get them through the long winter and spring, and most early households kept a stoneware crock in the basement to fill with salt-brined beef in the fall. Before chemical preservatives began to be used to cure meat, old-fashioned Yankee home-corned beef was a grayish pink color and was often saltier than today's pinky-red corned beef. A few ardent traditionalists still prefer homemade Maine "gray-cured" beef.

Yankee Pot Roast with a Fresh Face

Pot-roasting less-than-tender cuts of beef has been a mainstay formula of Down East cooks for generations, and the long, slow simmering truly does result in meltingly tender, flavorful meat with gravy that is perfect winter fare. In this recipe, I update the concept by cooking the root vegetables separately so they retain their color and texture, and by then adding lots of garlic to the stew and a big handful of fresh herbs to finish, thus giving the pot roast a "fresh face." Serve with boiled potatoes or Mashed Mainers (page 90), a salad, and perhaps a refreshing spoonful of Common Ground Apple-Cranberry Salsa (page 227). Then, why not finish with Grape Nuts Pudding (page 273) or slices of Graham-Cracker Cream Pie (page 246)?

5	garlic cloves
1	chuck or rump roast, 3 1/2–4 pounds
1	bay leaf
	Salt and freshly ground black pepper
2	tablespoons olive oil
1	large onion, chopped
2	tablespoons all-purpose flour
1	teaspoon paprika
2	cups beef broth or 1 can (14 1/2 ounces) beef broth, plus 1/4 cup water
1	cup dry red wine
3	tablespoons chopped fresh thyme, plus thyme sprigs
6	carrots, peeled and cut about 2 inches long and 1/2-inch wide
4	parsnips, peeled and cut into 1/2-inch slices
1 1/2	cups frozen pearl onions
1	tablespoon butter
1/4	cup chopped fresh flat-leaf parsley

1. Cut one of the garlic cloves into thin slivers. Make small slits all over the meat and insert the slivers. Crumble or chop the bay leaf as fine as possible, mix with salt and pepper to taste, and rub over the meat.

2. Heat the oil in a large Dutch oven over medium-high heat. Add the meat and cook until browned on all sides, 10 to 15 minutes. Remove to a plate, leaving the drippings in the pan.

3. Reduce the heat to medium. Add the onion to the pan and cook, stirring frequently, until it begins to soften, about 5 minutes. Chop the remaining 4 garlic cloves fine, add to the onions, and cook for 5 minutes. Sprinkle on the flour and paprika and cook, stirring, for 2 minutes.

4. Whisk in the broth and wine and bring to a boil. Return the meat and any accumulated juices to the pot, add 3 sprigs of the thyme, and cook, covered, over low heat, until the meat is tender, about 2 hours. Spoon off the excess fat that has risen to the surface. (The beef can be cooked up to 2 days ahead and refrigerated, in which case any fat can be lifted off the surface. Reheat in the sauce.)

5. Cook the carrots in a large saucepan of boiling salted water for 5 minutes. Add the parsnips and pearl onions and continue to cook until all the vegetables are tender, about 15 minutes. Drain, reserving 1 cup of the cooking water. Add the butter, toss to coat, and season with salt and pepper to taste. (The vegetables can be cooked up to 2 hours ahead and reheated in a microwave.)

6. Cut the meat into thin slices across the grain on a cutting board and arrange on a serving platter. Bring the pan sauce to a boil, adding any vegetable cooking water as necessary to thin it to a pouring consistency. Stir in the parsley and chopped thyme.

7. Arrange the cooked vegetables around the meat, spoon the herb gravy over, garnish with thyme sprigs, and serve.

Marjorie Standish on Pot Roasting

If there is a universal way of cooking beef in Maine, it has to be pot roast. There is a choice as to the cut of beef, a choice of utensil to cook it in, a choice of seasoning and a choice of cooking it on top of the stove or in the oven. If there is left-over pot roast, then it may be cut into smaller pieces, combined with gravy and made into a meat pie topped with either biscuits or pastry. If hash is what you have in mind, chop it with cold, boiled potatoes.

— Marjorie Standish, *Cooking Down East*

Grilled Spice-Brined Pork Tenderloin with Heirloom Tomato Salad

Boneless pork tenderloins are available at some farmers' markets in Maine — or in the meat case at the supermarket, of course! Tenderloins are a perfect candidate for brining (soaking in a spiced salt solution for a few hours) because the process helps the lean meat retain moisture and it also injects flavor. If they are not overcooked, pork tenderloins will be buttery-tender, and the smoky grilled meat is beautifully complemented by this height-of-summer salad made with juicy, right-from-the-vine heirloom (or otherwise) tomatoes.

SPICE-BRINED PORK

4 cups cold water

½ cup kosher salt

1 tablespoon crumbled dried rosemary

2 teaspoons mustard seeds, crushed (see Note)

2 teaspoons whole black peppercorns, crushed (see Note)

2 bay leaves, each broken in half

2 pork tenderloins, 12 ounces each

1½ tablespoons olive oil

Freshly ground black pepper

4—6 SERVINGS

1. Combine the water and salt in a large, deep bowl, stirring to dissolve the salt. Add the rosemary, mustard seeds, peppercorns, and bay leaves. Add the pork, turn to coat, and refrigerate, covered, for at least 2 hours, or for up to 12 hours.

2. To make the salad, toss the tomatoes with the onion, olives, and garlic in a large bowl. Add the olive oil, vinegar, salt, pepper, and pepper flakes and mix well. Set aside at cool room temperature for at least 1 hour, or refrigerate for several hours.

3. Build a medium-hot barbecue fire or preheat a gas grill to medium-high. Remove the pork from the brine, rinse thoroughly, and pat dry with paper towels.

4. Rub or brush with the oil and season generously with the pepper. Grill, turning to brown all sides, until almost but not quite cooked through in the center, 15 to 20 minutes. An instant-read thermometer inserted in the center should register no more than 145°F when it comes off the grill.

5. Let the pork sit, loosely covered, for 10 minutes. Cut into ½-inch slices.

6. Toss the tomato salad with the arugula. Spoon over or around the pork to serve.

   Note: *Use a mortar and pestle to crush the mustard seeds and peppercorns or put in a sealed plastic bag and pound with a mallet.*

HEIRLOOM TOMATO SALAD

3   cups diced juicy ripe tomatoes, preferably a mix of red and yellow (about 2 pounds)

1   medium-small white or red sweet onion, diced

½   cup pitted imported black olives

1   large garlic clove, finely chopped

⅓   cup olive oil, preferably extra-virgin

2   tablespoons balsamic vinegar

½   teaspoon salt, or to taste

¼   teaspoon freshly ground black pepper, or to taste

¼   teaspoon dried red pepper flakes

2   cups arugula, roughly torn if large

Betwixt the Fat and the Lean

In the past 20 years or so, pork breeders, responding to consumer demands for lower-fat meat, have been producing pork that is much leaner — and, some would say, meaner, because leaner cuts are less flavorful and more prone to drying out when cooked. Now major pork producer Smithfield Foods, Inc., has chosen to test-market a "new" higher-fat pork in Maine. "This is more of pork the way it used to be — tastier with a little bit of fat on it," says a company spokesperson. "Our lean pork never caught on in Maine as much as around the rest of the country. This is for customers who want to treat themselves occasionally with the fattier, more flavorful type of meat."

Shaker Roast Pork Loin with Apple-Sage Gravy

Inhaling the aroma of roasting meat in winter and listening to its gentle sputter makes one feel rich in all things good. Like all New England Shakers, Maine's Sabbathday Lake community (the only surviving Shakers) are exemplars of goodness, too, applying their philosophy of truth, simplicity, and attention to detail to all aspects of life in their self-sustaining community. This recipe is based on one from *Shaker Your Plate* by Sister Frances Carr (The Shaker Society, 1985).

1   boneless pork loin, 3 to 4 pounds

2   garlic cloves, cut into slivers

2   tablespoons grainy mustard

2   tablespoons olive oil

3   tablespoons chopped fresh sage, plus sage sprigs

1–2 tablespoons butter, if necessary

2   tablespoons all-purpose flour

1½ cups apple cider or apple juice

1   cup chicken broth

2   tablespoons lemon juice (juice of medium lemon)

Salt and freshly ground black pepper

6—8 SERVINGS

1. With a small sharp knife, make slits all over the pork and insert the slivers of garlic.

2. Stir together the mustard, oil, and 1 tablespoon of the sage in a small bowl. Spread the paste all over the meat and arrange some sprigs of sage leaves on the top. Place the roast, fat-side up, on a rack in a shallow metal roasting pan, cover loosely with foil, and set aside at room temperature for 1 hour.

3. Preheat the oven to 425°F.

4. Remove the foil, place the roast in the preheated oven, and immediately reduce the temperature to 325°F. Roast for about 20 minutes per pound and then begin checking the internal temperature; for example, if the roast weighs 3 pounds, begin checking after 1 hour. An instant-read thermometer inserted in the thickest part should register 150°F. When the meat is done, transfer the roast to a platter, cover loosely with foil, and allow to rest while making the gravy.

5. Straddle the roasting pan with drippings on two stove burners. You should have 2 tablespoons of fat in the pan; if not, add the butter to make up the difference. Sprinkle the flour over the drippings and cook over medium heat, stirring, for 2 minutes. Add the cider and broth and bring to a boil over high heat, stirring to dissolve any browned bits in the bottom of the pan. Stir in the remaining 2 tablespoons of sage and the lemon juice, and season with the salt and pepper to taste.

6. Pour any accumulated meat juices on the platter into the gravy. Carve the meat into ½-inch-thick slices, garnish with sage sprigs, and pass the gravy in a sauceboat at the table.

Cider Story

"Sweet cider" is the unadulterated juice from apples squeezed through a press. If the juice is filtered and then pasteurized to stop its natural fermentation process, it becomes apple juice. If alcohol is allowed to develop in the cider, after a while it turns into hard cider. Cider, both sweet and hard, was by far the most popular drink in colonial New England, from Maine to Connecticut. Everyone drank it, adults and children alike. President John Adams, who lived to be 91, prided himself on drinking a pitcher every morning. These days, cider mills all over Maine, using equipment ranging from antique wooden presses to modern hydraulic rigs, still turn out thousands of gallons of cider every fall. Families and field-tripping school children make pilgrimages to inhale the spicy, sweet, musky apple aroma in the pressing room and to watch as presses exert the equivalent of one hundred tons of pressure on a fleshy mound of apples, sending a flood of amber juice cascading into huge vats. Everyone leaves with plastic jugs of the just-made drink, which will keep in the refrigerator for a week or so before it gets fizzy and starts to ferment.

Venison with Cranberry-Chipotle Pan Sauce

You can control the spiciness in this hot 'n' tart sauce that is a perfect accent for venison. The heat comes from chipotles, smoked jalapeños that come packed in small cans in adobo sauce (see Note). Much of the fire is in the seeds, so if you like things less spicy, scrape out the seeds before mincing.

CRANBERRY-CHIPOTLE SAUCE

1	cup fresh or frozen cranberries
3/4	cup honey
2	tablespoons water
1	tablespoon butter
3	garlic cloves, minced
1	small chipotle chile in adobo, minced (see Note)

Salt

VENISON AND FINISH

1	tablespoon butter
1	tablespoon olive oil
4	venison steaks, sirloin, or top round (6–7 ounces each)

Salt and freshly ground black pepper

1/2	cup red wine
1/2	cup walnut pieces, lightly toasted (see Note)

4 SERVINGS

1. To make the Cranberry-Chipotle Sauce, combine the cranberries with the honey and water in a medium-sized saucepan. Bring to a boil, stirring, then reduce the heat to medium, and cook, uncovered, stirring occasionally, until the cranberries begin to burst, about 5 minutes.

2. Melt the butter in a small skillet over low heat. Add the garlic and cook until softened, about 3 minutes. Stir in the minced chipotle. Scrape the garlic-chipotle mixture into the cranberry mixture and season with salt to taste. (The sauce base can be made up to a day ahead and refrigerated. Return to room temperature before using.)

3. Heat the butter and olive oil in a large skillet over medium-high heat. Season the venison with the salt and pepper to taste. When the oil is hot, add the steaks and cook until well-browned on the bottom, about 3 minutes. Turn and cook to desired degree of doneness, about 2 minutes longer for medium-rare. (Do not overcook; venison is dry if cooked much beyond this stage.) Transfer to a warm platter and tent with foil while finishing the sauce.

4. Add the wine to the skillet and bring to a boil, stirring up the browned bits in the bottom of the pan. Stir in the Cranberry-Chipotle Sauce mixture and simmer for 1 minute to reduce and thicken slightly. Pour the pan sauce over the steaks, sprinkle with the nuts, and serve.

Note: *After the can of chipotles is opened, transfer remaining contents to a plastic container and freeze for future use. To toast the walnuts, spread the walnuts in a dry skillet and cook over medium heat, stirring frequently, until almost one shade darker, about 4 minutes.*

MOOSE POINT TAVERN

Moose Point Tavern used to be the main lodge for Henderson Camps, a famous 19th-century sporting camp built on the shores of Big Wood Lake in Jackman, in Maine's North Woods. Carolann Ouellette, who now owns and runs the restaurant, is dedicated to retaining the essence of the old sporting camp atmosphere, and, indeed, when you enter the timbered, tin-ceilinged room you feel transported back to those days. The welcome is warm and the atmosphere is relaxed — just as it was when the Henderson family ran the place. Depending on the season, you can sit on an expansive deck and take in the spectacular lake and mountain view, or have a cocktail in the bar in front of the open hearth brick fireplace. Then to dinner.

Starters at Moose Point range from such down-to-earth offerings as buffalo wings and beer-battered onion rings to mussels steamed with wine and garlic, "made-in-Maine" crab cakes, and duck tenders with a Maine raspberry sauce. Entrées include curry and maple-glazed pork medallions, a grilled steak with India pale ale marinade, orange and basil seared salmon, and this fabulous venison with a cranberry and chipotle sauce. Carolann proudly features Maine-grown and Maine-made ingredients, which are highlighted on the menu. House-made desserts such as cheesecake with local berries and a rich chocolate "decadence" are well worth the calories.

Sporting Camp Cookery

Alice Arlen's *Maine Sporting Camp Cookbook* (Down East, 2004) features 11 recipes for venison (including goulash, pot roast, stew, sautéed strips, pie, and meat loaf), many suggestions for what to do with wild game birds (wild duck baked on a plank, woodcock in hot sauce, grouse nuggets, fried partridge sandwich), moose made into chili and a seven-layer casserole, a deviled elk stew, and . . . for stalwart wild game devotees, roast woodchuck and bear liver and onions.

Choice of Venison

"Got your deer yet?" is the standard greeting in the fall among the confraternity of Maine hunters. Hunters and their families whose freezers are stocked with wild venison know and prefer the wild, slightly gamey flavor of Maine's white-tailed deer meat. However, farmed venison is also very much an option. Maine has several dozen venison farms, and raising deer is a viable agricultural industry. Farmed, or "fallow," deer have rather luxurious lifestyles compared to their wild cousins. Because they don't run, and are fed on the likes of grain, hay, apples, pumpkins, and other garden produce, the meat is mild in flavor, and, though lean, is tender and succulent if not overcooked.

THE BETHEL INN

The Bethel Inn could easily have been the movie set for the holiday classic *White Christmas*. Standing serenely on Bethel's town common, in the heart of Maine's gentle western mountains, the sprawling 80-year-old inn (which also has a health club, golf course, and cross-country ski trails) is the archetypal New England hostelry. The lobby is spacious and welcoming, and the fire-lit dining room epitomizes country elegance.

And the food is good! Chef James Byron's menu lists all the sorts of classics that one might expect in such a setting — then branches out with such appetizers as smoked duck galantine or pan-fried corn cakes with smoked country bacon. Entrées include the full range of seafood, meat, fowl, and game dishes such as Maple-Mustard Venison Medallions.

Maple-Mustard Venison Medallions

This venison preparation is my adaptation of one of The Bethel Inn's wonderful winter specialties. The chef serves it with roasted red bliss potatoes and glazed squash.

8–12 (depending on size) eye round venison medallions (2–2 ½ ounces each)

¼ cup pure maple syrup, preferably Maine-made (see Mail-Order Sources, page 277)

1 tablespoon walnut oil (optional)

2 tablespoons water

Salt and freshly ground black pepper

2 tablespoons olive oil

4 tablespoons butter

2 tablespoons minced shallots (about 2 large)

1 cup beef broth

1 cup dry red wine

1½ tablespoons grainy Dijon mustard

4 SERVINGS

1. Place the meat between sheets of plastic wrap and pound to an even ½-inch thickness.

2. Whisk together the maple syrup, walnut oil, if desired, and water in a shallow dish. Add the venison medallions, turn to coat, and set aside to marinate for about 2 hours.

3. Remove the venison from the marinade, pat dry with paper towels, and season on both sides with salt and pepper to taste. Reserve the marinade.

4. Heat the olive oil in a large skillet over medium-high to high heat. Cook the meat, in batches if necessary, until just seared on both sides but still pink within, 1 to 2 minutes per side. (Be careful not to over-cook or the meat will become dry and tough.) Remove to a platter and tent loosely with foil to keep warm.

5. Reduce the heat to medium. Add 2 tablespoons of the butter to the skillet. Add the shallots and cook for 2 minutes. Add the broth, wine, and reserved marinade. Bring to a boil, stirring up browned bits in the bottom of the pan, and cook briskly until the liquids have reduced by about half, about 5 minutes. Whisk in the mustard. Cut the remaining 2 tablespoons of butter into small bits and whisk into the sauce. Season with salt and pepper to taste.

6. To serve, spoon some sauce in a pool on each plate, place the meat atop the sauce, and spoon a little more over the meat. Pass any remaining sauce at the table.

Chicken Breasts with Morels, Leeks, and Cream

Every year in Maine, knowledgeable local people forage morels: the mushroom of spring. With their dark brown, pitted, conical caps, some say morels look like a sponge on a stick, but they taste divine, with a rich, woodsy flavor that harkens back to the earth from which they spring. Morels are beautifully showcased in this dressed-up chicken dish that combines them with leeks, cream, and some good white wine. Accompany the meal with the same Riesling, and serve the chicken with such seasonal sides as the Oven-Roasted Asparagus (page 60) or Sauté of Fiddleheads, Sugar Snaps, and Baby Carrots (page 61).

4 skinless, boneless chicken breast halves, about 5 ounces each

Salt and freshly ground black pepper

3 tablespoons all-purpose flour

3 tablespoons butter

5 slender leeks, thinly sliced (white and pale green parts only)

8 ounces (about 3 cups) morel mushrooms, trimmed and halved, if large (see Note)

1 cup slightly sweet white wine, such as Riesling

1 cup heavy cream

1½ tablespoons lemon juice (juice of ¾ medium lemon)

2 tablespoons chopped fresh flat-leaf parsley

4 SERVINGS

1. Season the chicken with salt and pepper and dredge in the flour, shaking off the excess.

2. Heat the butter in a large skillet over medium heat. Cook the chicken, covered, until golden brown on both sides, about 8 minutes total. Remove to a plate, leaving the drippings in the pan.

3. Add the leeks, cover the pan, and cook for 5 minutes.

4. Uncover, add the mushrooms, and cook, stirring occasionally, until the mushrooms release their aroma and start to wilt, about 3 minutes.

5. Add the wine, raise the heat to high, and boil briskly until reduced by half, about 3 minutes.

6. Add the cream, return the chicken and any accumulated juices to the pan, reduce the heat to medium, and simmer, uncovered, until the sauce is lightly reduced and thickened and the chicken is no longer pink, 5 to 10 minutes.

7. Squeeze in the lemon juice and season with salt and pepper to taste. (The dish can be made up to 4 hours ahead and refrigerated. Reheat gently before serving.)

8. Sprinkle with the parsley and serve.

   Note: *Dried morels are an excellent substitute. Use about a handful. To reconstitute, pour boiling water over them and soak for an hour or so. And if you can't get morels, substitute porcini, portabella, or almost any other wild or cultivated mushroom.*

— A Mushroom Niche —

Candice and Dan Heydon have parlayed their 10 acres of hardscrabble oak forest in Damariscotta into a thriving mushroom business. Starting in 1989, with a Maine extension course in mushroom growing, the couple quickly educated themselves in mycological matters and started using their oak logs to grow shiitake mushrooms.

The Oyster Creek Mushroom Company began with a single log but now uses 4,000 logs in a huge greenhouse, and produces more than 25,000 pounds of shiitakes annually. In addition, Oyster Creek hires fungi freelancers from all over the state — people who are knowledgeable in the ways of the wild mushrooms growing in their particular area.

Starting in spring, as soon as the snow leaves the ground, pickers start showing up at the couple's back door with boxes of treasure — first morels, followed by other species, such as hens of the woods, matsutake, boletes, and chanterelles, most of them gathered in the northern parts of the state. The Heydons carefully double check the mushrooms they buy from foragers. "We can easily sell everything we can grow ourselves, along with everything people bring us."

Lemon-Thyme Chicken

Fresh thyme grows beautifully in Maine. Of course, you can buy it now all winter long, but when it first greens up in early summer, I love to pluck the fragrant branches and use it with abandon. This simple chicken sauté showcases the herb beautifully. And if you add some spring peas and Mashed Mainers with Mint (page 90), you've got yourself a really lovely dinner.

4	skinless, boneless chicken breast halves (about 5 ounces each)
3	tablespoons all-purpose flour
1	tablespoon plus 2 teaspoons chopped fresh thyme, plus sprigs for garnish
½	teaspoon salt
½	teaspoon freshly ground black pepper
2	tablespoons olive oil
1	tablespoon plus 2 teaspoons butter
1	cup chicken broth
2	tablespoons lemon juice (juice of medium lemon)
½	teaspoon sugar
8	thin lemon slices

4 SERVINGS

1. Place the chicken between two sheets of plastic wrap and use the bottom of a small heavy pot or the smooth side of a mallet to pound the chicken an even ½-inch thick. On a plate, stir together the flour, 1 tablespoon of the thyme, salt, and pepper. Dredge the chicken in the seasoned flour, shaking off the excess.

2. Heat the oil and 1 tablespoon of the butter in a very large skillet. When the oil is hot, add the chicken to the pan and cook, turning once, until golden outside and white but still juicy within, 10 to 15 minutes. Remove to a platter, leaving the drippings in the pan. Tent the chicken with foil to keep warm.

3. Add the broth and the remaining 2 teaspoons thyme to the skillet, raise the heat to high, and cook, stirring up browned bits from the bottom of the pan, until the liquid is reduced and lightly thickened, about 3 minutes. Add the lemon juice and sugar and simmer for 1 minute. Cut the remaining 2 teaspoons butter into small pieces and whisk into the sauce.

4. Arrange the lemon slices atop the chicken, pour the sauce over, garnish with the thyme sprigs, and serve.

Country Fair Garlic Barbecue Chicken

During the middle part of the twentieth century, Maine was a big chicken producer (in fact, defunct chicken barns are part and parcel of the mid-coast landscape), but now Pine Tree State birds are raised mostly for the dominant egg industry. When Maine chickens were in their heyday, lots of them ended up slow-grilling to juicy perfection over huge charcoal grills at country fairs around the state. Barbecued chicken, mopped with a simple garlicky basting sauce, is still a staple at such events. We buy some every year at the Blue Hill Fair (made famous in E.B. White's *Charlotte's Web*) and take it home to eat on the deck with Maine Potato Salad with Egg and Pickles (page 64), a sliced tomato salad, and perhaps Mixed Summer Fruit Cobbler (page 253) for dessert.

1   cup cider vinegar

½   cup vegetable oil

½   cup water

2   garlic cloves, finely chopped

1   tablespoon salt

1   teaspoon freshly ground black pepper

1   teaspoon paprika

Roasting chicken (3 pounds), cut into 8 pieces

4 SERVINGS

1. Combine the vinegar, oil, water, garlic, salt, pepper, and paprika. Add the chicken pieces, turn to coat, and set aside at cool room temperature, or refrigerate, for about 1 hour.

2. Preheat the oven to 325°F.

3. Remove the chicken from the marinade with tongs and arrange on a rimmed baking sheet or roasting pan. Reserve the marinade. Roast for about 25 minutes, or until the chicken looks about half cooked. (The recipe can be prepared to this point up to several hours ahead. Refrigerate the chicken and marinade.)

4. Build a moderate charcoal fire or preheat a gas grill to medium. Pour the reserved marinade into a small saucepan and bring to a boil over high heat. Boil for 1 minute.

5. Grill the chicken, skin-side down, for about 10 minutes, or until the skin is nicely brown. Brush with marinade, turn, and cook until the juices run clear, 10 to 15 minutes. Brush with marinade again and remove from the grill.

6. Serve the chicken warm or at room temperature.

Charlotte at the Blue Hill Fair

When they pulled into the Fair Grounds, they could hear music and see the Ferris wheel turning in the sky. They could smell the dust of the race track where the sprinkling cart had moistened it and they could smell hamburgers frying and see balloons aloft . . . The children grabbed each other by the hand and danced off in the direction of the merry-go-round, toward the wonderful music and the wonderful adventure and the wonderful excitement, into the wonderful midway where there would be no parents . . . Mrs. Arable stood quietly and watched them go. Then she sighed. Then she blew her nose.

"Do you really think it's all right?" she asked.

"Well, they've got to grow up some time," said Mr. Arable. "And a fair is a good place to start, I guess."

— E.B. White, *Charlotte's Web*

Farmer with a Vision

Eliot Coleman sometimes refers to himself as a "backwards farmer" because at his Four Season Farm on Cape Rosier in mid-coast Maine, he begins much of his planting in the fall. Coleman, whose books and lectures have inspired thousands of small farmers in Maine — and, indeed, around the world — and his wife, Barbara Damrosch, a well-known author of gardening books, have turned the normal northern New England growing season upside down by designing a system of hoop houses and special plant covers that mimic perpetual spring in the dead of winter.

"It's like magic to lift up a plant cover when there's snow on the ground and see lettuce growing and radishes sprouting. I never get tired of it." Nor do his devoted customers, who dote on Four Season's "candy carrots," so called because of their intense natural sweetness; the small, round white turnips; the slender leeks; and a perfectly balanced mesclun mix that might include beet greens, a number of lettuces, frisée, claytonia, spinach, and arugula.

Chicken Roasted with Farm Vegetables

Several small farmers around the state of Maine are raising free range, organic, hormone-free chickens to supply good restaurants and sell through local outlets. One such small producer is Maine-ly Poultry in Warren. In fact, demand is so high that these farms could sell a lot more than they can produce. Not only are the chickens a better choice for the health-conscious, but they taste really wonderful — especially when roasted to golden perfection surrounded by caramelized root vegetables like the ones from Eliot Coleman's Four Season Farm.

1 chicken, 3 to 4 pounds

1 lemon

1 onion, quartered

4 garlic cloves

4 tablespoons extra-virgin olive oil

Salt and freshly ground black pepper

4 carrots, peeled and cut into 2-inch lengths

4 red-skinned potatoes cut into 1 1/2-inch chunks

4 turnips, peeled and cut into 1 1/2-inch chunks

4 garlic cloves

1 tablespoon chopped fresh rosemary leaves, plus sprigs for garnish

1/2 pound green beans, trimmed and steamed until barely tender

4 SERVINGS

1. Preheat the oven to 450°F.

2. Gently pull up the breast skin of the chicken. Cut half the lemon into thin slices and insert under the skin. Put the onion and remaining half lemon into the chicken cavity. Drizzle with 1 tablespoon of the olive oil and season inside and out with salt and pepper to taste. Tie the legs together with kitchen twine. Place the chicken on a rack in a large roasting pan and scatter the carrots, potatoes, turnips, and garlic around it. Sprinkle with more salt and pepper, drizzle with 2 tablespoons of the remaining olive oil, and sprinkle with the rosemary.

3. Roast for 20 minutes. Reduce the oven temperature to 325°F. Shake the pan to redistribute the vegetables, brush the chicken with the remaining tablespoon of oil, and return to the oven. Continue to roast, basting once or twice and shaking the pan or turning the vegetables, until an instant-read thermometer registers 165°F in the thickest part of the thigh, 40 to 50 minutes longer. Add the green beans to the vegetable mix about 5 minutes before the chicken is done.

4. Remove the chicken and let it rest for 10 minutes before carving. Arrange the carved chicken on a platter. Remove the lemon half from the cavity, squeeze it over the vegetables, and arrange the vegetables around the chicken. Garnish with the rosemary sprigs and serve.

Shaker Chicken Stew with Scallion Dumplings

"Nothing seems to bring people closer together than the act of sharing food," says Sister Frances Carr of Maine's Sabbathday Lake Shaker community. In her 1985 book, *Shaker Your Plate*, Sister Carr puts forth the Shaker philosophy that focuses on "plain, wholesome food . . . simple, but painstakingly prepared." This chicken stew with scallion-flecked dumplings is an adaptation of one of her exemplary recipes. Selling their wonderful home-grown and dried herbs is one of the ways that the Shaker community supports itself (see Mail-Order Sources, page 277), and I bet if you made this dish with their dried thyme, you'd notice the difference.

CHICKEN STEW

5 cups chicken broth

3 ½ pounds bone-in chicken thighs, excess fat removed (see Note)

1 medium onion, thinly sliced

2 celery ribs, thinly sliced

1 large bay leaf, broken in half

2 teaspoons dried thyme

2 ½ cups baby carrots (about ¾ pound)

Salt and freshly ground black pepper

SCALLION DUMPLINGS

1 ½ cups all-purpose flour

1 ½ teaspoons baking powder

½ teaspoon salt

2 tablespoons minced scallions or chives

3 tablespoons chilled solid vegetable shortening, cut into 5 pieces

½ cup plus 1 to 2 tablespoons whole, low-fat, or skim milk

4—6 SERVINGS

1. To make the Chicken Stew, bring the broth to a boil in a large soup pot or Dutch oven. Add the chicken, onion, celery, bay leaf, and thyme. Reduce the heat to medium-low and simmer, covered, until the chicken is about three-quarters cooked, 15 to 20 minutes. Add the carrots and continue to cook until the chicken is no longer pink, about 10 minutes longer. Remove from the heat.

2. Remove the chicken to a plate and, when cool enough to handle, strip off the skin, remove the meat from the bones, and cut into 2-inch chunks. Return the chicken meat to the broth and season with salt and pepper to taste.

3. To make the Scallion Dumplings, whisk together the flour, baking powder, and salt. Stir in the scallions. Work the shortening into the flour mixture, using your fingertips or a fork, until most of the pieces are about the size of small peas. Add ½ cup of the milk and stir with a fork until the dough comes together in a sticky mass. If the mixture seems dry, add some or all of the remaining milk.

4. Return the stew to a simmer. Dip a tablespoon into the simmering liquid, scoop out a rounded spoonful of dumpling dough, and drop it into the simmering stew. Repeat with the remaining dough, forming 12 to 14 dumplings. Cover the pot and simmer over low heat until the dumplings look shiny on top and are firm to the touch, about 15 minutes. Serve into shallow soup bowls.

Note: *If time is short, use about 1¾ pounds skinless, boneless thighs and cook for about half the time.*

Shaker Advice for Doing Good

**Do all the good you can,
In all the ways you can,
To all the People you can,
In every place you can,
At all the times you can,
As long as ever you can.
— Framed motto hung in the Maine
Sabbathday Lake community dining room**

Spicy Chicken Big Mamou

One of the anything-but-standard items on the menu of the A-1 Diner is this spicy, warming chicken mamou, the recipe for which was contributed by an A-1 waitress with a Cajun past.

4 tablespoons olive oil

1 large onion, chopped

3 garlic cloves, finely chopped

1 teaspoon dried thyme

½ teaspoon dried basil

½ teaspoon red pepper flakes

½ teaspoon freshly ground black pepper

½ teaspoon white pepper

1 can (28 ounces) crushed or puréed tomatoes

1 cup chicken broth

1 tablespoon sugar

1 tablespoon Worcestershire sauce

1¾ pounds boneless skinless chicken thighs, cut into 2-inch chunks

2 tablespoons mixed Cajun pepper seasoning (see Note)

Salt (optional)

1 bunch scallions, thinly sliced

Cooked white rice

6 SERVINGS

1. Heat 2 tablespoons of the oil in a large pot over medium heat. Add the onion and cook, stirring frequently, for 6 minutes. Add the garlic and cook, stirring, for 1 minute. Add the thyme, basil, pepper flakes, black and white pepper, and cook, stirring, for 1 minute.

2. Add the tomatoes, chicken broth, sugar, and Worcestershire sauce. Bring to a boil, reduce the heat to medium-low, and simmer, uncovered, until slightly reduced, about 20 minutes.

3. Season the chicken on all sides with the Cajun seasoning. Heat the remaining 2 tablespoons oil in a large skillet over medium to medium-high heat. Add the chicken and cook, turning once, until browned. Scrape the contents of the skillet into the sauce.

4. Simmer, uncovered, over medium-low heat, stirring occasionally, until the chicken is tender and no longer pink, about 30 minutes. Taste and season with salt, if desired. Stir in half the scallions, spoon the sauced chicken over the rice, and sprinkle with remaining scallions.

Note: *Use one of the Cajun spice mixtures of cayenne, other peppers, and herbs, or make your own by combining 1 teaspoon salt, ¾ teaspoon white pepper, ¾ teaspoon black pepper, ½ teaspoon cayenne pepper, 2 teaspoons ground cumin, 1 teaspoon dried thyme, and 1 teaspoon dried basil.*

THE A-1 DINER

The A-1 Diner in Gardiner is an ancient but well-preserved specimen of the dining-car diner. Inside, it's got wooden booths, laminate-top tables, and leatherette-seated stools at the counter, as well as a quilted steel wall and perfectly preserved tiles on the floor.

The place is such a wonderfully authentic vintage set piece that you'd probably be happy just to stop in for a look and a cup o' joe. But don't.

Co-chefs and -owners Mike Giberson and Neil Anderson are serious about their food, serving unusually delicious fare three meals a day. Baked beans, corned beef hash, biscuits, and mashed potatoes are homemade. Standards like meatloaf and fried chicken are there on the menu, but so are more upscale items like Creole Beans and Rice, Salmon with Pesto, and Eggplant Saffron Custard Gratin.

Spice-Trade Chicken Curry

The Maine table has been enlivened by the exotic spices of the Far East for a couple of centuries. Curries of various types, brought to New England coastal towns by English seamen, were a particular favorite. And they still are. Along about February or March, when the outside world is still brown and chill, I begin to crave curries — for their bright color as well as their powerful flavors. This one is sharp with spice, but mellowed and enriched by the coconut milk in the sauce.

2 tablespoons vegetable oil

1½ pounds skinless, boneless chicken thighs, cut into 2-inch chunks

Salt and freshly ground black pepper

1½ teaspoons cumin seeds

2 large onion, chopped

1 green bell pepper, chopped

3 garlic cloves, chopped

2 tablespoons peeled and grated or finely chopped fresh ginger (2-inch piece)

2 jalapeño chiles, chopped

3 tablespoons good-quality curry powder (see Note)

1 can (14½ ounces) unsweetened coconut milk

1 large tomato, seeded and finely chopped

3 tablespoons lime juice (juice of 2 medium limes) plus additional lime wedges

6 scallions, thinly sliced

¼ cup coarsely chopped fresh cilantro

Cooked jasmine or basmati rice

Chutney of your choice (optional)

4 SERVINGS

1. Heat the oil in a very large skillet or Dutch oven over medium-high heat. Season the chicken with salt and pepper to taste and sprinkle with the cumin seeds. Cook the chicken in the oil until nicely browned on all sides, 6 to 8 minutes. Remove with a slotted spoon to a plate, leaving the drippings in the pan.

2. Add the onions, green pepper, and garlic to the drippings and cook, stirring frequently, until softened, about 5 minutes. Add the ginger, jalapeños, and curry powder and cook, stirring, for 1 minute.

3. Add the coconut milk and tomato and return the chicken to the sauce. Bring to a boil, reduce the heat to low, and simmer, uncovered, until the chicken is very tender, about 30 minutes, adding water to the sauce if it begins to look in danger of sticking. (The curry can be cooked up to a day ahead and refrigerated. Reheat before finishing.)

4. Stir in the lime juice and adjust the seasonings to taste. Scatter with the scallions and cilantro and arrange the lime wedges around. Serve with the rice and pass a bowl of chutney, if desired.

Note: *Use a good-quality curry powder or a combination of standard curry powder and one of the newer curry spice blends, such as red curry powder.*

Turkey Cutlets with Crispy Cider-Corn Bread Dressing

Make this for supper when you're craving the flavors of Thanksgiving dinner but aren't the least bit interested in roasting a 20-pound bird. Of course, you need cranberry sauce. You could use store-bought whole-berry sauce, or make Cooked Cranberry-Pear Conserve (page 230). But then just add baked sweet potatoes and a green vegetable for a delicious autumnal meal.

1¼ pounds turkey cutlets, cut about ½-inch thick

Salt and freshly ground black pepper

2 teaspoons poultry seasoning mix, such as Bell's

4 tablespoons butter

1 large celery rib, chopped

1 small onion, chopped

1¾ cups packaged crumbled cornbread stuffing mix (about 4 ounces)

1 cup apple cider or apple juice

1 tablespoon chopped fresh sage

4 SERVINGS

1. Season the turkey cutlets with salt and pepper to taste and 1½ teaspoons of the poultry seasoning. Melt 2 tablespoons of the butter in a large skillet over medium heat. Add the turkey and cook in a single layer, in two batches if necessary, until barely colored and just cooked through, about 2 minutes per side. (Do not overcook at this point, or the turkey will be dry.) Remove the cutlets and arrange in a single layer in a shallow 2-quart broiler-safe baking dish. Leave the drippings in the pan.

2. Preheat the broiler.

3. Melt the remaining 2 tablespoons butter in the same skillet. Add the celery and onion and cook until lightly browned and softened, about 5 minutes. Add the stuffing mix, cider, sage, and remaining ½ teaspoon poultry seasoning and stir until the liquid is absorbed but the stuffing is still quite moist, about 3 minutes. Season with salt and pepper to taste.

4. Spoon the stuffing over the turkey. (The dish can be made up to an hour or two ahead and set aside at cool room temperature.)

5. Broil, 4 to 5 inches from the heat, until the stuffing is golden and crispy around the edges, 2 to 4 minutes.

Bell's Seasoning

In the 1860s, Willie Bell from Boston dreamed up the concept of an all-purpose seasoning blend that could be used for everything from turkey stuffing to oysters. This was a man well ahead of his time, predating by more than a century the myriad seasoning blends now crowding our spice shelves. Willie convinced his mother, who was a good cook, to help him, and they experimented with herbs from their kitchen garden, coming up with the formula that became Bell's Seasoning. A combination of powdered rosemary, oregano, sage, ginger, marjoram, thyme, and pepper, Bell's is still packaged in a distinctive yellow cardboard box with a colorful turkey on the front, and it's still the poultry seasoning of choice for most Yankees.

Hashed Turkey with Dried Cranberries

This is an updated turkey hash made with sweetened dried cranberries, which are one of my favorite "new" New England ingredients. The cranberries are dried with just enough added fructose to make them palatable, without sacrificing their pleasingly sour edge. The hash is the perfect vehicle for leftover turkey (or chicken), or you can make it with rotisserie-cooked turkey from the deli. I'd suggest a salad of dark leafy greens or steamed broccoli, and perhaps a plate of Crisp Ginger-Almond Wafers (page 272) to finish.

4 SERVINGS

4   cups cooked, unpeeled red-skinned potatoes, cut into ½-inch cubes

4   cups (1 pound) diced cooked turkey or chicken

6   scallions, thinly sliced

¾   cup dried sweetened cranberries

2   tablespoons chopped fresh sage (or 1 tablespoon crumbled dried sage leaves), plus fresh leaves for garnish (optional)

¾   teaspoon salt, or to taste

½   teaspoon coarsely ground black pepper

1   cup half-and-half or light cream

3–4 tablespoons olive oil

1. Toss together the potatoes, turkey, scallions, cranberries, sage, salt, and pepper in a large bowl. Drizzle with ½ cup of the half-and-half and toss to mix well.

2. Heat 3 tablespoons of the oil in a very large (about 12-inch), heavy skillet, or two medium skillets over medium-low heat. Add the hash mixture and use a spatula to press it down evenly. Cover the pan and cook for 15 minutes, uncovering to stir well every few minutes. Uncover, raise the heat to medium, and cook, stirring often, until the hash is crusty and rich golden brown, 8 to 10 minutes longer. If the hash seems dry, add the remaining tablespoon of oil during the last few minutes of cooking.

3. Just before serving, stir the remaining ½ cup half-and-half into the hash. Taste, adding more salt if desired. Garnish with the sage leaves, if desired, and serve.

Cranberries Down East

Mainers have come to expect more from local cranberry growers. Maine cranberry growers use a different variety of cranberries than do farmers in, say, Massachusetts. The result is a larger, more colorful and flavorful berry.

— Nan Bradshaw, owner of Bradshaw's Cranberry Farm in Dennysville, Washington County

Politics and Pie

Every small town in Maine holds a town meeting once a year, for which residents turn out for an hourslong session to hash out school budgets and debate road appropriations. On the Cranberry Isles, town business is mixed with community pleasure in the form of a community lunch organized by the Great Cranberry Isles Ladies Aid Society. One recent year, they served up a feast of chicken, biscuits, and approximately 20 homemade pies.

Seared Duck Breast with Cumberland Pan Sauce

Whether you get duck breasts from your friendly neighbor the bird hunter or buy farm-raised breasts from a supermarket, this rich, flavorful meat merits a special dinner.

GARLIC MARINADE

¼ cup olive oil

2 garlic cloves, crushed

2 tablespoons orange juice (juice of small orange)

2 tablespoons chopped fresh rosemary

1 tablespoon soy sauce

½ teaspoon freshly ground black pepper

4 skinless, boneless duck breasts (6 ounces each) (see Note)

CUMBERLAND PAN SAUCE

1 tablespoon butter

1 tablespoon olive oil

2 tablespoons finely chopped shallots (2 large shallots)

1 cup port

¼ cup orange juice (juice of medium orange)

3 tablespoons red currant jelly

2 tablespoons red wine vinegar

1½ tablespoons grainy Dijon mustard

1 tablespoon chopped fresh rosemary, plus sprigs for garnish

Half an orange, sliced thinly, slices halved

Salt and freshly ground black pepper

1. To make the Garlic Marinade, whisk together the olive oil, garlic, orange juice, rosemary, soy sauce, and pepper in a large bowl. Add the duck breasts, turn to coat, and refrigerate for at least 2 hours, or overnight.

2. Remove the duck from the marinade and pat dry with paper towels.

3. To make the Cumberland Pan Sauce, heat the butter and oil in a very large skillet over medium-high heat. Brush some of the oil/butter mixture on the duck. When the pan is hot, cook the duck until seared (browned) outside and medium-rare within, 2 to 3 minutes per side, depending on thickness. Remove to a plate and tent with foil to keep warm, leaving the drippings in the pan.

4. To finish the sauce, add the shallots to the skillet and cook, stirring, for 1 minute. Add the port, orange juice, and jelly and cook briskly until the jelly melts. Whisk in the vinegar, mustard, and rosemary and cook until the sauce is slightly reduced and thickened, about 4 minutes. Add the orange slices and season with the salt and pepper to taste.

5. Slice the duck on the diagonal, arrange on plates, spoon the sauce over, and serve.

Note: *If you use wild duck, allow 2 to 3 breast halves per person, depending on their size. Since the wild meat is especially lean, be very careful not to overcook it.*

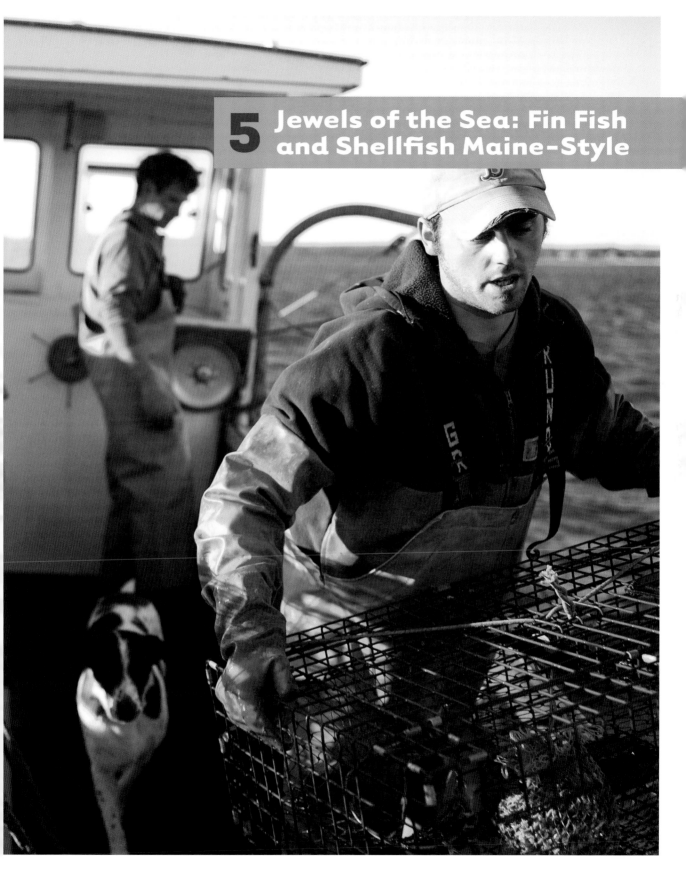

Roasted Whole Striped Bass with Lemon and Pesto

Wild striped bass, or "stripers," have been staging something of a comeback recently. Once threatened by commercial fishing and pollution, these beautiful large, silvery, black-striped fish are now being caught in summer by sports fishermen in New England rivers and bays. Striped bass are also being farmed, and those fish are usually in the 1½-pound range. The flesh of stripers is firm, meaty, and utterly delicious — and is perfectly complemented by a brushing with garlicky herb pesto as it roasts at a high heat.

2   whole striped bass, 1½ pound each, or one larger fish, cleaned

1   cup or so South Paris Mint-Walnut Pesto (page 85) or other pesto

Thin lemon slices

Mint or parsley sprigs, or both, for garnish

4 SERVINGS OR MORE, IF ROASTING A LARGER FISH

1. Preheat the oven to 500°F. Grease a baking dish (large enough to hold the bass) with oil.

2. Rinse and dry the bass thoroughly and cut 3 or 4 slashes in each side, right down to the bone. Place in the prepared dish and brush inside and out generously with the pesto. Arrange the lemon slices down the center.

3. Roast until the fish is opaque down to the bone and flakes easily when tested with a fork at the thickest part, 15 to 20 minutes for smaller fish, 25 to 35 minutes for larger fish.

4. Remove to a platter, garnish with the mint, and serve.

Island Recipe

Orr's Island native Walter Leeman professes that "God's greatest gift to mankind is the sow hake" [a very large, not-terribly-well-known fish] and boasts that he can stretch one fish to feed himself four consecutive dinners. "I'll fry it the first night, corn it the second [an old-fashioned preparation of salting the hake and serving it with fried salt pork bits, chopped onions, vinegar, and boiled potatoes], make hash the third, and my favorite fish cakes are last." I have opened Walter's refrigerator on many occasions over the past twenty years and have never seen it devoid of hake in its various stages of the four-day meal plan.

— Linda Greenlaw, *Recipes from a Very Small Island*

Oven-Roasted Cod with Prosciutto-Garlic Topping

Although it has become somewhat scarce, cod is still a favorite fish in Maine. I love it cooked this way, roasted at a high heat, with this salty, herby, lemony, garlicky topping, which gets crispy and delicious in the hot oven, and is the perfect foil for the clean, neutral flavor of cod. You could actually use any white fish for this — halibut would be great, for instance, or monkfish or catfish or sea bass or . . . Though the recipe is simple, it's elegant enough to be the centerpiece for a special meal. Serve it with a rice pilaf, steamed baby summer squash and, to finish, something fruity, like Mixed Summer Fruit Cobbler (page 253), or, in cooler months, Farm Stand Apple Crisp with Walnut-Oat Crunch (page 254).

PROSCIUTTO-GARLIC TOPPING

4 SERVINGS

1/2   cup (about 2 ounces) chopped prosciutto

1/4   cup chopped fresh flat-leaf parsley

3   tablespoons chopped fresh basil

1   large garlic clove, minced

2   teaspoons coarsely grated or chopped lemon zest

1/4   teaspoon coarse-ground black pepper

COD

2   tablespoons olive oil

4   cod fillets, about 6 ounces each

Salt and freshly ground black pepper

3/4   cup dry white wine

1. To make the Prosciutto-Garlic Topping, toss together the prosciutto, parsley, basil, garlic, lemon zest, and pepper in a small bowl.

2. Preheat the oven to 500°F. Brush a shallow rimmed baking sheet or baking pan with some of the oil. Place the fish in the pan and season with salt and pepper to taster. Sprinkle with the topping, patting it on evenly. Drizzle with the remaining oil and pour the wine around the fish.

3. Roast until the fish is no longer translucent, flakes easily with a fork, and the topping is crispy and browned, about 5 minutes for every 1/2 inch of thickness.

4. Serve on individual plates or on a platter with the pan juices spooned over the fish.

Salt Codfish Cakes with Bacon

This is basically my grandmother's codfish cake recipe, the one I remember with nostalgic affection from my childhood. Grandmother Allie Hayward was a Bermudian, my grandfather, a Connecticut Yankee, and in both places dried salt cod played a major culinary role for centuries. After a couple of decades of scarcity, salt cod is again readily available, especially in locales with a substantial Portuguese or Caribbean population. Codfish and potatoes, like my grandparents' "bicoastal" marriage, are natural partners, with the tangy saltiness of the fish smoothed and tempered by the neutral starchiness of potatoes.

1   pound boneless salt cod

2   pounds russet, Yukon gold, or all-purpose potatoes, peeled and cut into 2-inch chunks

4   tablespoons butter

½   teaspoon freshly ground black pepper

⅓–½ cup half-and-half or light cream

Salt (optional)

8   slices bacon

Olive oil or butter, if necessary, for cooking

2   tablespoons chopped fresh parsley

4 SERVINGS

1. Soak the cod in a large dish in cold water to cover overnight, changing the water twice.

2. Drain, place the cod in a saucepan or large skillet, add water to cover, and bring to a boil. Simmer over medium-low heat until the fish is soft and flakes easily with a fork, 15 to 20 minutes. Drain and, when cool enough to handle, strip off and discard any skin and remove any bones.

3. Cook the potatoes in a large pot in salted water to cover until they are tender, about 20 minutes. Drain well and put through a ricer or return to the pot and mash with a potato masher or large fork. Add the flaked cod, butter, and pepper and beat with a wooden spoon, adding enough half-and-half to make a smooth but stiff mixture. Season with salt, if desired (keeping in mind that the bacon will add a bit more saltiness).

4. Shape into 8 to 12 cakes, ½-inch thick each. (The cod cakes can be shaped up to several hours ahead and refrigerated.)

5. Cook the bacon in a large skillet over medium heat until crisp, about 10 minutes. Remove and drain on paper towels, leaving the drippings in the pan.

6. Cook the codfish cakes over medium heat in the bacon drippings (in two skillets or two batches if necessary), supplementing the bacon fat with a bit of the oil or butter to keep them from sticking. Cook until golden brown and heated through, 3 to 4 minutes per side.

7. Break the bacon strips in half, place over the cod cakes, sprinkle with the parsley, and serve.

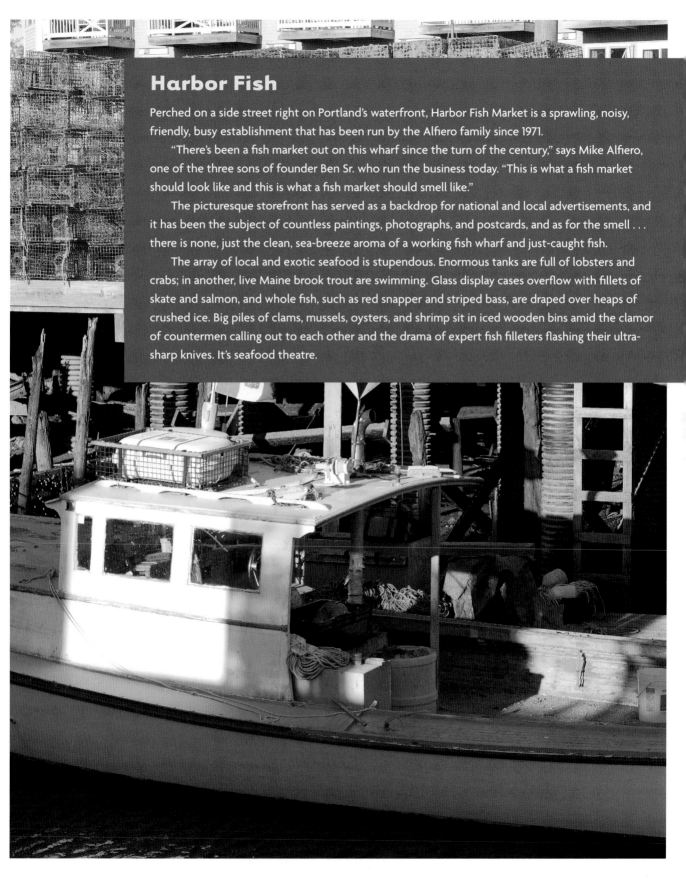

Harbor Fish

Perched on a side street right on Portland's waterfront, Harbor Fish Market is a sprawling, noisy, friendly, busy establishment that has been run by the Alfiero family since 1971.

"There's been a fish market out on this wharf since the turn of the century," says Mike Alfiero, one of the three sons of founder Ben Sr. who run the business today. "This is what a fish market should look like and this is what a fish market should smell like."

The picturesque storefront has served as a backdrop for national and local advertisements, and it has been the subject of countless paintings, photographs, and postcards, and as for the smell . . . there is none, just the clean, sea-breeze aroma of a working fish wharf and just-caught fish.

The array of local and exotic seafood is stupendous. Enormous tanks are full of lobsters and crabs; in another, live Maine brook trout are swimming. Glass display cases overflow with fillets of skate and salmon, and whole fish, such as red snapper and striped bass, are draped over heaps of crushed ice. Big piles of clams, mussels, oysters, and shrimp sit in iced wooden bins amid the clamor of countermen calling out to each other and the drama of expert fish filleters flashing their ultra-sharp knives. It's seafood theatre.

Findon's Haddock

The probably apocryphal version of the story is that finnan haddie, which is smoked and lightly salted haddock, was invented in Findon, near Aberdeen, Scotland, when a warehouse full of haddock caught fire and inadvertently smoked the entire catch of the day.

However, Sandra Oliver, a Maine food historian, says the more likely (though less dramatic) story is that Findon's fishwives beheaded and split small haddock (haddie), lightly salted them, and then hung them in the chimney "where the peat reek rose." This domestic curing method was probably common in Scotland by 1800, and during the nineteenth century, demand for Findon (which got slurred to "finnan") haddie grew so strong that the curing process became a commercial venture in Britain and also in New England.

Says Oliver, "You sometimes draw a blank look in the seafood departments of southern New England markets when you ask if they have finnan haddie, but not so here in Maine. We

Baked Seafood-and-Herb-Stuffed Haddock

Oh, isn't stuffed fish a lovely party dish? It always feels so special and guests are so appreciative of the bit of extra effort it involves. The extra treat in this herby stuffing is some chopped fresh shrimp, which contribute their pretty color as well as some additional flavor. Since haddock fillets are a little too thick to roll comfortably, the fish are cut in half to create a sandwich for the savory stuffing. If you do have thinner fillets (sole or flounder, for example) you can make rolls and secure them with a toothpick. How about accompaniments such as roasted red-skinned potatoes, skinny green beans, and a light lettuce salad?

½ cup (1 stick) butter

¼ cup finely chopped celery (½ rib)

¼ cup chopped onion (½ medium onion)

¼ cup chopped scallions (2 scallions)

¼ cup chopped shelled and deveined Maine shrimp, about 1 ounce

1½ cups fresh breadcrumbs (see Note)

3 tablespoons chopped fresh flat-leaf parsley

½ teaspoon salt for the stuffing, plus more to season the haddock

¼ teaspoon freshly ground black pepper for the stuffing, plus more to season the haddock

2–3 tablespoons plus ½ cup dry white wine

4 haddock fillets (6–8 ounces each)

Lemon wedges

4 SERVINGS

1. Heat 2 tablespoons of the butter in a large skillet over medium heat. Add the celery, onion, and scallions and cook, stirring frequently, until the celery is quite soft, 5 to 6 minutes.

2. Add the shrimp and cook, stirring, until they turn pink, 2 to 3 minutes. (If the shrimp are cooked, simply stir them in and heat through.)

3. Stir in the breadcrumbs, parsley, salt, and pepper. Sprinkle with the 2 tablespoons of the white wine, adding the third tablespoon if needed to make the stuffing hold together. (The stuffing can be made up to 1 day ahead and refrigerated.)

4. Grease a large baking dish with butter. Preheat the oven to 400°F.

5. Cut each fillet crosswise to make a total of 8 pieces. Arrange 4 pieces in the baking dish and season lightly with salt and pepper to taste. Divide the stuffing over the fish, pressing to make an even layer, and top with the remaining fish. (The recipe can be prepared to this point up to 8 hours ahead and refrigerated.)

6. Melt the remaining 6 tablespoons butter in a small saucepan and whisk in the remaining ½ cup wine. Pour over the fish, then season the tops lightly with salt and pepper to taste. Bake until the fish flakes easily when tested with a fork in its thickest part and the stuffing is heated through, 20 to 30 minutes, depending on the thickness of the fish. Garnish with the lemon wedges and serve.

Note: *Tear 3 slices of good-quality bread into pieces and whir in a food processor to make breadcrumbs.*

Politically Incorrect at the Empire Diner

Old Roger Sperry's favorite special had always been Deep-Fried Haddock with Tartar Sauce, Whipped Potatoes with Beef Gravy, a side of Apple Sauce and Parker House Rolls. It was also his firm conviction that there wasn't much point in fighting a world war if you were going to come home and start serving things in *hoisin* sauce — whatever that was.

— Richard Russo, *Empire Falls*

THE BROOKLIN INN

The Brooklin Inn is a small, friendly, low-key hostelry in Brooklin, Maine, that also happens to have a fabulous dining room. Innkeepers Chip and Gail Angell are members of Chef's Collaborative, a national network that promotes sustainable cuisine by celebrating local, seasonal, and artisanal cooking.

"We try to know who raised, grew, picked, or caught all the food you eat here," says Chip.

The menu changes daily and boasts that "all our meat and produce is organic, if not local; and local, if not organic." Local farmers, producers, and ice cream makers are proudly listed. Such first courses as local mussels Dijon, crab cakes on mizuna leaves, heirloom tomatoes with manchego cheese, and roasted beet salad prove the point. Main courses vary, and include chicken under a brick with shiitake risotto, local bouillabaisse, and duck with a fig glaze.

Desserts are such updated classics as berry crisps with locally made ice cream, a delicate steamed chocolate pudding, and fabulous fruit tarts.

Milk-Poached Finnan Haddie with Hard-Cooked Eggs

At the Brooklin Inn, this wonderful dish of locally smoked haddock with potatoes and hard-cooked eggs is served (usually in colder weather) with wilted local rainbow chard.

1½ pounds smoked haddock

2½ cups whole milk

8 small red-skinned potatoes, halved

1 tablespoon arrowroot

4 hard-cooked eggs, thinly sliced

Freshly ground black pepper and salt

Parsley sprigs for garnish

4 slices good-quality white sandwich bread, toasted and cut into quarters (toast points)

4 SERVINGS

1. Place the haddock in a large, nonreactive (see Note) skillet, pour the milk over it, and let soak for 1 hour. Place the pan over medium-high heat, bring to a gentle boil, reduce the heat to low, and simmer, uncovered, until the fish flakes easily with a fork, 15 to 20 minutes.

2. Meanwhile, cook the potatoes in a saucepan of boiling salted water to cover until tender, about 15 minutes. Drain.

3. Grease a shallow 2- to 2½-quart baking dish with butter. Preheat the oven to 400°F.

4. Remove the haddock from the milk with a slotted spoon, break into large chunks, removing any bones, and layer in the bottom of the prepared dish. Arrange the cooked potatoes around the edge.

5. Reheat the milk over medium heat. Spoon some hot milk into a small bowl and whisk in the arrowroot, then whisk the arrowroot mixture back into the milk in the skillet. Pour the lightly thickened sauce over the haddock, then scatter the eggs over the top. Season with pepper and salt to taste. The haddock could be salty enough. (The dish can be prepared ahead to this point and set aside at cool room temperature for a couple of hours or refrigerated.)

6. Bake the haddock until it flakes easily with a fork and is golden brown on top, about 15 minutes. Garnish with the parsley and serve with the toast points.

   Note: *Stainless steel and enameled cast iron are nonreactive. Avoid aluminum and uncoated iron.*

PRIMO

When Melissa Kelly and Price Kushner opened Primo in Rockland, Maine, in 2000, the culinary world took notice — and beat a path to their door. Located in a renovated 110-year-old house south of town, Primo has five cozy country dining rooms and an upstairs bar built out of old doors from the original house. Extensive organic gardens surround the restaurant; they furnish the kitchen with vegetables, fruits, and inspiration for the dazzling, mostly Mediterranean-style food.

Every day at Primo, there is a new menu, always with a couple of fabulous wood-fired, thin-crust pizzas; several appetizers (for example, wild nettle soup, ginger-glazed pork belly, wood-oven roasted Nantucket bay scallops, fresh goat cheese wrapped in grape leaves and grilled); a couple of pastas (house-made); and such main dishes as grilled duck breast with a celeriac-pear purée, scaloppine of pork in a fresh sage sauce, and grilled swordfish atop smoked paprika semolina gnocchi.

Desserts are amazing. Imagine the likes of lemon soufflé tart with fresh blackberries, orange-scented crème caramel with vanilla poached cranberries, and homemade gelato.

Seared Halibut on Native Corn and Lobster Risotto

If you can't get local or extremely fresh halibut, you could be consoled with the corn and lobster risotto — great on its own — that accompanies Primo's rendition of Maine halibut.

NATIVE CORN AND LOBSTER RISOTTO

4 SERVINGS

1   ear of corn

1   tablespoon butter

1   tablespoon olive oil

2   tablespoons chopped onion

2   large garlic cloves, minced

1   cup Arborio rice

1/2   cup dry white wine

3   cups chicken, vegetable, or lobster stock (see Note), or a combination, plus more if necessary

1/2   cup fresh shelled peas (from about 1/2 pound in the pod)

3/4   cup diced cooked lobster meat (about 3 ounces)

2   tablespoons grated Parmesan cheese

Salt and freshly ground black pepper

1   tablespoon chopped fresh parsley

1   tablespoon chopped fresh tarragon

SEARED HALIBUT

4   pieces (6 ounces each) halibut fillet

Salt and freshly ground black pepper

1   tablespoon olive oil

1. To make the risotto, stand the husked ear of corn on end and use a sharp knife to remove the kernels. Set aside.

2. Heat the butter and the oil in a medium-large, heavy saucepan. Add the onions and cook over medium heat until they begin to soften, about 3 minutes. Add the garlic and cook, stirring, for 1 minute. Add the rice and stir to coat with the butter and oil. Add the wine, raise the heat to high, and cook, stirring, until the liquid evaporates, 1 to 2 minutes.

3. Meanwhile, heat the broth in a saucepan.

4. Add one-third of the warm broth to the rice and cook, stirring almost constantly, until most of the liquid has absorbed, about 5 minutes. Repeat with another third of the broth. Add the last third of the broth, along with the corn and peas, and cook until most of the liquid is absorbed and the rice is swollen and tender but still firm to the bite, about 5 minutes. Set aside, partially covered.

5. Preheat the oven to 500°F.

6. Season the halibut on both sides with salt and pepper to taste. Heat the oil in a large ovenproof skillet over medium-high heat. When the oil is hot, add the fish. Do not move the pieces until they begin to brown, 2 to 3 minutes. Turn the fish and place the whole pan in the oven for about 5 minutes or until they flake easily with a fork.

7. To finish the risotto, reheat over low heat, adding a bit more broth if necessary. Stir in the lobster meat and cheese and season with salt and pepper to taste.

8. To serve, spoon risotto onto plates and lean the fish on the risotto at an angle. Sprinkle with the parsley and tarragon and serve.

Note: *You can make a simple lobster stock by simmering lobster bodies in water to cover and then straining out the solids.*

Mackerel with Caper and White Wine Sauce

Lately, the kitchen at Street & Co. has been cooking up the fresh local mackerel in all sorts of delicious ways. This treatment, in which the fish is split and filled with a Mediterranean-inspired stuffing, is one they deemed most successful. It might be served with a mélange of roasted vegetables on the side.

4 SERVINGS

SAVORY STUFFING

1	cup breadcrumbs
6	tablespoons butter
1	tablespoon minced shallot (1 large shallot)
1	garlic clove, minced
2	tablespoons currants, finely chopped
2	tablespoons finely chopped kalamata olives
2	tablespoons sun-dried tomatoes, finely chopped

MACKEREL AND SAUCE

4	mackerel (1 pound each)
1	cup bottled clam juice or chicken broth
1	cup dry white wine
¼	cup (½ stick) butter
¼	cup drained capers
1½	tablespoons lemon juice (juice of ¾ medium lemon)
	Salt and freshly ground black pepper
2	tablespoons olive oil

1. To make the Savory Stuffing, toast the breadcrumbs in a medium-sized skillet over medium heat until one shade darker, 3 to 4 minutes. Remove to a bowl. In the same skillet, heat the butter. Add the shallots and garlic and sauté over medium heat for 2 minutes. Add to the breadcrumbs, along with the currants, olives, and sun-dried tomatoes. Toss to combine.

2. To prepare the mackerel, scale and butterfly the fish by cutting down through the backbone, opening up the fish, and removing the bones. (Better yet, ask the fish market to do this.) Leave the skin intact and the head on. Open the fish up like a book so it lies quite flat. Refrigerate until ready to cook. Repeat with the remaining mackerel.

3. Preheat the oven to 400°F.

4. To make the sauce, combine the clam juice and wine in a medium-sized saucepan. Bring to a boil and cook briskly until the liquid is reduced by about half, about 5 minutes. Add the butter, capers, and lemon juice, and swirl until the butter melts.

5. Season the mackerel with salt and pepper to taste. Heat the oil in two ovenproof skillets over medium-high heat. Place the mackerel in the pans flesh-side down and cook until the flesh is golden brown, about 2 minutes. Turn and cook skin-side down for 2 minutes.

6. Spoon the stuffing into the head cavities and roast in the oven until the stuffing is heated through, the mackerel skin is crispy and brown, and the fish flakes easily when tested with a fork, about 5 minutes. Transfer to a platter or dinner plates.

7. Meanwhile, reheat the sauce. When the mackerel are cooked, pour the sauce over them and serve.

STREET & CO.

Sometimes, when you're strolling the dimly lit cobbled back streets of Portland's Old Port, you'd swear you had time-traveled back into an earlier century. Wharf Street, where Street & Co. resides, is just such a lane. But when you step through the doors into the warmly lit, welcoming, and very twenty-first century ambience of this restaurant, you're happy to be in the here and now.

Street & Co. specializes in seafood (especially local seafood) cooked simply, but often with the bold and garlicky seasoning notes of the Mediterranean. A raw bar featuring well-iced Maine clams and oysters runs along the back of the room, and the kitchen is open — all the better to watch the half-dozen or so young chefs do their beautifully choreographed dance at the stoves. There's a regular menu and a specials menu, which is printed up each day. So you might order your tuna or sole or scallops grilled or blackened or broiled, or be interested in something more elaborate, like sea bass with mussels and garlic, grilled local squid tossed with a puttanesca sauce, or one of the latest mackerel recipes.

Grilled Fourth-of-July Salmon with Chive Egg Sauce

In early Maine days, when the state's larger rivers — the Kennebec, Androscoggin, Penobscot — ran rich with salmon, Independence Day was rung in with the fruits of the early summer season. The traditional celebratory meal consisted of salmon with egg sauce, fresh green peas, tiny new potatoes, and strawberry shortcake for dessert. This is a slightly updated version of the salmon. Classically, the egg sauce is made with a white sauce base, which I believe tends to obscure the other flavors, so mine is a simple wine and cream base. You must — those are strict instructions — have fresh peas with this meal. You'll need about three-quarters of a pound of peas in their pods for each person, so share the labor by turning it into a communal shelling bee.

CHIVE EGG SAUCE

3	tablespoons butter
2	tablespoons minced shallots (2 large shallots)
1/2	cup bottled clam juice
1/2	cup dry white wine
1	cup heavy cream
1/2	teaspoon salt
1/4	teaspoon freshly ground black pepper
2	hard-cooked eggs, coarsely chopped
1	tablespoon lemon juice (juice of 1/2 medium lemon)
3	tablespoons snipped fresh chives

GRILLED SALMON

6	salmon steaks or fillets, 6–7 ounces each
2	tablespoons olive oil

Salt and freshly ground black pepper

Chive spears (with purple flowers attached if possible)

Lemon wedges

1. To make the Chive Egg Sauce, melt the butter in a medium-sized saucepan over medium heat. Add the shallots and cook for 1 minute. Add the clam juice and wine, bring to a boil, and cook briskly until reduced by about one-third, 2 to 3 minutes. Add the cream and simmer over medium heat until slightly reduced and thickened, about 2 minutes. Season with the salt and pepper. Add the eggs and lemon juice and stir gently so as not to break up the egg yolks too much. (The sauce can be made up to 24 hours ahead and refrigerated. Reheat in a microwave and stir in the chives before serving.) Gently stir in the chives.

2. Brush the grill rack with oil. Build a moderately hot charcoal fire or preheat a gas grill to medium-high.

3. Brush the salmon on both sides with the oil and season with the salt and pepper to taste. Grill the fish, turning carefully once with a large spatula, until the flesh just turns opaque in the thickest part and flakes easily when tested with a fork, about 5 minutes per 1/2 inch of thickness. (If you like your salmon more on the rare side, reduce the cooking time.) Transfer to a serving platter and garnish with the chive spears and lemon. Pass the Chive Egg Sauce in a sauceboat for spooning over the salmon.

Smelts for Breakfast

Smelt fishing is a rite of early spring in Maine. It's done at night, when the smelts are migrating from their saltwater home upriver to spawn. After dark, if you go out to streams and inlets in the middle of nowhere, you'll sometimes find little orbs of lantern or firelight and people standing around with long-handled fishing nets. If you're lucky, the water will be roiling with small (they measure four to six inches) sparkling silver smelts. If the smelts are on the smaller side, they're cooked whole — rolled in seasoned flour and fried — if larger, they're cleaned by quickly twisting off the head and pulling out the innards. Although smelts freeze well, they're best eaten fresh — for breakfast, with the fingers.

BRADFORD CAMPS

Bradford Camps' guests arrive via float plane to remote Munsungun Lake west of Ashland, one of the most scenic areas of northeastern Maine. They're warmly greeted by camp owners Karen and Igor Sikorsky and shown to one of several vintage log cabins on the lake. After settling in, guests meet one of Bradford's certified Maine guides, who might take them trout or salmon fishing or partridge (grouse) hunting. Or they can swim, hike, canoe, kayak, or just relax on the porch. And eat.

Meals are served in the homey main lodge and generous, well-cooked meals they are. Breakfasts: the stuff of legend. Eggs all ways, bacon, sausages, muffins, pancakes, homemade toast, and just-caught trout. Lunches are packed or served in the lodge. After a day on the water or in the woods, Igor and Karen offer cocktails on the porch, cooled with ice cut from the lake each winter. Saturday night dinner is usually bean-hole beans and all the fixins (see page 132). Other nights' meals consist of such soul-satisfying fare as roast pork chops or pork loin, roast turkey with all the trimmings, prime rib, and fried chicken or fish, all served with salads and vegetables from their garden, and home-baked pie or cake for dessert.

A typical testimonial from a satisfied guest: "Bradford Camps is truly a gem! The food is delicious and everyone creates a warm, relaxed atmosphere. Karen and Igor run this camp with expertise, generosity, and a fun-loving spirit. Thank you!"

Pan-Fried Trout

At Bradford Camps, cook Donna Beloin fries their just-caught trout in bacon fat, so you'll need to plan to cook up some bacon and eat it with the meal (breakfast, lunch, or supper) or substitute half butter, half vegetable oil as the frying medium.

8 small brook trout (about 8 ounces each), or 4 pan-sized trout (about 1 pound each), cleaned

1/2 cup milk

1/2 cup all-purpose flour

3/4 teaspoon Old Bay or other seafood seasoning mix

1/2 teaspoon salt

1/2 teaspoon freshly ground black pepper

4 tablespoons bacon fat (see Note)

Lemon wedges

4 SERVINGS

1. Rinse the trout and trim off the fins with kitchen shears. Place the milk in a shallow dish. In another shallow dish, stir together the flour, Old Bay seasoning, salt, and pepper.

2. Heat the bacon fat in two medium-large skillets. Dip the trout in the milk and dredge in the flour mixture, shaking off the excess. Cook over medium to medium-high heat until well browned and crisp on the first side, 3 to 4 minutes. If the fish curls up, which very fresh trout tend to do, press down with a spatula so it cooks evenly. Turn and cook on the second side until browned and crisp and the flesh flakes easily when tested with a fork at the thickest part, 3 to 5 minutes. Do not overcook, or the trout will lose flavor.

3. Remove from the pan, garnish with the lemon wedges, and serve.

A Fisherman's Supper

Jeff McEvoy, of Weatherby's Camps in Grand Lake Stream, says, "If the client has caught a salmon the guide will grill that in a fold-up grill on the open fire. They may have some chicken on hand as well. They boil up onions and potatoes, and generally have homemade bread, sweet pickles, and a homemade dessert. Fresh guide's coffee is made by mixing up coffee grounds with raw egg — shell and all — and adding that to the coffeepot on the fire. You boil it up and then take it off the fire, let the grounds and eggshell settle to the bottom, and then serve it up."

— Alice Arlen, *The Maine Sporting Camp Cookbook*

THOMASTON CAFÉ

Several national publications have discovered The Thomaston Café. "A real gem," *Discoveries* magazine reports. Says the *New York Times:* "enduringly Yankee, with a modern flair." *Down East* magazine says "every town should have a restaurant like the Thomaston Café." Run by German-born Herbert Peters and his wife, Eleanor, the café has a friendly, casual feel that is indeed quintessentially Yankee, but much of the food has something of a European accent.

Fresh local ingredients star. Blueberry buckwheat pancakes are topped with Maine maple syrup. Lunch features are quesadillas made with local organic chicken, fresh Maine crab cakes (almost entirely fresh crab, hardly any filler), salads of local organic greens and homemade soups. At dinner, the lights dim and you can order the likes of seared diver scallops with wilted greens, Israeli couscous with local wild mushrooms, or their signature dish, scrumptious lobster ravioli in a light wine and cream sauce. Every town should be so lucky.

Dilled Fish Hash

This dilled fish hash, which is available for breakfast or lunch at Thomaston Café, uses local haddock, just as another hash variety, wild mushroom hash, is made with mushrooms from a Damariscotta farm.

4	tablespoons butter
1	medium onion, diced
1	celery rib, chopped
1/2	cup heavy cream
1	pound haddock, or other firm white fish fillet
2	eggs
2 1/2–3	cups coarse fresh breadcrumbs (see Note)
1 1/2	tablespoons chopped fresh dill
1	tablespoon Dijon mustard
1	teaspoon grated lemon zest
1	tablespoon lemon juice (juice of 1/2 medium lemon)
1/2	teaspoon salt
1/4	teaspoon white pepper
	Lemon wedges

4 SERVINGS

1. Melt the butter in a large, heavy skillet over medium heat. Add the onion and celery and cook, stirring occasionally, until softened, about 8 minutes. Add the cream and the haddock, bring to a boil, reduce the heat to medium, and cook, covered, until the haddock is opaque, about 10 minutes. Set aside to cool. Use a fork to flake the haddock.

2. Lightly beat the eggs in a large bowl. Add 2½ cups of the breadcrumbs, dill, mustard, lemon zest and juice, salt, and pepper. Add the fish mixture and combine with a fork. Refrigerate the mixture for at least 1 hour, or overnight. If necessary, add enough of the remaining breadcrumbs to make the mixture firm enough to be shaped into cakes.

3. Shape the mixture into 8 cakes, each about ½-inch thick. Brush a griddle or large skillet with oil (use two pans if necessary to keep the cakes in a single layer) and heat over medium-high heat. Cook the cakes until nicely browned on both sides and heated through, 5 to 8 minutes. Serve with the lemon wedges.

Note: *Tear 6 slices of good-quality bread into pieces and whir in a food processor to make breadcrumbs.*

Julia's Good Fish Advice

Julia Child, who awakened a couple of generations of American cooks to the pleasures and proper techniques of good cooking, gives her usual clear, precise, no-nonsense advice on how to buy fresh fish. "Look into its eyes," advises Julia. "Make sure they're clear, never sunken. Touch the fish to make sure it's not slimy. Inspect the gills for good color. And sniff, sniff, sniff. If the fish is already wrapped in plastic, tear it off and smell the fish at the checkout counter before you bring it home. It should have a clean, non-fishy aroma, without a hint of ammonia. Once home, store it on ice or in the coldest part of the refrigerator. Cook it and eat it as soon as possible."

Classic Steamed Clams with Broth

Here's the classic method of steaming soft-shell clams — and, in my opinion, it's the best and only way. No gussying up with beer or onions or wine or herbs or whole spices — just the pure, primal, salty-sweet flavor of the clams themselves, with only a quick pass through broth and melted lemon butter for enhancement. You can serve steamers as the centerpiece of the meal, with maybe a salad to follow, or do them as an hors d'oeuvre (in which case this recipe would serve about eight people). Spread newspapers out on a picnic table, provide plenty of napkins and cold beer (Atlantic Brewing's Blueberry Ale would be a good choice), and enjoy the taste of seaside summer. And at the end of the feast, in a final grand gesture, true clam aficionados will want to drink down the last of the briny steel-gray broth.

4 quarts soft-shell (steamer) clams, scrubbed and soaked (see About Clams, opposite)

½ cup water

½ cup (1 stick) butter

1 tablespoon lemon juice (juice of ½ medium lemon)

4 SERVINGS

1. Rinse the clams. Put them in a large pot with the water. Cover and bring to a boil over high heat. Reduce the heat to medium-low and cook for 5 minutes. Check the clams; if they are all open, remove from the heat. If some are still closed, continue to cook for a few minutes until all open.

2. Melt the butter in a small saucepan, stir in the lemon juice, and pour into two small bowls.

3. Using a slotted spoon, transfer the clams to two serving bowls. Discard any clams that have not opened. Pour the broth (the clams exude a lot of liquid, so there should be a goodly amount) into one or two bowls, leaving any mud or sediment behind.

4. To eat the steamers, most people first pull off the black skin clinging to the edge of the clam and surrounding the neck. Next, holding it by the neck, dip the clam in broth, swishing it around to rinse and reheat, then dunk in the lemon butter, and, finally, pop into your mouth. Encourage people to sip the last of the broth, leaving, of course, any sediment behind.

About Clams

All clams are either hard-shell or soft-shell, and within each category, the smaller clams are more tender than the larger. The smallest hard-shells, such as littlenecks, (usually less than 2 inches across) are highly prized, both for eating raw or for cooking. The largest hard-shells, which run from 3 to 6 inches across, are called quahogs (pronounced *ko-hogs*) or chowder clams, and are best minced and used in chowders. Likewise, with soft-shells — also called steamers, because that is the way they're usually cooked — the smaller clams are more desirable for eating whole.

Buying. The clams must be alive when you buy them. Hard-shells are shut up quite tight and, if they're dead, you can move their shells apart. Live soft-shells react visibly when touched, retracting their necks and closing more tightly, although they're never closed all the way; hence, the name "gapers."

Storing. Don't store clams in sealed plastic or in fresh water. Just put them in a bowl and store in the refrigerator, where they should stay alive for several days — although the sooner you cook and eat them, the better.

Cleaning. Hard-shell clams require only a quick scrub with a stiff brush. Soft-shells often contain lots of sand or mud. Jasper White, noted Boston chef, recommends soaking them in big bowls of cold salted water for several hours, gently lifting them from one bowl to the other, changing and swishing the water, and repeating the process until the water is almost clear of any sediment. Any tiny amounts of remaining mud can be gotten rid of by dunking the clams in the broth they're served with.

Portuguese Clams with Linguiça

A few Portuguese fishermen made it up into Maine in the eighteenth and nineteenth centuries and stayed to settle and raise families, although not in anywhere near the numbers that established themselves in towns and cities along the Massachusetts and Rhode Island coasts. More and more Portuguese and Spanish ingredients, however, (spicy linguiça and chourico sausage, bacalao [dried salt cod], and smoked Spanish paprika, for example) are showing up in Maine markets, perhaps because lots of chefs are enamored of these intense Mediterranean flavors. Linguiça and chourico are both garlicky, spicy smoked pork sausage, and for all practical purposes they're interchangeable. Polish kielbasa is a good substitute.

¼ cup extra-virgin olive oil

3 Turkish bay leaves

½ pound linguiça or chourico, sliced about ½-inch thick

1 large onion, chopped

1 medium yellow or orange pepper, chopped

4 garlic cloves, finely chopped

2½ cups diced seeded tomatoes (about 1¾ pounds; canned are fine, drained of juice)

1 cup dry white wine

½ teaspoon liquid hot pepper sauce, such as Frank's, or to taste

Salt and freshly ground black pepper

4 dozen littleneck clams, scrubbed (see About Clams, page 187)

2 tablespoons chopped fresh cilantro

2 tablespoons chopped fresh flat-leaf parsley

4 SERVINGS

1. Heat the oil in a very large, deep skillet over medium heat. Add the bay leaves and cook over medium heat, turning with tongs, until they are one shade darker, about 2 minutes.

2. Push the bay leaves to one side and add the linguiça, onion, bell pepper, and garlic to the pan. Cook, stirring occasionally, until the linguiça browns lightly and the vegetables begin to soften, about 8 minutes.

3. Add the tomatoes and wine, raise the heat to high, and cook briskly, uncovered, until the liquid is reduced by about half, about 3 minutes. Season with the liquid hot pepper sauce and salt and pepper to taste. It should be spicy, but not overwhelmingly so. (The sauce can be prepared up to 2 days ahead and refrigerated. Reheat before proceeding.)

4. Add the clams to the sauce, cover the pan, and cook over medium heat until the shells open and the meat is just barely firm, about 10 minutes.

5. Spoon the clams and sauce into shallow soup plates, sprinkle with the cilantro and parsley, and serve.

Blue Hill Crab Boil

Why, I keep asking, don't more Mainers eat steamed crabs the way they do lobster? True, the local sand or rock crabs aren't quite as large as most Maryland blue crabs and, therefore, require more work to pick out the succulent, sweet meat, but still . . . Finally, I did come across a few folks who do a crab "boil" (actually the crabs are steamed) with Maine crabs — and, not coincidentally, they're all Maryland transplants, like my friend Leslie Walton. "We cover the table with newspaper and then with brown paper bags and just sit down with the crabs and a cold beer. They're fantastic," says Leslie. The simple lemon-lime mayo dipping sauce is my own addition, and it's strictly optional.

1–2 teaspoons Old Bay or other seafood seasoning mix

8–12 live crabs (about 1 pound each), or more crabs if they are smaller (see Note)

½ cup mayonnaise

1 teaspoon grated lemon zest

½ teaspoon grated lime zest

2 teaspoons lemon juice (juice of ⅓ medium lemon)

2 teaspoons lime juice (juice of about ½ medium lime)

¼ teaspoon cayenne pepper

4 SERVINGS

1. Bring about 1½ inches of water to a boil in one very large pot or two medium-sized pots and add the seafood seasoning. If the crabs' pincer claws are not pegged, use long tongs or wear gloves while handling them. Place the crabs, undersides down, in the pot(s). Cover, return to a boil, reduce the heat to medium, and steam until the crabs are bright orange-red and the meat in the largest claw is no longer translucent, 10 to 15 minutes.

2. Meanwhile, stir together the mayonnaise, lemon zest, lime zest, lemon juice, lime juice, and cayenne.

3. Drain the crabs in a colander and heap them onto a platter to serve. To eat the crabs, begin by cracking and pulling off the top shell. Twist off the claws and tap them gently with a mallet to crack the shells without crushing the meat. Remove the meat with picks. Break the bodies into sections and pull out the meat with your fingers or a pick. Dip into the lemon-lime mayo.

Note: *If using Maine crabs, the sand (or peekytoe) crabs contain more meat. With rock (or Jonah) crabs, most of the meat is in the large claws. Of course, this recipe also works beautifully with blue crabs or other edible varieties of the crustacean.*

Maine Crab Nomenclature

When you ask Maine fishermen what kinds of crabs they catch, the answer often comes back "just Maine crabs." Much of the Maine crab that ends up as crab cakes in high-end restaurants is called "Maine peekytoe" on restaurant menus. This name is probably a corruption of "picked (meaning crooked) toe," referring, in Maine dialect, to the crab's bent front legs. Peekytoe crabs are also called sand crabs, and they are a smaller cousin of the West Coast Dungeness. To further confuse matters, there is a similar-looking Maine crab called a rock crab or Eastern Jonah crab. The meat in rock crabs resides mostly in the claws, and it is less flavorful than peekytoe meat. I have hardly ever seen live crabs for sale in Maine. If you'd like to get some for your crab boil, it's best to inquire about them where you get your fresh lobsters. Lobster fishermen sometimes save crabs for "picking," and if they know someone is looking to buy some, they'll probably be able to provide.

Cundys Harbor Crab Cakes on Local Greens Vinaigrette

Summer and fall are the best seasons for crabmeat in Maine. That's when the "Fresh Crabmeat Today" signs go up from Cundys Harbor all the way up the coast to Eastport. The smallish sand or rock crabs crawl into traps with the lobsters and, instead of tossing them back overboard, Mainers have developed a well-regulated cottage industry of steaming, chilling, and painstakingly picking out the sweet crabmeat. This is my favorite crab-cake formula. It uses crushed Saltine crackers (not too many) and a light hand with seasonings so that the delicate sweet crab flavor can shine through. Of course any other good lump-style crab will work beautifully, whether from Maryland, Louisiana, or the West Coast.

1/2 cup mayonnaise

1   egg

2   tablespoons finely chopped chives or scallions

2   tablespoons chopped flat-leaf parsley

1 1/2 tablespoons Dijon mustard

1/4 teaspoon freshly ground black pepper

1   cup crushed Saltine crackers (about 30 crackers; see Note)

1   pound fresh lump-type crabmeat, picked over to remove any cartilage

1   tablespoon lemon juice (juice of 1/2 medium lemon)

3–4 tablespoons olive oil or vegetable oil

4   handfuls mixed mesclun greens

About 1/4 cup Simple Shallot Vinaigrette (page 58) or other vinaigrette

Lemon wedges

4 SERVINGS

1. Line a baking sheet with waxed paper.

2. Whisk together the mayonnaise, egg, chives, parsley, mustard, and pepper in a large bowl. Stir in the cracker crumbs. Add the crabmeat and lemon juice and stir gently but thoroughly to combine. (It's nice if some larger lumps of crabmeat remain intact.)

3. Shape the mixture into 8 patties, about 1/2-inch thick each, and place on the prepared baking sheet. Refrigerate for at least 30 minutes or up to 6 hours, covered, until the cakes are firm.

4. Heat the oil over medium heat in two large skillets. Cook the crab cakes, uncovered, until nicely browned, 3 to 5 minutes. Turn, cover the pan, reduce the heat to medium-low, and cook until the undersides are golden and the cakes are hot in the center (cut into one and test with a knife), about 5 minutes.

5. Mound the greens on four plates or a serving platter and drizzle lightly with the vinaigrette. Serve the crab cakes on top of the greens and garnish with the lemon wedges.

Note: *You can substitute unsalted common crackers or fresh or dry breadcrumbs — just add about 1/2 teaspoon salt to the mixture.*

Simple Steamed Maine Lobster

Lobster is Maine's crowning glory, the stunning jewel in its seafood crown. Among the countless ways to enjoy eating lobster — as an hors d'oeuvre tidbit on a pick; composed into a gorgeous summer salad; heaped into a butter-grilled roll; simmered in a stew; stuffed back into its beautiful red shell and baked — probably the most spectacular is the utterly straightforward, basic steamed Maine lobster with melted butter. It has everything: It feels opulent, yet is essentially simple; it's glamorous, yet hands-on and primitive; it's photo-op beautiful at the beginning of the meal and satisfyingly messy at the end. Above all, a perfectly steamed lobster has an incomparable taste: briny-sweet, rich, leaving the flavor of the sea and summer on the tongue.

1½ tablespoons salt

4   live lobsters, at least
     1¼ pounds each

½   cup (1 stick) butter, melted

1–2 tablespoons cider vinegar,
     white wine vinegar, or lemon
     juice (optional; see Note)

4 SERVINGS

1. Fill a large (4- to 5-gallon) kettle or two smaller pots with about 1½ inches of water. Add the salt to the water and bring to a boil. Meanwhile, as an optional step, place the lobsters in the freezer for 15 minutes to numb them.

2. Grasp the lobsters around their middle (I wear rubber gloves when handling them) and plunge them head first into the pot. Immediately cover the pot and return to a boil. Reduce the heat to medium and steam until the lobsters are done, approximately 10 minutes per pound. When fully cooked, the lobsters are bright red, and a sharp tug on one of their antennae pulls it out readily. If in doubt, break one of the lobsters apart where the body meets the tail. The meat should be creamy white, with no translucence.

3. Remove the lobsters from the pot with tongs and transfer to a colander in the sink. Place on plates and serve as-is, or, if desired, perform either of the following refinements: Use the tip of a small knife to punch a hole between the lobster's eyes and hold it over the sink to drain off excess liquid. Place the lobster on its back on a cutting board and use a large knife to split the lobster down through the underside and drain.

4. Divide the melted butter into two small bowls and add the vinegar, if desired, to one or both of the bowls.

   Note: *While the vinegar or lemon juice addition is not classic, I like the way it balances out the richness of both butter and lobster meat.*

To Buy and Cook Lobsters (*Homarus americanus*)

Hard- vs. soft-shell. Lobsters molt (shed their shells) several times a year. After molting, the shell begins to harden and the meat inside grows to fill the new shell. Because of the timing of their life cycle, most lobsters we eat in the summer are newly molted soft-shells, or are at some stage between soft- and hard-shelled. Very soft-shelled lobsters ("shedders") have very little meat and are watery, with somewhat spongy claw meat. Very hard-shelled lobsters are packed tightly with meat and their shells have calcified so much that major carpentry is often needed to open them. I find that the meat in hard-shells can often be tough. Hence, my preference is for lobsters with shells somewhere in between soft and hard, tending, when in doubt, to the soft side.

Storing. Lobsters must be alive before they go into the pot. When they die, they release gastric enzymes that begin to deteriorate the meat. If cooking live lobsters within 3 to 4 hours of purchase, simply store them in a bag in the coldest part of the refrigerator. Do not store them on ice or in tap water. For longer storage, wrap each lobster loosely in damp newspaper and store in the coldest part of the refrigerator — usually the bottom shelf. Hard-shells can be stored for a day or so; soft-shells are more perishable and often die if held overnight.

Steaming vs. boiling. Lobsters can be boiled in a large pot of salted boiling water, but I prefer to steam them in just an inch or so of water. Steaming has several advantages: It's safer and easier than dealing with a huge cauldron of boiling water; the water returns to a boil faster so timing is more accurate; it's less messy because there are fewer boilovers; and — most important — the lobsters have better flavor because they are less diluted with water.

Pots. Bigger is better. A large speckled enamel canning pot is ideal for cooking four lobsters, but really any large (such as 4- to 5-gallon capacity) pot will do nicely. Or use two smaller pots. The material doesn't need to be heavy-gauge metal — in fact, water will boil faster in a lighter-weight vessel.

Cooking. Run about 1½ inches of water into the pot and add about a tablespoon of salt. Bring the water to a boil. (Meanwhile, you can put the lobsters in the freezer for 15 minutes to numb them, making them less active when they hit the heat.) When the water is boiling, place the lobsters in the pot head first. Immediately clamp the lid back on tightly and return to a boil over high heat. Reduce the heat to medium to medium-high and steam according to the guidelines below until the shells turn bright red. (Another test for doneness is to tug on one antennae. If it pulls out relatively easily, the lobster is cooked.) Hard-shell lobsters take the longer cooking times.

1 pound — 9 to 10 minutes

1¼ pounds — 12 to 14 minutes

1½ pounds — 14 to 16 minutes

1¾ to 2 pounds — 17 to 19 minutes

THE MAINE DINER

The Maine Diner, painted a cheery blue and white and with flags flying from its roof, is perched handily on Route 1 in Wells, just a short hop off the interstate. Myles Henry and his brother Dick are savvy hosts, greeting locals and tourists, managing any crowds, and enthusiastically promoting their 25-year-old establishment. In addition to tons of seafood specialties, they feature such quintessential diner fare as baked pea beans, homemade mac 'n cheese, hot turkey sandwiches, chicken pot pie, salmon pie, and, for dessert, all manner of homemade pies, crisps, and . . . a delicious molassesy Indian pudding.

Lobster Pie

"It's just not practical to offer whole boiled lobster dinners at a diner," explains The Maine Diner co-owner Myles Henry. "So that's why we concentrate on serving lobster every *other* way — lobster stew, lobster salad rolls, lobster clubs, lobster quiche, and, probably our most famous dish, this rich cracker crumb-topped lobster pie, which has been in our family for many years."

4 lobsters, 1½ pounds each, rinsed

1 tablespoon salt, plus more for seasoning the stuffing

¾ cup (1½ sticks) butter, plus 4 tablespoons, melted

2 cups crushed Ritz crackers (48 crackers)

1 large lemon plus additional lemon wedges

Salt and freshly ground black pepper

Fresh parsley sprigs

4 SERVINGS

1. Bring about 2 inches of water to a boil in a large pot. Add the salt to the water and plunge the lobsters in, heads down. Return to a boil, reduce the heat to medium, and steam, covered, for 12 minutes. Drain, reserving about ½ cup of the cooking water.

2. When cool enough to handle, pick the meat out of the lobsters, working over a bowl to catch any juices. Remove and reserve the green tomalley. Cut the meat into 1½-inch chunks.

3. Preheat the oven to 425°F.

4. Heat the ¾ cup butter in a large skillet over medium-high heat. Add the cracker crumbs and cook, stirring often, until heated through. Stir in the reserved tomalley. Grate 2 teaspoons of zest from the lemon and squeeze the juice. Add both to the skillet. Add enough reserved lobster juices and cooking water to make a mixture that is about as moist as turkey stuffing. Season with the salt and pepper to taste.

5. Divide the lobster meat among four individual 8-ounce ramekins or transfer to a shallow 1½-quart baking dish. Cover with the cracker mixture, patting it on evenly. (The recipe can be prepared to this point up to 8 hours ahead and refrigerated. Remove from the refrigerator an hour or so before baking.)

6. Bake until the top begins to brown and the lobster is heated through, 10 to 15 minutes. Garnish with the parsley and lemon wedges, and serve with the melted butter alongside.

Note: *At The Maine Diner, they use lemon juice only, but I like the sharpness of the zest as a balance to the richness of the crumbs.*

HIDDEN TREASURES: MAINE POUNDS IN-THE-ROUGH

Around the turn of the 20th century, when summer "rusticators" started arriving in Maine in large numbers, some savvy fishermen turned their lobster "pounds" (referring to impoundments along the shore where live lobsters were stored) into outdoor eateries. Wood-fired cooking cauldrons were set up so that visitors could buy their fresh lobsters, watch them being cooked on the spot in the open air, and then settle down at an outdoor picnic table for a feast "in-the-rough."

Today, the state still boasts at least a couple dozen of these wonderful lobster-pound restaurants, scattered along the coast and also inland, along the tourist highways (where the lobsters are now stored in tanks). Many still have outdoor cookers, although most are now fired with propane.

Here's the standard eat-in-the-rough protocol: Dress casually, and bring a sweater and some bug spray. Step up to the window and place your order. Your lobster is then stuck into a sturdy string bag, along with corn-on-the-cob, steamers, or mussels if you've ordered them, and the bag goes in the cooker. You take your place at a picnic table to wait, usually 20 minutes or so, while your dinner cooks. The glorious food, which will usually be presented on large, sturdy paper plates, arrives, and you don your plastic bib and plan your attack. Half an hour later, lobster satiated, you use your handi-wipe to clean your lobstery hands — and perhaps order a slice of blueberry pie. It's in-the-rough Nirvana.

Some of the in-the-rough places have inside seating — most do not. Most don't have liquor licenses, so it's usually okay to BYOB. Call before you go to get directions. These favorites of mine are listed south to north. All numbers are in the 207 area code.

Chauncey Creek Lobster Pier, Kittery Point, 439-1030. Yay! Here's your first chance to devour a lobster dinner across the state line into Maine. It's a charming dock on a tree-shrouded estuary.

Two Lights Lobster Shack, Cape Elizabeth, 799-1677. Eat your shore dinner at picnic tables on the rocks between two majestic lighthouses (or, on foggy days, hunker down in a cozy indoor dining room).

Harraseeket Lunch and Lobster, South Freeport, 865-4888. The Coffin family boasts both fishermen and cooks, who bring the "bugs" to their wharf and cook them for you right there. Close to busy Freeport, but feels like a world away.

Five Islands Lobster Company, Georgetown, 371-2990. A group of shacks cluster on a wooden dock overlooking one of the prettiest harbors on the coast. Five Islands has been called the Platonic ideal of a Maine lobster pound.

Boothbay Region Lobstermen's Co-op, Boothbay Harbor, 633-4900. Situated across the harbor from downtown Boothbay, this pound offers no-frills lobster dinners served at picnic tables under a simple shelter.

Shaw's Fish and Lobster Wharf, New Harbor, 677-2200. A large, bustling establishment with a full menu of fried seafood as well as seawater-boiled lobsters. Sit outdoors or in, and watch the always-interesting action on the working fishing wharf.

Round Pond Lobster Co-op, Round Pond, 529-5725. This co-op wholesales lobsters for fishermen on the busy harbor and also cooks the crustaceans up for you, along with simple shore dinner accompaniments.

Cod End Cookhouse, Tenants Harbor, 372-6782. The wharf houses a retail fish market as well as the cookhouse, which serves up some of the best lobsters and fried seafood on the coast.

Waterman's Beach Lobsters, South Thomaston, 596-7819. Cited by the James Beard Foundation as an example of a classic lobster pound, this family-run place is consistently excellent.

Young's Lobster Pound, East Belfast, 338-1160. With their wholesale and retail businesses, the Young family brings reliably fresh seafood to this part of the coast and cooks it for you here in this no-frills operation.

Dennett's Wharf, Castine, 326-9045. The full-service restaurant sits on prime harborfront real estate in this quintessential New England village. Eat on the deck and watch the yachts and lobster boats go by.

Eaton's Lobster Pool, Little Deer Isle, 348-2383. Off the beaten path, but worth the journey to this old place on a gorgeous, pristine cove. Full menu.

Tidal Falls Lobster Kettle, Hancock, 422-6457. The property has been acquired by a nature conservancy, but the simple restaurant still operates. Eat your lobster while watching the reversing falls, as well as the osprey and eagles soaring overhead.

Trenton Bridge Lobster Pound, Trenton, 667-2977. The oak-fired kettles are always steaming at this popular pound at the bridge just before crossing over onto Mt. Desert Island.

Beal's Lobster Pier, Southwest Harbor (Mount Desert Island), 244-7178. Right on the large working pier overlooking busy Southwest Harbor, this classic place offers some fried seafood as well.

Thurston's Lobster Pound, Bernard (Mount Desert Island), 244-7600. Order your string-bag-cooked shore dinner and sit at picnic tables on a double tier of decks facing across beautiful Bass Harbor. Excellent chowders here, too.

Lobster History

Before the 1800s, lobsters were so abundant you could simply pick them off the beach — but people who could afford to, didn't. Lobsters were considered a low-class food, and prisoners were forced to eat them three times a week. Or the lobsters were fed to the chickens. In the mid-19th century, fishermen began lobstering by boat and, after that, the lobster's relative scarcity produced increased demand for the crustacean. Fishing "smacks," boats equipped with large circulating wells of seawater holding thousands of pounds of lobsters, ferried the live crustaceans from sparsely populated Maine down to Boston's large lobster-hungry populace.

How the Lobster Got Its Shell

It is apparent to serious shellfish eaters that in the great evolutionary scheme of things crustaceans developed shells to protect them from knives and forks.

— **Calvin Trillin,** *Alice, Let's Eat*

To Eat a Lobster

- Grasp the lobster with one hand on the body and one hand on the tail and twist to break in two. Even if the lobster has been drained, some liquid will probably gush out, so hold it over your plate.
- I start with the tail. First remove the flat flippers at the end and pull them between your teeth, as you would an artichoke leaf, to get any meat. (Soft-shells won't have much.)
- If the tail hasn't been split, poke the meat out with your finger or a knife. Discard the black intestinal vein running down the center. Dip the meat into melted butter and eat.
- Twist off the two large claw legs where they meet the body. Twist off the pincer claws. Using a nutcracker, crack the claws and the knuckles. The claw meat is easy to get at; sometimes the knuckle meat — some of the sweetest — needs to be poked out with a lobster pick or your little finger.
- If you pull the small legs through your teeth, sometimes you'll get a bit of meat. There are also small nuggets in the joints where the legs meet the body.
- Tucked away in the body is the soft green tomalley, or the lobster's equivalent of a liver, and, if the lobster is a female, the bright pink roe, or coral. Some consider these morsels, particularly the rich-tasting tomalley, to be the very best parts of all.

Pan-Seared Scallops with Dill Citronette

Large, sweet, meaty sea scallops are a fabulous once-in-a-while treat. Some scallops, however, are soaked in a phosphate-type preservative that adds liquid and an off-flavor, so be sure to try to buy "dry pack" scallops. The trick to pan-searing scallops is to make sure they don't touch each other in the pan, because if they do, juices are likely to run out and they won't brown properly. Here, the seared scallops are sauced with a delicious (and ultra-quick) citrusy pan sauce. Such a centerpiece star calls for a good supporting cast that might include a curried rice pilaf, Trio of Autumn Greens (page 91), and perhaps Dark and Sticky Gingerbread with Maple Whipped Cream (page 266) to finish.

1½ pounds sea scallops, tough muscle removed from side of each if necessary

Salt and freshly ground black pepper

3 tablespoons olive oil

2 tablespoons butter

¼ cup finely chopped shallots (about 3 shallots)

½ cup dry white wine

2 teaspoons grated lemon zest

2 tablespoons lemon juice (juice of medium lemon)

1 teaspoon grated lime zest

1 tablespoon lime juice (juice of about ¾ lime)

1 tablespoon chopped fresh dill, plus sprigs for garnish

4 thin lemon slices, halved, for garnish

4 SERVINGS

1. Pat the scallops dry with paper towels. Sprinkle the scallops on both sides with salt and pepper to taste.

2. Warm a serving platter. Heat 2 tablespoons of the oil and the butter in one large or two medium-sized skillets over medium-high heat. When the oil is hot, place the scallops in the pan(s) in a single layer, without touching. Cook until the scallops are seared and golden on both sides, turning carefully once with tongs, 4 to 6 minutes total. Remove to the prepared platter and cover loosely with foil while making the pan sauce.

3. Add the remaining 1 tablespoon of oil to the pan and cook the shallots over medium heat for 1 minute, stirring. Add the wine, bring to a boil, stirring and scraping up any brown bits, and cook for 1 minute. Add the lemon zest and juice, the lime zest and juice, and dill and simmer for 1 minute.

4. Drizzle the scallops with the pan sauce, garnish with the dill sprigs and lemon slices, and serve.

Mussels Steamed with Leeks and Mustard Cream

This is a sublime and really quite elegant way to treat the once-lowly mussel. Hopefully you have access to nice clean mussels, preferably farm-raised, so when you buy them they're without grit, barnacles, or wiry beards. All you need for a perfectly lovely meal is a salad — either Mixed Greens with Simple Shallot Vinaigrette (page 58) or Green Bean, Walnut, and Feta Salad (page 65) — some crusty country bread for sopping up all the luscious sauce, and, depending on the season, Cranberry-Pear Crisp with Almond Topping (page 265) or Springtime Strawberry Rhubarb Crumble-Topped Pie (page 238) for dessert.

3　tablespoons butter

3　slender leeks, thinly sliced (white and pale green parts only)

3　garlic cloves, finely chopped

4　pounds mussels, scrubbed (debearded if necessary; see Note)

1　cup dry white wine

2　bay leaves

1½ cups heavy cream

1　tablespoon coarse-grain Dijon mustard

3　tablespoons chopped fresh flat-leaf parsley

2　tablespoons chopped fresh tarragon

Salt and freshly ground black pepper

4 SERVINGS

1. Melt the butter in a very large, deep skillet or saucepan over medium-low heat. Add the leeks and cook until softened, about 10 minutes. Add the garlic and cook, stirring, for 2 minutes. Remove from the heat and set aside.

2. Combine the mussels, wine, and bay leaves in a large pot, cover the pan, and bring to a boil. Reduce the heat to medium, and cook until the shells open, 4 to 8 minutes, depending on size. Using a slotted spoon, transfer the mussels to a bowl, discarding any that don't open. Let the cooking liquid settle for a few minutes, then pour the clear broth into a glass measure, leaving any sediment behind.

3. Pour the broth into the skillet with the leeks, add the cream and mustard, and bring to a boil over high heat, whisking to dissolve the mustard. Cook, uncovered, until the liquid reduces by about one-third, about 5 minutes. (The recipe can be made several hours ahead to this point. Cover the mussels and cream mixture and refrigerate separately. Bring to a boil before proceeding with step 4.)

4. Add the mussels in their shells to the skillet and stir in the parsley and tarragon. Heat gently until the mussels are heated through, 2 to 4 minutes. Season with the salt and pepper to taste.

5. To serve, divide the mussels and sauce among four large, shallow soup dishes.

   Note: *To debeard mussels, pull out the dark threads that protrude from the shell. Do this just before cooking; mussels die when debearded.*

Farming Mussels

Mussel farming is a thriving business in Maine. Growers are seeding the beautiful black bivalves on ropes that hang down from floats and rafts, and harvesting them when they're of a smallish uniform size. Since they feed on plankton, never going near the muddy bottom, farmed mussels are cleaner than their wild counterparts, with never a trace of grit and without those pesky wirelike beards. They are also meatier than wild mussels because they haven't had to spend as much energy developing protective shells. Successful mussel farms operate up and down the Maine coast, including in Casco Bay near Portland, in midcoast Tenants Harbor, in Blue Hill's Salt Pond, and in the Isle au Haut Thoroughfare.

Broiled Herb-Crumbed Sea Scallops

Large sea scallops fished from Maine waters are wonderful cooked this way — broiled, with a simple herbed crumb topping. The buttery crumbs protect the sweet, lean scallop meat from the drying effects of the heat, plus the crumbs add richness, texture, and flavor, but not so much as to overpower the delicate taste of the bivalve. My suggestions for accompaniments here would be Classic Scalloped Potatoes (page 86), steamed asparagus or broccoli, and something like a plate of Spiced Hermit Bars (page 269) or Crisp Ginger-Almond Wafers (page 272) and winter fruit for dessert.

4 SERVINGS

6 tablespoons butter

1 large garlic clove, minced

2 cups fresh breadcrumbs (see Note)

2 tablespoons chopped fresh flat-leaf parsley

1/2 teaspoon grated lemon zest

2 teaspoons lemon juice (juice of about 1/4 lemon)

1/4 teaspoon salt for the crumbs, plus more for the scallops

1/4 teaspoon freshly ground black pepper for the crumbs, plus more for the scallops

1 1/2 pounds sea scallops, tough muscle removed from side of each if necessary

8 lemon wedges

1. Melt the butter in a medium-sized skillet over medium heat. Add the garlic and cook, stirring, for 1 minute. Add the breadcrumbs, raise the heat to medium-high, and cook, stirring almost constantly, until they begin to toast and turn very pale golden, about 2 minutes. (They will also cook in the broiler, so toast lightly here.) Remove from the heat and stir in the parsley, lemon zest and juice, salt, and pepper.

2. Adjust the broiler rack so it is 4 to 5 inches from the heat source; pre-heat the broiler. Grease a large, shallow baking pan (such as a broiler pan without the slotted top) or rimmed baking sheet with oil.

3. Arrange the scallops in a single layer in the pan and season lightly with salt and pepper. Sprinkle with the seasoned crumbs, patting them on so they adhere to the scallops. Broil until the crumbs are richly browned and the scallops have just lost their translucence, 5 to 7 minutes.

4. Serve with the lemon wedges to squeeze over the scallops.

   Note: *Tear 4 slices of good-quality bread into pieces and whir in a food processor to make breadcrumbs.*

Scallop Fisherman's Dividend

Have you ever tasted a raw scallop right out of the ocean? I think they're even better than raw clams or oysters. Prettier, too. You pop off the shell, pick the scallop up with your fingers, and down it goes.

— Paul Sewell, fisherman

SCALA
BREAD
2.95

Semolina
ROLLS
.60 ea.
OR
6 FOR
$3.00

Maine's Eggs

Brown eggs are the preferred egg in Maine and much of the rest of New England. There is even a Brown Egg Council, and its president explains that brown eggs gained a foothold in Maine and the rest of New England back in the days of the China trade. Clipper ship captains sailed to Asia and brought back hens and roosters indigenous to that part of the world, which happened to be red or brown birds that laid brown-shelled eggs. (White-shelled eggs come only from white birds.) Rhode Island Reds, as some of these chickens came to be known, were large and hardy birds, well equipped to withstand New England winters, and before the days of refrigeration, Yankees became partial to brown eggs because they knew they were local, and therefore fresher. The sentiment continues today. Maine has a large commercial egg industry, with its hub in Turner, in the central part of the state.

Breakfast Cheese Strata

This one-dish egg- and cheese-layered casserole makes an ideal breakfast or brunch dish — perfect for those visiting house guests, which, in Maine, make rather frequent appearances during the summer months. Everybody loves this dish, and it has the always-welcome do-ahead feature: you can put it together the evening before, stick it in the refrigerator, and it's all ready to bake in the morning. For breakfast, you could subtract the optional scallions, or, when it's going to be a brunch dish, add other sautéed vegetables (such as peppers or zucchini), or even layer in about half a pound of cooked and crumbled breakfast sausage.

12 slices good-quality firm white sandwich bread, or 12 ounces Italian bread, preferably day-old

3–4 tablespoons butter, softened

2 1/2 cups (about 10 ounces) grated medium-sharp Cheddar cheese

3 thinly sliced scallions, or 3 tablespoons snipped fresh chives (optional)

4 eggs

2 1/2 cups whole or low-fat milk

1 teaspoon Dijon mustard

1/2 teaspoon salt

1/8 teaspoon freshly ground black pepper

Paprika

6 SERVINGS

1. Grease a 9-inch square baking dish or other 2½-quart baking dish with butter.

2. Cut the crusts off the bread and spread the slices with butter. Cut each slice into 3 strips. Layer half the bread in the bottom of the prepared dish and sprinkle with half the cheese and half the scallions, if desired. Repeat with the remaining bread, cheese, and scallions.

3. Whisk together the eggs, milk, mustard, salt, and pepper in a large bowl. Pour the egg mixture evenly over the bread. Cover and let stand for at least 1 hour, or cover and refrigerate for as long as 8 hours.

4. Preheat the oven to 350°F.

5. Bake the strata, uncovered, until it is evenly puffed and golden and a knife inserted near the center comes out clean, 55 to 60 minutes. Sprinkle lightly with paprika and serve immediately from the casserole.

Maple French Toast

A dribble of maple syrup in the egg-milk soaking mixture not only adds good smoky flavor, but helps this French toast to brown to a rich, dark hue. Good firm, chewy bread, ideally from a local artisan loaf, makes all the difference. If you try this with soft, flimsy sandwich bread, the French toast will be limp and soggy.

3/4 cup whole milk

3 eggs

3 tablespoons pure maple syrup, plus more for serving

Pinch of ground cinnamon

3 tablespoons unsalted butter

4 slices (cut 1/2- to 3/4-inch thick) good-quality bread, halved if easier to fit in pan

4 SERVINGS

1. Whisk together the milk, eggs, maple syrup, and cinnamon in a glass pie dish or other shallow dish.

2. Melt 1½ tablespoons of the butter in a large, heavy skillet over medium to medium-high heat. Dip 2 slices of bread into the egg mixture, letting excess drip off, and place in the pan. Cook until the undersides are a crusty golden brown, 2 to 3 minutes. Turn and cook until the bottom sides are firm and flecked with brown, about 2 minutes. Repeat with the remaining butter, bread, and egg mixture.

3. Serve hot with butter and maple syrup.

Maine Maple Sunday

More than 100 Maine maple producers — many of whom call themselves *sugarmakers* — open the doors of their sugarhouses one Sunday every March and invite the public to join them in their rite of spring. It's a chance to see firsthand how 40 gallons of clear sap is evaporated into just one gallon of golden syrup. In addition to syrup sampling, some other typical activities include making sugar on snow (if there's clean snow), sleigh or wagon tours of the sugarbush, and tasting such goodies as maple cotton candy, maple jelly, maple baked beans, syrup on biscuits, and maple apple crisp.

Waxing Rhapsodic about Maple

Maple sugar is the great New England contentment ... It sits so sweetly and lightly on the tongue that it never cloys the palate. It is delicate, and it has body, in its pure early spring rendering, that is almost ethereal.
— Fred Halliday, *The New England Food Explorer*

Oversize Golden Pancakes with Blueberry Option

Farm-fresh eggs — preferably organic — with their deep orangey-yellow yolks, taste so wonderful and contribute such beautiful color to the dishes they're in, that it's really worth seeking them out. In Maine, we can get fresh eggs at farmers' markets or at roadside stands in farming districts, or you can buy free-range eggs at whole foods markets. They make a huge difference in these pancakes. You can make them plain. Or, when blueberries are in season (or you have some frozen berries), choose the blueberry option.

1¼ cups whole, low-fat, or skim milk, plus more for thinning, if necessary

2   eggs

3   tablespoons unsalted butter, melted

1½ cups all-purpose flour

2   tablespoons sugar

2   teaspoons baking powder

½   teaspoon salt

1   cup (½ pint) blueberries (see Note)

Additional butter

Pure maple syrup

4 SERVINGS

1. Whisk together the milk, eggs, and melted butter in a small bowl.

2. In a large bowl, whisk together the flour, sugar, baking powder, and salt. Pour the milk mixture into the flour mixture and whisk gently, until the flour is just moistened. Do not overmix, or the pancakes can be tough.

3. Heat a lightly oiled cast iron griddle or skillet over medium heat. Make a small test pancake to check the heat of the pan and the consistency of the batter. Add a bit more milk if the batter does not spread sufficiently to make a pancake, and regulate heat if necessary.

4. For each pancake, spoon out a generous ¼-cup of batter onto the griddle, making 2 or 3 at a time (or make them any other size you want). If using the blueberries, sprinkle a couple of tablespoons over the batter. Cook until the undersides are golden and the tops are pocked with small holes, 1 to 2 minutes. Turn carefully with a spatula and cook until the undersides are lightly browned, about 1 minute.

5. Serve immediately with the butter and maple syrup, or keep warm in a slow (200°F) oven while using the remaining batter.

   Note: *If using frozen berries, spread out on paper towels and blot excess moisture before sprinkling over pancakes.*

Dried Blueberry Oatmeal Scones

Dried (or dehydrated) blueberries, which are more and more available, are a wonderful way to enjoy Maine's preeminent fruit all year long. Their pleasantly chewy, raisin-like texture and concentrated flavor makes them ideally suited for adding to baked things, and their tartness perfectly enhances these rich, crumbly oat scones.

1   cup plus 2 tablespoons all-purpose flour

1/2   cup quick-cooking or one-minute rolled oats (see Note)

2   tablespoons plus 2 teaspoons sugar

2   teaspoons baking powder

1/2   teaspoon salt

4   tablespoons cold unsalted butter

1/2   cup dried blueberries (about 3 ounces)

1/4   cup whole or low-fat milk

1   egg

1. Preheat the oven to 375°F.

2. Combine the flour, oats, 2 tablespoons of the sugar, baking powder, and salt in a food processor. Pulse once or twice to blend. Cut the butter into several chunks and distribute over the flour mixture. Pulse until most of the butter is about the size of small peas. Add the blueberries and pulse once to mix.

3. Measure the milk into a glass measuring cup, add the egg, and whisk lightly to blend. With the motor running, pour the liquid through the feed tube and process in short bursts until the dough begins to clump together. (To make by hand, whisk together the flour, oats, sugar, baking powder, and salt in a large bowl. Add the butter and use your fingers to rub the mixture together until most of the dough is the size of small peas. Stir in the blueberries. Add the milk and beaten egg all at once and stir with a pastry spatula or wooden spoon.)

4. Scrape the dough onto a floured board, knead once or twice, gather into a ball, and pat into a disc about 9 inches in diameter and 1/2-inch high. Using a large knife, cut into 8 pie-shaped wedges and place about 1 inch apart on an ungreased baking sheet. Sprinkle with the remaining 2 teaspoons sugar.

5. Bake in the center of the preheated oven until the scones are an even pale golden brown, about 18 to 20 minutes. Serve warm.

   Note: *Do not use regular old-fashioned rolled oats or instant oatmeal in this recipe.*

Martha's Marvelous Blueberry Muffins

My sister Martha has lived in Maine for more than 25 years, which means she is beginning to almost qualify as a bona fide Mainer. Martha has always loved to cook and bake with Maine's seasonal best (she is a dedicated Portland Farmers' Market shopper), and muffins are one of her specialties. She makes them with whatever fruit is currently in season, and when the first wild Maine blueberries show up, she makes these muffins, which we call, simply, "Martha's Marvelous."

2 cups all-purpose flour

1/3 cup sugar

1/4 cup packed light brown sugar

2 teaspoons baking powder

3/4 teaspoon salt

3/4 cup whole or low-fat milk

2 eggs

5 tablespoons unsalted butter, melted

1 cup blueberries (1/2 pint)

12 MUFFINS

1. Preheat the oven to 400°F. Grease a 12-cup muffin tin (1/2 cup capacity for each muffin) with butter or line with paper liners.

2. Set a medium-mesh sieve over a large bowl and measure the flour, sugar, brown sugar, baking powder, and salt into the sieve. Use your fingers or a wooden spoon to push the flour-sugar mixture through the sieve. (This removes the lumps from the brown sugar and blends the dry ingredients.)

3. Whisk together the milk, eggs, and melted butter in a small bowl. Pour the egg mixture into the flour mixture and stir gently just until the dry ingredients are moistened. (Do not overmix or the muffins will be tough; the batter should still look slightly lumpy.) Fold in the blueberries.

4. Spoon the batter into the muffin tins, filling each cup about three-quarters full.

5. Bake until the muffins are golden brown and springy to the touch, 18 to 22 minutes. Cool in the tin for 5 minutes before removing. Serve warm.

Maine Johnnycake (Corn Bread)

In Rhode Island, johnnycake (often spelled jonnycake) is a flat, unleavened cornmeal pancake, but in Maine, johnnycake (always spelled with the "h") is the old name for corn bread — regular baking powder-raised corn bread. Many old-timers still call it johnnycake or johnnybread, and I'm adding my vote, too, for keeping the name alive. My recipe for this always-welcome addition to supper is pretty much the classic formula, with the exception of the little bit of black pepper, which I think adds interest.

1¼ cups all-purpose flour

¾ cup yellow cornmeal

2 tablespoons sugar

1 tablespoon baking powder

¾ teaspoon salt

¼ teaspoon freshly ground black pepper

1 cup whole, low-fat, or skim milk

1 egg

4 tablespoons unsalted butter, melted, or ¼ cup vegetable oil

MAKES ONE 9-INCH PAN OF CORN BREAD OR 12 CORN MUFFINS

1. Preheat the oven to 425°F. Grease an 8- or 9-inch square baking pan with butter (see Note).

2. Whisk together the flour, cornmeal, sugar, baking powder, salt, and pepper in a medium-sized bowl.

3. Whisk together the milk, egg, and butter in a small bowl. Pour the milk mixture into the flour mixture and stir gently but thoroughly to combine. Scrape the batter into the prepared pan and smooth the top.

4. Bake until the bread is pale golden brown and a tester inserted in the center comes out clean, 18 to 22 minutes. Cut into squares and serve hot.

   Note: *For muffins, grease a 12-cup muffin tin.*

— French Flatbreads

Ployes (rhymes with boys) are pancake-like buckwheat flatbreads. They are a French tradition that lives on in French-Acadian households in Maine, especially in Aroostook County. At Bouchard Family Farm in Fort Kent, a ployes recipe has been passed down from the French-speaking exiles who arrived in the Saint John River Valley in the eighteenth century. The Bouchards even sell a ployes mix so you can stir up some batter and make the pancakes at home. (See Mail-Order Sources, page 277.)

Grange Supper Baking Powder Biscuits

The skilled volunteers who cook and bake for Maine's public suppers do it with a restrained undertone of friendly competition — particularly when it comes to baked goods. At the suppers put on by North Blue Hill's Halcyon Grange, Flossie Howard's melt-in-the-mouth biscuits have reigned supreme for many years. I wouldn't try to compete (or compare), so this is my tried-and-true biscuit recipe, which has also received some modest acclaim. I think the combination of vegetable shortening and butter gives the biscuits both flavor and a tender crumb.

2   cups all-purpose flour

1   tablespoon baking powder (see Note)

3/4   teaspoon salt

1   teaspoon sugar

3   tablespoons cold unsalted butter, cut into chunks

3   tablespoons cold vegetable shortening, cut into chunks

3/4   cup cold whole, low-fat, or skim milk

ABOUT 16 BISCUITS

1. Preheat the oven to 450°F.

2. Combine the flour, baking powder, salt, and sugar in a food processor. Process for about 10 seconds to blend. Distribute the chunks of butter and shortening over the flour and pulse 8 to 10 times, until most of the shortening is about the size of small peas. With the motor running, slowly pour the milk through the feed tube. Stop the machine when the dough begins to clump together. (To make by hand, whisk together the flour, baking powder, salt, and sugar in a large bowl. Add the butter and shortening and use your fingers to rub the mixture together until most of the shortening is the size of small peas. Add the milk all at once and stir with a fork to make a soft dough.)

3. Turn out the dough onto a lightly floured board, gather into a ball, and knead about 5 times, until smooth. Roll or pat out to an even ½-inch thickness. Using a 2-inch cutter or a floured glass, cut the biscuits and arrange on an ungreased baking sheet. (For crusty sides, place about 2 inches apart; for soft-sided biscuits, place no more than ½ inch apart.) Reroll the scraps once and cut. (The biscuits can be shaped up to 3 hours ahead. Refrigerate, loosely covered.)

4. Place the baking sheet in the preheated oven and immediately reduce the temperature to 400°F. Bake for 12 to 15 minutes, or until the biscuits are well risen and are pale golden. Serve hot or warm.

Note: *You can substitute 2 teaspoons Bakewell Cream and 1 teaspoon baking soda.*

Maine's Own Leavening

In many Maine households there is only one biscuit recipe — the one printed on the back of the bright yellow and blue tin of Bakewell Cream. This unique leavening agent was created during World War II when a shortage of cream of tartar prompted a Bangor chemist to concoct a substitute so that Mainers could keep right on baking their beloved biscuits, shortcakes, and cobblers.

Bakewell Cream, whose main ingredient is "acid sodium pyrophosphate," is similar to cream of tartar in that it must be mixed with baking soda to activate the leavening action. Bakers loved the way Bakewell Cream raised their biscuits to new heights, and the product is still the preferred leavener for many Mainers. As Bakewell Cream's recipe booklet states, "It makes a superior, almost no-fail biscuit, even for a heavy-handed amateur cook."

— What's for Suppah? —

The public supper is a more than 200-year-old institution in Maine that not only refuses to fade away, but is more popular than ever. On any given weekend in any season in any corner of the state, you are likely to find at least a couple of fund-raising suppers listed in the paper or advertised on signs posted in front of the grange or church hall where the supper will be held, with names like "Boiled Dinner Supper," "Hunter and Harvest Supper," and "Turkey and Ham and Roast Beef Supper." You'll see "Spaghetti Supper" and the occasional "Seafood Chowder Supper." But it's the Bean Supper that really reigns supreme in Maine.

Here's the typical menu: baked beans, of course, usually both large beans (yellow eyes or Jacob's cattle) and small beans, such as pea beans; various other casseroles, such as American chop suey, mac 'n' cheese, or chili; coleslaw; pickles; and homemade breads, such as Grange Supper Baking Powder Biscuits

(page 212) or Saturday-Night Supper Steamed Brown Bread (opposite). Friendly competition prevails among the volunteer cooks — which is all to the benefit of the paying guests. For dessert, it's often blueberry or strawberry shortcake (during berry season) or pies. Slices are sometimes lined up as you enter the hall so you get to choose dessert first. And what a choice it is! Will it be blueberry or apple or pumpkin or graham cracker cream or lemon sponge or chocolate cream or custard or . . . ? One way of choosing is to just close your eyes and point.

Public suppers are democratic. You sit at long communal tables and all paying customers are welcome, young or old, local or "from away." By the end of the supper, as coffee is sipped, all traces of Yankee reserve have melted away, and everyone savors the pleasure of participating in this uniquely American shared experience.

Saturday-Night Supper Steamed Brown Bread

Old-time Mainers sometimes called this "rye 'n' injun" bread (the "injun" referring to the cornmeal, because all things corn were associated with Native Americans). Others just called it brown bread. You can actually buy brown bread in a can, which you then heat by steaming, and it isn't bad. But this homemade version is absolutely delicious — plus, making it is kind of a fun project. In New England, steamed brown bread was (and still is) a traditional accompaniment to Saturday night's baked beans.

½   cup cornmeal

½   cup rye flour (see Note)

½   cup whole-wheat flour

1   teaspoon baking soda

½   teaspoon salt

1   cup buttermilk or sour milk
    (see Note)

⅓   cup molasses

½   cup raisins (optional)

1 LOAF (6—8 SERVINGS)

1. Grease a 13- to 14-ounce coffee can with butter. Bring a kettle of water to a boil.

2. Whisk together the cornmeal, rye flour, whole-wheat flour, baking soda, and salt in a large bowl. Add the buttermilk and molasses and whisk until well blended. Stir in the raisins, if desired. Scrape into the prepared coffee can and cover tightly with foil.

3. Place the coffee can into a deep pot (with lid) and pour the boiling water in to come halfway up the can. Cover the pot, bring the water to a boil, reduce the heat to low, and steam for about 1½ hours, or until a skewer inserted in the center comes out clean.

4. Use oven mitts to lift the can out and cool on a rack for 10 minutes. Tap the bread out of the can (or remove the bottom with a can opener and push the bread out). Serve warm or at room temperature. (The bread reheats well in the microwave.)

Note: *A good place to find rye flour (as well as the other flours) is in organic or whole-foods stores, where they're sold in bulk. To make sour milk, add 2 teaspoons white vinegar or lemon juice to 1 cup whole or low-fat milk and let stand for 10 minutes.*

Shaker Pumpkin-Walnut Bread

Sister Frances Carr of Maine's Sabbathday Lake Shaker community published *Shaker Your Plate* in 1985. It's a cookbook filled with recipes for simple goodness, which is the Shakers' motto. This autumnal pumpkin bread — moist and flavorful — is based on a similar recipe by Sister Carr. It's the slight amount of cornmeal in the batter that gives the bread its delightful, ever-so-slightly-gritty crunch.

1   cup coarsely chopped walnuts

1¼ cups all-purpose flour

¼   cup cornmeal

1   teaspoon baking powder

1   teaspoon salt

½ teaspoon baking soda

½ teaspoon ground cinnamon

¼ teaspoon ground allspice

¼ teaspoon ground nutmeg

2   eggs

1   cup canned pumpkin purée (not sweetened pumpkin pie filling)

1   cup sugar

½ cup vegetable oil

⅓ cup water

¼ cup packed brown sugar, preferably dark brown

1 LOAF (ABOUT 20 SLICES)

1. Preheat the oven to 350°F. Grease a 9-by-5-inch loaf pan with butter.

2. Spread the walnuts out into a dry skillet and toast over medium heat, stirring frequently, until one shade darker, about 4 minutes.

3. Whisk together the flour, cornmeal, baking powder, salt, baking soda, cinnamon, allspice, and nutmeg in a medium-sized bowl.

4. In a large bowl, using an electric mixer or whisk, beat together the eggs, pumpkin purée, sugar, oil, water, and brown sugar. Add the flour mixture and whisk or beat on medium speed until well-blended. Stir in the toasted walnuts. Scrape the batter into the prepared pan.

5. Bake until the bread shrinks from the side of the pan and a tester inserted in the center comes out clean, about 1 hour. Cool in the pan for 10 minutes; then invert onto a rack and cool completely. (The bread can be wrapped and stored in the refrigerator for up to 3 days, or frozen for up to 1 month.) Cut into slices to serve.

Wind and Sun Farm Partially Whole Wheat Sandwich Bread

Katey Burns and Dan Huisjen produce some of my favorite farmers' market items at their Wind and Sun Farm in Brooksville: a variety of baby organic vegetables, tender pea shoots, rich duck eggs, a slow-toasted granola, and this fantastic partially whole wheat sandwich loaf. The secret to its tender but chewy crumb and sweetly yeasty flavor lies in using excellent quality bread flours (see Note), and in the deliberately slowed-down rising times. "I give the dough a power nap before the kneading step," says Katey. "This gives the flour more opportunity to develop its deep, complex flavor."

2   tablespoons plus 3½ to 4 cups unbleached white bread flour (see Note)

1   package (¼ ounce) active dry yeast

2   teaspoons sugar

½   cup plus 2 cups warm tap water (105°F–115°F)

1½ cups whole wheat bread flour (see Note)

1   tablespoon salt

MAKES TWO 8½-BY-4½-INCH LOAVES

1. For the sponge, combine 2 tablespoons of the white flour, yeast, sugar, and ½ cup of the water in a large mixing bowl or the bowl of a large stand mixer. Let stand until bubbly, about 5 minutes. Add the remaining 2 cups water and the whole wheat flour, and whisk until smooth. Cover and set aside at room temperature until this loose sponge rises slightly, 20 to 30 minutes.

2. Stir in the salt and begin adding the white flour, a cup at a time, mixing with a wooden spoon or a dough hook, if using a stand mixer, until the dough is fairly firm and only slightly sticky. Now stop the mixing and let the dough rest for 30 minutes before finishing the kneading.

3. On a lightly floured board, knead the dough (or use the dough hook attachment to the stand mixer), adding more flour as necessary, until the dough is smooth and elastic. (This will take 5 to 10 minutes.) Cover and let rise in an oiled bowl or the mixer bowl until doubled in bulk, 1 to 1½ hours.

4. Grease two 8½-by-4½-inch loaf pans with oil or butter. Punch the dough down, turn out onto a lightly floured board, and divide into two equal portions. Shape into two loaves and place, seam side down, in the prepared pans. Set aside and let rise until almost doubled, 30 to 45 minutes.

5. Preheat the oven to 350°F. Bake the loaves in the preheated oven for about 45 minutes, until they are lightly browned and sound hollow when tapped. Turn out onto a wire rack and cool completely before slicing. (The bread can be wrapped well and stored in the refrigerator for two days or so, or frozen for up to 1 month.)

Note: *Bread flour, which is made of hard, high protein wheat, is the preferred flour when you want a chewy, crusty bread. Katey uses King Arthur unbleached bread flour (available in supermarkets) and Morgan's Mills Organic whole wheat bread flour or the new Maine-grown flour from Aurora Mills in Aroostook County (see Mail-Order Sources, page 277).*

Baker-Farmer Connection

Jim Amaral of Borealis Breads (one of the pioneering artisan bread bakeries in Maine) was intent on trying to create an "all-Maine bread." When Amaral couldn't find the Maine-grown wheat he desired, he approached Matt Williams, an Aroostook County farmer, who agreed to grow one winter wheat and two spring wheats for the bakery. Now, Aroostook Wheat, a whole-wheat loaf with an amazing earthy interior and firm, crisp crust, is one of Borealis' most popular breads. "What we're trying to do is create a loaf that tastes like Maine," Amaral explains. Considering that this bread is nothing more than flour, water, and salt, and their own starter made from more of the wonderful flour, it does indeed.

Skillet Rhubarb-Ginger Chutney

Old-fashioned chutney recipes called for simmering the fruit-spice mixture for upwards of two hours, which results in a very thick, dense compote. The contemporary cook is usually after something lighter, in which the identity of the primary ingredient remains recognizable. This rhubarb chutney is done in less than 30 minutes, start to finish — and it lasts at least two weeks in the refrigerator. It'll be gone before that, though — eaten with any hot or cold roast meats, especially ham or pork, or spread on smoked turkey sandwiches.

4 cups sliced rhubarb (about 1⅓ pounds)

1½ cups sugar

1 small onion, chopped

½ cup water

⅓ cup white wine vinegar or cider vinegar

1 tablespoon peeled and minced fresh ginger (about 1-inch piece)

2 whole cloves

1 small dried hot red chile or ½ teaspoon dried red pepper flakes

½ teaspoon salt

MAKES ABOUT 2 CUPS

1. Combine the rhubarb, sugar, onions, water, vinegar, ginger, cloves, chile, and salt in a wide, deep, nonreactive skillet (see Note). Turn the heat to high and bring to a boil, stirring occasionally.

2. Reduce the heat to medium-low to low and cook the chutney, uncovered, at a slow simmer, stirring occasionally, until most of the liquid is gone and the sauce is syrupy, about 30 minutes. (Add water during the cooking process if the mixture looks dry or is in danger of scorching.)

3. Remove the dried chile and cloves. Cool to room temperature, transfer to plastic containers or jars, and refrigerate. Use within 2 weeks.

Note: *Stainless steel and enameled cast iron are nonreactive. Avoid aluminum and uncoated iron.*

Robert Frost on Picking Blueberries in Maine

You ought to have seen how it looked in the rain,
The fruit mixed with water in layers of leaves,
Like two kinds of jewels, a vision for thieves.

— "Blueberries," *North of Boston*

Small Batch Blueberry Preserves

I love to capture the essence of summer fruits, but am not all that keen on standing over a huge steaming kettle in August or dealing with the sometimes-daunting admonitions of water-bath processing. So I've turned to putting up just a few jars of Maine's prized blueberries at a time and storing them in the refrigerator, from which they disappear long before they have a chance to spoil.

2 cups Maine lowbush blueberries or larger highbush blueberries

1⅓ cups sugar

1 tablespoon lemon juice (juice of ½ medium lemon)

¼ teaspoon butter

Half a cinnamon stick

2½ tablespoons liquid pectin

MAKES 3 HALF-PINT JARS

1. Combine the berries, sugar, lemon juice, butter, and cinnamon stick in a wide, heavy saucepan or medium-sized deep skillet. Use a potato masher to crush the blueberries to release their juice.

2. Bring the mixture to a full rolling boil over high heat, stirring almost constantly. Boil for 1 minute. Add the pectin, return to a boil, and boil for 1 minute, stirring. Remove from the heat.

3. Discard the cinnamon stick. Ladle the mixture into clean glass canning jars or other jars. Cool to room temperature (preserves will thicken as they cool), cover, and refrigerate for up to 2 weeks.

Variation: *You can use the same proportions and method with almost any berry, including strawberries, raspberries, or blackberries.*

Blueberries for Sal

Her mother walked slowly through the bushes, picking blueberries as she went and putting them in her pail. Little Sal struggled along behind, picking blueberries and eating every single one.

— Robert McCloskey, *Blueberries for Sal*

Tomato Tasting Week

Maine's farms are bursting with tomatoes! What until recently was celebrated as Tomato Tasting Day in Maine has stretched into an annual Tomato Tasting Week at close to 50 farms and farmers' markets. During the week in August, the farmers invite folks to stop by for tastes of the newest crop of successful multicolored heirlooms, with such descriptive names as Green Zebra, Cherokee Purple, Yellow Pear, White Wonder, and Black Krim.

Maine Summer Salsa Fresca

It takes a while to happen in Maine, but when tomatoes start to arrive in mid-August in all their multicolored profusion, no one can resist eating them at every meal. One thing I do with dead ripe local tomatoes is chop them up and make salsas of several varieties. This is my version of simple, all-purpose fresh tomato salsa, good scooped up with tortilla chips or spooned atop grilled fish or chicken or baked beans or eggs or stirred into soup or . . . .

2   cups chopped seeded ripe tomatoes (2 medium tomatoes)

1   cup chopped sweet onion, such as Vidalia, or red onion (1 large onion)

1   cup chopped green bell pepper (1 large pepper)

2   tablespoons lime juice (juice of 1 large lime)

1   jalapeño or serrano chile, chopped fine (see Note)

1   teaspoon salt

1/3 cup chopped fresh cilantro

1. Combine the tomatoes, onion, bell pepper, lime juice, jalapeño, and salt in a large bowl. Stir to combine. Set aside at room temperature for at least 1 hour, or refrigerate for up to 8 hours. Return to room temperature before serving.

2. Spoon off any excess accumulated liquid, add the cilantro, adjust the seasonings to taste, and serve.

Note: *If fresh hot chiles aren't available, use a pickled jalapeño, or substitute about ½ teaspoon liquid hot pepper sauce.*

Stonewall Success

In 1991, Jonathan King and James Stott, two friends who were waiters, cooks, and avid gardeners, set up a card table at their local farmers' market, displaying the few dozen vinegars and jams they had finished hand labeling just a few hours earlier. Less than 10 years later, Stonewall Kitchen (named for the graceful stone walls that surrounded their original farm) boasts more than 6,000 accounts nationwide, a staff of well over 200, and a new 55,000-square-foot headquarters in York, Maine. The company, which consistently wins taste and packaging awards, makes not only delicious jams, jellies, preserves, chutneys, vinegars, marinades, and sauces, but also now sells lines of kitchen, garden, and home accessories.

Down East Dilly Beans

Affectionately known as "dilly beans" in Maine, these tongue-tingling pickles constitute something of a small cottage industry in the Pine Tree state. You see locally made dillies for sale at just about every farm stand and tourist-oriented food emporium in the state. Since I am convinced that part of their charm is in the way they look, standing neatly upright packed into their glass jars, I have written this recipe accordingly. As with all the pickle recipes in this book, you can treat these dilly beans as a refrigerator pickle. Or, if you like, you may process the jars, while they're still hot, in a boiling-water-bath canner according to the canner's directions.

---

2 pounds green beans

3 ½ cups cider vinegar

1 ¾ cups water

About 8 small dried hot chiles

2 tablespoons kosher salt

2 teaspoons mustard seeds

4 garlic cloves, peeled and halved

About 8 large fresh dill sprigs

MAKES ABOUT FOUR 1½-PINT JARS

1. Bring a large pot of water to a boil. Trim the stem ends of the beans so they fit standing upright into 1½-pint glass jars (see note). Blanch the beans in the boiling water for exactly 1½ minutes. Drain into a colander, then plunge into a bowl of ice water. Pack the beans upright into clean 1½-pint jars.

2. Combine the vinegar, water, chiles, salt, and mustard seeds in a medium-sized nonreactive saucepan (see Note). Bring to a boil for 1 minute, stirring to dissolve the salt.

3. Divide the garlic and dill among the jars and pour the hot vinegar mixture over the beans, leaving about ½-inch of headspace. Cool to room temperature, cover, and refrigerate for at least 12 hours, or for up to 2 weeks.

   Note: *If you don't care about using jars, simply toss the blanched beans with the hot liquid and seasonings in a large bowl and then refrigerate, covered. Stainless steel and enameled cast iron are nonreactive. Avoid aluminum and uncoated iron.*

Pickle Queen

Members of the Stanchfield family have farmed their acreage in Milo, in the central part of Maine, for five generations. When Wilma Stanchfield started selling her pickles, it was just as a sideline, but the business has grown into a healthy and viable one. "We still grow almost all of the ingredients for our pickles and relishes right here on the farm," says Wilma. "Freshness is key. We pick the vegetables and pack them just as fast as we can. Not much more than 24 hours from the garden to the jar is the goal." Stanchfield Farms pickles asparagus, cauliflower, beans, beets, fiddleheads, zucchini — and, of course, cucumbers, pickled half a dozen ways.

Green Tomato Refrigerator Pickles

After Maine gardens have pumped out all the sweet, juicy ripe tomatoes they can muster, gardeners in Maine are usually left with quite an abundance of green (or unripened) tomatoes, because of our earlyish fall and shorter days. The green tomatoes sit on windowsills or get wrapped in newspaper in hopes of ripening, or they can shine in a brief star turn of their own by being turned into such tasty delicacies as fried green tomatoes (thickly sliced, dredged in seasoned flour, and pan fried) or these scrumptious — and very simple — refrigerator pickles.

1	pound green tomatoes
1	medium onion
2	tablespoons salt
½	cup distilled white or cider vinegar
½	cup water
⅓	cup sugar
1	teaspoon whole mustard seeds

MAKES 1 ½ PINTS

1. Core the green tomatoes, halve, and cut into thin slices. Halve and slice the onion. Combine the tomatoes and onion with the salt in a large bowl; toss very thoroughly to make sure the salt is distributed evenly. Add a handful of ice cubes and toss again. Cover and set aside at room temperature for 2½ to 3 hours.

2. Drain the tomato mixture in a colander, pushing down to extract as much liquid as possible.

3. Combine the vinegar, water, sugar, and mustard seeds in a medium saucepan. Bring to a boil over high heat, stirring to dissolve the sugar. Add the drained tomato mixture, return to a boil, and remove from the heat. Cool in the saucepan, then transfer the pickles with the liquid to plastic containers or jars and refrigerate until cold, about 1 hour. The pickles will keep in the refrigerator for at least 3 weeks.

Raye's Mustard

The Raye family has been grinding mustard in the same Eastport, Maine, location since 1903. Originally set up to produce mustard sauces for Maine's growing sardine industry, the company still creates mustards that are stone ground from whole seeds on the last surviving stone mustard mill in this country.

Sadly, the sardine industry no longer flourishes, but Raye's continues to satisfy the country's ever-increasing appetite for flavorful, high-quality condiments. The mustard mill is also a working museum, and visitors are welcome.

Common Ground Apple-Cranberry Salsa

With its wonderfully fresh-tasting crunch, piquant flavor, and beautiful colors, this tasty salsa showcases fall ingredients, such as the ones featured at Maine's famed Common Ground Fair. It's a natural accompaniment to roasted meats and chicken, but also makes a great hors d'oeuvre, served with a soft creamy chèvre or cream cheese, and crackers. If you like things hotter, don't scrape out the jalapeño seeds and ribs before you chop the pepper.

ABOUT 3 CUPS

1   large, crisp sweet apple, such as McIntosh, unpeeled, cored, and cut into 1-inch chunks

3/4   cup fresh cranberries (3 ounces)

3   tablespoons lime juice (juice of 2 medium limes)

2   tablespoons honey

2   tablespoons olive oil

1   small onion, chopped

3/4   cup chopped orange bell pepper (about 1 medium pepper)

1/2   cup chopped fresh cilantro

1   garlic clove, finely chopped

1   fresh or pickled jalapeño chile, minced

1   teaspoon salt

Freshly ground black pepper

1. Pulse the apple chunks and cranberries in a food processor until chopped medium-fine but not puréed. Do not overprocess.

2. Toss the apple-cranberry mixture with the lime juice, honey, and oil in a mixing bowl. Stir in the onion, bell pepper, cilantro, garlic, jalapeño, and salt. Season with the black pepper to taste.

3. Set the salsa aside at room temperature for at least 1 hour to allow the juices to release and the flavors to marry. Alternatively, the salsa can be stored in the refrigerator for a day or so.

Heatin' Up

Mainers have developed a yen for the hot stuff. More than a dozen little companies in the state are taking the chill off winter by producing hot sauces in infinite variety, and they've given themselves fun lovin' names like Firegirl, Flaming Gourmet, Mother's Mountain, Heat Me Up, and Burn Me Good.

GREEN PEPPER Jelly · CRABAPPLE Jelly · STRAWBERRY Jelly · Tomato Jelly · MINT Jelly · GRAPE Jelly · RASPBERRY Jelly

SQUASH · TOMATOES · Cut Yellow Beans · JULIENNE CARROTS · BEET GREENS

...MON ...SAUCE · PEARS · TOMATO SAUCE ONIONS AND GREEN PEPPERS · SUCCOTASH · TOMATO SAUCE ZUCCHINI AND ... · PARSNIPS

Yellow ...

Grandmother's Cellar

[Grandmother] stopped longest in front of her hanging shelves where the jellies, jams, and preserves gleamed red, purple, and yellow in the lamp-light. She took time to count the jars of jelly and to sort the preserves. When she found that her sweets were lasting well, she selected a jar of wild strawberries or pickled pears to go with the supper biscuits.

— Esther E. Wood, *Country Fare*

WATERMELON PICKLES · MUSTARD PICKLES · PICKLED BEETS · Golden Glow PICKLES

Raw Cranberry-Clementine Relish

I like to have two cranberry sauces on the Thanksgiving dinner table — a cooked one, such as the Cooked Cranberry-Pear Conserve (page 230), and a raw relish. This relish, which goes together in about five minutes, has stirred more comment and praise than many a more complicated dish on the feast table. And its agreeably crunchy texture and tart, horseradish-spiked flavor is the perfect addition to the post-prandial turkey sandwich.

1   bag (12 ounces) fresh
    cranberries

2   smallish clementines, cut into
    1-inch chunks, seeds discarded

³⁄₄ cup sugar

¹⁄₄ cup orange marmalade

3   tablespoons prepared
    horseradish

MAKES ABOUT 3 CUPS

1. Pulse the cranberries and clementines in a food processor until they are chopped medium-fine. (Do not overprocess to a purée.) Transfer to a bowl.

2. Stir in the sugar, marmalade, and horseradish and mix well. Cover and refrigerate for at least 3 hours, or for up to a week. Serve cool or at room temperature.

— Cranberries Way Down East

Cranberries, a native American fruit, were harvested by Maine Indian tribes and later by European settlers who established a small commercial cranberry industry in the state in the early 1900s. The industry went into decline, but was reborn around 1989, and now upwards of 40 farms are growing the tart scarlet fruits in bogs, most of which are located in Down East Maine's Washington County. Nan Bradshaw of Bradshaw's Cranberry Farm in Dennysville, says, "Mainers have come to expect more from local growers. We use a different variety of cranberries than they do in Massachusetts, and the result is a larger, more colorful and flavorful berry."

Cooked Cranberry-Pear Conserve

Based on the research I've done on the subject, a preserve and a conserve seem to refer pretty much to the same thing — that is, fruit cooked and preserved with sugar. I've called this a conserve because I happen to like the old-fashioned sort of ring to the name, but you can call it plain old cranberry sauce if you like. The pear adds a bit of different texture and the ginger makes it sparkle on the tongue.

1   bag (12 ounces) fresh cranberries

1   firm, flavorful pear, such as a Bosc, peeled, cored, and chopped

3/4   cup sugar

2/3   cup dry vermouth or white wine

2   tablespoons chopped crystallized ginger

MAKES ABOUT 3 CUPS

1. Combine the cranberries, pear, sugar, and wine in a large saucepan or deep skillet. Bring to a boil over high heat, stirring to dissolve the sugar. Reduce the heat to medium-low and simmer, uncovered, until the cranberries pop and the sauce is lightly thickened, 10 to 15 minutes. (Do not cook the mixture until it is dry, as it will thicken up considerably as it cools.) Stir in the ginger.

2. Transfer to covered containers and refrigerate for at least 4 hours, or up to 5 days. Bring to room temperature before serving.

Nineteenth-Century Maine Island Life

From June, when the scent of wild strawberries filled the air, until late summer, when the last of the raspberries, blackberries, and blueberries were gone, the girls went berrying. In the fall, they gathered cranberries in the bog back of the sea beach. Then Hannah and the girls made jams and jellies, and pies as well from the apples of the red asktrakhan tree. Hannah taught the girls how to make butter and cheese, soap and candles, bread, Indian pudding, and a good chowder.

— Barbara Cooney, *Island Boy*

Kenneth Roberts' Ketchup Confessions

Maine sea captains brought tomato seeds from Spain and Cuba . . . and the good cooks in the families experimented with variants of the ubiquitous and somewhat characterless tomato sauce of Spain and Cuba. Such was the passion for my grandmother's ketchup in my own family that we could never get enough of it. We were allowed to have it on beans, fish cakes and hash, since those dishes were acknowledged to be incomplete without them; but when we went so far as to demand it on bread, as we often did, we were peremptorily refused, and had to go down in the cellar and steal it — which we often did. It has a savory, appetizing tang to it that seemed to me to be inimitable. I became almost a ketchup drunkard, for when I couldn't get it, I yearned for it.

— Kenneth Roberts,
Trending into Maine

Pickled Pumpkin

Fall means mounds of pumpkins, of course, and this pickle is a delicious way to preserve a taste of the season. Small "baby" or sugar pumpkins now make an annual appearance in markets and roadside stands, and their more tender flesh is eminently suitable for pickling. The pumpkin cubes simmer in a spiced vinegar-sugar syrup until tender and translucent, emerging as a toothsome delight that is somewhat akin to watermelon pickle.

1–1 1/2 pounds pumpkin

2 tablespoons kosher salt

2 cup plus 1/4 cup cold water

3/4 cup cider vinegar

2/3 cup sugar

2 slices unpeeled fresh ginger

1 thick slice lemon peel

Half a cinnamon stick

MAKES ABOUT 2 CUPS

1. Cut the pumpkin into large wedges, scrape out the seeds, and peel with a vegetable peeler or small paring knife. Cut into 1-inch cubes.

2. Dissolve the salt in 2 cups of the cold water in a bowl. Add the pumpkin, stir to combine well, and set aside, covered, for at least 6 hours, or overnight. Drain in a colander and rinse well.

3. Combine the vinegar, sugar, the remaining 1/4 cup water, ginger, lemon peel, and cinnamon stick in a medium-sized, nonreactive saucepan (see Note). Bring to a boil, stirring to dissolve the sugar, and add the pumpkin. Reduce the heat to low and cook, covered, until the pumpkin is tender and translucent, 15 to 20 minutes.

4. Cool the pickled pumpkin in its syrup to room temperature, transfer to covered containers or jars, and refrigerate for at least 12 hours, or for up to 2 weeks.

Note: *Stainless steel and enameled cast iron are nonreactive. Avoid aluminum and uncoated iron.*

Pickle History

Pickles play an important role in Maine's culinary history. Because pickling was one of the few ways to preserve produce for the long winter months, the state's European settlers were ardent picklers, and pickling was part of the seasonal rhythm, like blacking the stove or stacking the wood pile. Before the invention of the canning process in the early nineteenth century, simple pickling was done by mixing up a brine solution of salt and vinegar and preserving cucumbers and other vegetables in a closed clay crock kept in a cold dark cellar.

7 Delectable Desserts

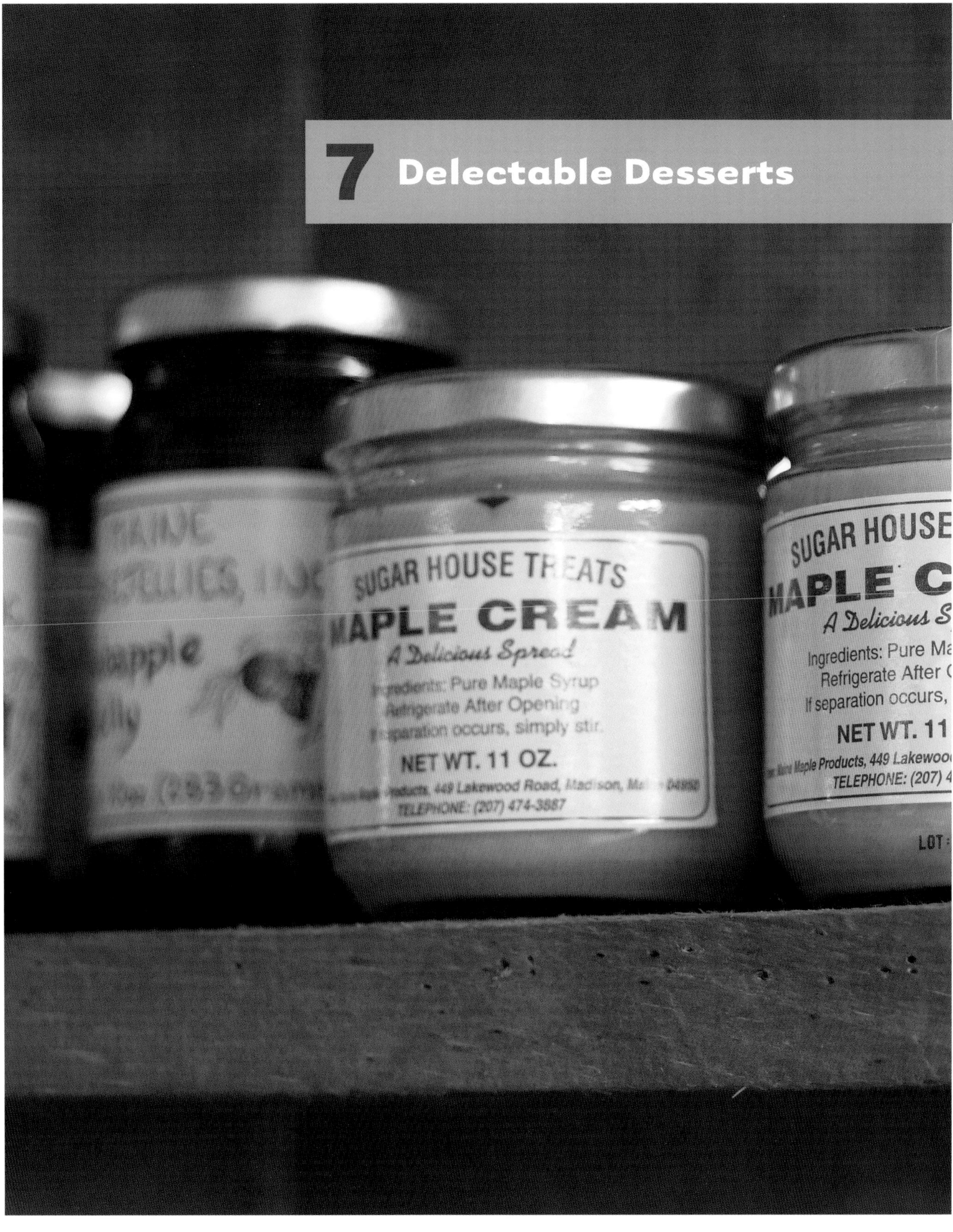

My Flaky Pie Pastry

This piecrust recipe uses half butter (for flavor) and half solid vegetable shortening (for crisper, flakier texture), and it's a great choice for just about any pie. If you need only a single crust, simply cut all the ingredients in half.

2½ cups all-purpose flour

1 teaspoon salt

1 teaspoon sugar

½ cup (1 stick) cold unsalted butter, cut into 8 pieces

½ cup cold solid vegetable shortening, cut into 8 chunks

6–8 tablespoons ice water

PASTRY FOR 1 DOUBLE-CRUST PIE

1. Combine the flour, salt, and sugar in a food processor. Pulse to mix. Distribute the butter and shortening over the flour and process in short bursts until most of the shortening is about the size of small peas. Sprinkle 6 tablespoons of the ice water over the mixture and pulse just until no dry flour remains and the dough begins to clump together. If the dough is too dry, sprinkle on the remaining 2 tablespoons of water and pulse again. (To make by hand, see page 236.)

2. Divide the dough in half and turn out onto two sheets of plastic wrap. Shape and flatten into two 5-inch discs, wrap, and refrigerate for at least 30 minutes. (Piecrust may be refrigerated up to 2 days, or frozen for up to 1 month.) Remove from the refrigerator 10 minutes before rolling out.

Standish's Sweet Memories

The very words "Maine cooking" start our memories flying backward . . . Our thoughts hover around the cookie jar and we remember sugar cookies, ginger snaps, brambles, hermits, filled cookies and hard gingerbread. We open our old tin cake boxes and see ribbon cake, applesauce cake, dried apple cake, sponge cake, walnut cake. They may be frosted, more often they are not. When a State of Mainer thinks of apple pie he sets his belt buckle forward a notch. He remembers the flaky pastry of his grandmother's day and the Northern Spies sliced into that pastry for his favorite pie.

— Marjorie Standish, *Cooking Down East*

Old-Fashioned Lard Crust

Lard, which is rendered and clarified pork fat, was the preferred (and sometimes the only available) shortening for generations of Maine pie makers. Lard makes a meltingly tender crust, although I prefer using it in combination with unsalted butter to balance its distinctive, mildly nutty flavor. This crust complements fruit fillings — especially apple, blueberry, and rhubarb — particularly well.

2 1/2 cups all-purpose flour

2 teaspoons sugar

1 teaspoon salt

1/2 cup cold or frozen lard, cut into 1/2-inch chunks

6 tablespoons cold unsalted butter, cut into 1/2-inch chunks

6–8 tablespoons ice water

PASTRY FOR 1 DOUBLE-CRUST PIE

1. Combine the flour, sugar, and salt in a food processor. Pulse to mix. Distribute the lard and butter over the flour and process in short bursts until most of the shortening is about the size of small peas. Sprinkle 6 tablespoons of the ice water over the mixture and pulse just until no dry flour remains and the dough begins to clump together. If the dough is too dry, sprinkle on the remaining 2 tablespoons of water and pulse again. (To make by hand, see below.)

2. Divide the dough in half and turn out onto two sheets of plastic wrap. Shape and flatten into two 5-inch discs, wrap, and refrigerate for at least 30 minutes. (Piecrust may be made ahead and refrigerated up to 2 days, or frozen for up to 1 month.) Remove from the refrigerator 10 minutes before rolling out.

— To Make Piecrust by Hand

If you don't have (or don't choose to use) a food processor to mix up piecrust, whisk together the flour, sugar, and salt in a large bowl. Cut the chilled shortening into 1/2-inch chunks and scatter over the flour. Using a pastry blender or two table knives or your fingertips (my preference), work together until most of the shortening is about the size of small peas. Sprinkle most of the ice water over the flour mixture and work with a large fork or your hands, adding more water by tablespoons, until the dough is evenly moistened and begins to clump together. Gather into a cohesive ball, flatten into discs, wrap and refrigerate.

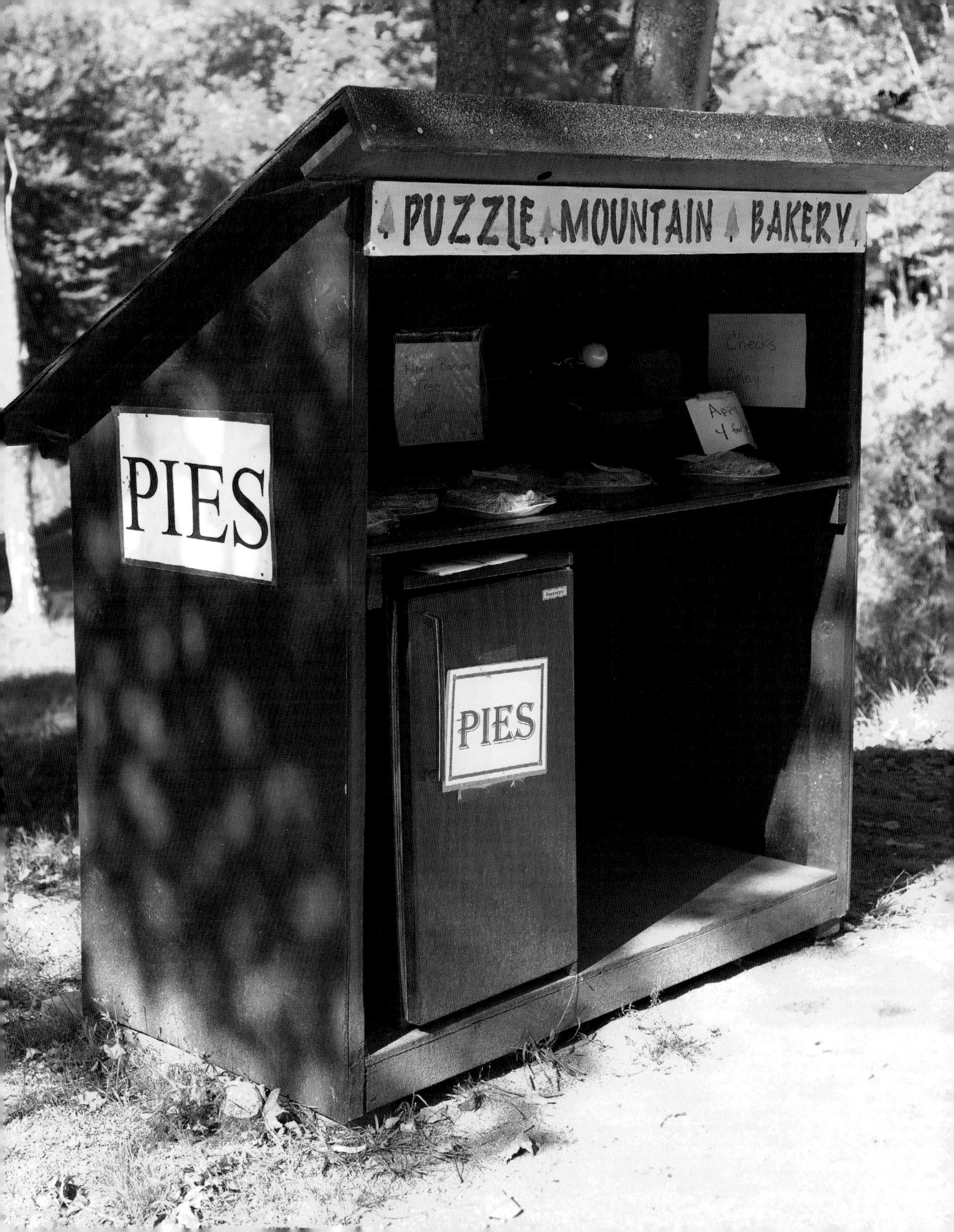
PUZZLE MOUNTAIN BAKERY
PIES
PIES

Springtime Strawberry Rhubarb Crumble-Topped Pie

Rhubarb is one of that small select group of ingredients (also comprising asparagus, fiddleheads, and dandelion greens) that is emblematic of spring in Maine. When you begin to see gardens burgeoning with clumps of elephant-ear-shaped rhubarb leaves, it's time for rejoicing. There are other uses for rhubarb — as sauce, in preserves and chutneys — but because it is so often baked into pies, it came to be known as the "pie plant." You could make this pie with all rhubarb (in which case you'd want to decrease the flour to 2½ tablespoons) but adding strawberries with their extra juiciness and sweetness is a classic springtime pie combo. If you prefer a pastry top, omit the prebaking and follow the instructions for crafting an apple pie (page 257), dotting the filling with butter before covering with the top crust.

My Flaky Pie Pastry (page 235) or Old-Fashioned Lard Crust (page 236) for a single-crust pie

CRUMBLE TOPPING

⅔ cup all-purpose flour

3 tablespoons light brown sugar

2 tablespoons granulated sugar

⅛ teaspoon salt

5 tablespoons cold unsalted butter

6—8 SERVINGS

1. On a floured surface, roll out the dough, working from the center in all directions until you have a 12-inch round. Fold the dough in half and ease it into a 9-inch pie pan with the fold in the center. Unfold the dough and fit the pastry into the pan. Trim and flute the edges and prick the crust all over with a fork. Freeze for at least 30 minutes.

2. Preheat the oven to 375°F.

3. Press a sheet of foil into the bottom of the pie shell. Bake for 20 minutes. Remove the foil and continue to bake for 5 to 8 minutes, until pale golden. If the pastry starts to puff up, press the bottom gently with a large spatula or oven-mitted hand to flatten. Fill immediately or cool on a rack.

One Man's Meat

We had stewed rhubarb for lunch. It was from stewed rhubarb that the gods got their idea for ambrosia.

— E.B. White, *One Man's Meat*

STRAWBERRY RHUBARB FILLING

2 ½ cups sliced rhubarb (about 1 pound) (see Note)

2 ½ cups hulled strawberries, halved or quartered if large (1 ¼ pints)

2   teaspoons lemon juice (juice of ⅓ medium lemon)

1   teaspoon pure vanilla extract

1   cup sugar

⅓   cup unbleached, all-purpose flour

¼   teaspoon salt

¼   teaspoon ground cinnamon

4. Meanwhile, make the crumble topping. Combine the flour, brown sugar, granulated sugar, and salt in a medium-sized bowl. Cut the butter into small pieces, scatter over the flour mixture, and use your fingers to work the mixture together until large, moist clumps form. (Large clumps make a more attractive finished topping.) Refrigerate until ready to use.

5. Combine the rhubarb and strawberries in a large bowl and toss with the lemon juice, and vanilla. Sprinkle with the sugar, flour, salt, and cinnamon, and toss to combine. Heap into the pie shell and sprinkle evenly with the crumble topping.

6. Bake until the topping is browned and the fruit juices bubble through, 1¼ to 1½ hours. Cool on a wire rack for at least 1 hour to allow juices to thicken further.

Note: *Cut the rhubarb into slices about 1 inch long. If the pieces are too small, they will "melt" while baking, losing all their identity.*

— Origins of Maine Cuisine

Maine's short northern growing season and harsh winters dictated a need for preserved foods, and salt pork, salted and smoked fish, pickled vegetables, and dried beans were essential elements in the diets of Mainers from all walks of life. As Europeans settled in and began to farm in earnest, their food-stuffs expanded to include chickens and turkeys, corned (salted) beef, deer and other wild game, pumpkins and winter squashes, cornmeal, potatoes and other root vegetables, and apples. They relied on maple sugar, syrup, and molasses for sweetening. (Of these, corn, beans, winter squash, and maple were introduced to the early settlers by the local Pasamaquoddy tribe and other Native Americans.) These raw ingredients were crafted into such familiar homespun dishes as fish and clam chowders, cod fish cakes, baked beans, coot stew, boiled dinner (turned next day into red flannel hash), johnnycake (corn bread), biscuits, steamed brown bread, pea soup, gingerbread, and pies made with a lard crust.

U-Pick Strawberry Shortcake with Egg Biscuit

Shortcake is one of America's most estimable contributions to the roster of the world's great desserts. Simplicity itself, shortcake, which requires little in the way of culinary expertise except for a light hand with the dough, is the epitome of good Yankee country cooking, and strawberry shortcake, made with dead-ripe, fragrant native berries, is probably the queen of all shortcakes. Whether gathered on hands and knees at a pick-your-own farm or bought from a roadside stand or farmers' market, in-season native strawberries are surely one of nature's most priceless seasonal offerings. This "short" (meaning very buttery) egg biscuit is made into one large cake for an impressive presentation to a large group. Although shortcake is best served warm, I do give instructions for preparing all the elements before guests arrive.

STRAWBERRY FILLING

2   quarts ripe strawberries, preferably local berries

1/3   cup sugar

2   teaspoons lemon juice (juice of 1/3 medium lemon)

8 SERVINGS

1. To make the strawberry filling, choose 8 pretty berries and set them aside. Hull the remaining berries. Place half of the berries in a large shallow bowl or on a large rimmed plate and crush them with a large fork or a potato masher. Slice the remaining berries and combine with the crushed berries. Stir in the sugar and lemon juice and set aside at room temperature for at least 30 minutes to allow the juices to flow. (The strawberry mixture can be prepared up to 6 hours ahead and refrigerated. Return to room temperature before serving.)

2. Preheat the oven to 450°F. Generously grease an 8-inch cake pan with butter.

3. To make the egg biscuit, pulse the flour, sugar, baking powder, and salt in a food processor to blend. Distribute the butter over the flour mixture and pulse until the mixture looks crumbly. Pour the milk into a glass measure and whisk in the egg. With the motor running, pour the milk mixture through the feed tube and process just until the dough begins to clump together. (To make by hand, whisk the dry ingredients together in a bowl, work in the cold butter with your fingertips, add the milk and egg, and stir with a large fork to make a soft dough.)

4. Scrape out onto a lightly floured surface, knead lightly a few times, and roll to an 8-inch round. (The dough can be prepared ahead and refrigerated. To make individual biscuits, see Note.)

EGG BISCUIT AND TOPPING

2   cups all-purpose flour

¼   cup sugar

4   teaspoons baking powder

½   teaspoon salt

½   cup (1 stick) cold unsalted
       butter, cut into about 12 pieces

½   cup whole or low-fat milk

1   egg

1½   cups heavy cream

2   tablespoons powdered sugar

3   tablespoons unsalted butter,
       softened

5. Transfer the dough to the prepared pan, patting it gently to the edges. Place in the oven and immediately reduce the oven temperature to 375°F. Bake until the shortcake is pale golden brown on top, 22 to 26 minutes. Cool in the pan on a rack for 10 minutes.

6. To make the topping, whip the cream with the powdered sugar in a medium to large bowl until it forms soft peaks. (This step can be done a couple of hours ahead; refrigerate the topping.)

7. To assemble, using a large spatula, transfer the shortcake to a large serving platter. Use a serrated knife to split the cake horizontally and lift off the top with a large spatula. Spread the bottom of the cake with the softened butter, spoon on about half the berry mixture, and spread with about half the whipped cream. Replace the top, spoon over the remaining berry mixture, and top with the remaining whipped cream. Decorate with the reserved berries. Cut into wedges to serve.

Note: *To make individual biscuits, roll the dough to about ¾-inch thickness and cut out 8 biscuits using a 2½-inch cutter. Arrange on a baking sheet and bake for 15 to 18 minutes.*

— Shortcake at the Fair

The Mountain Rebekah Lodge sells out of strawberry and blueberry shortcake every year at its booth at the Blue Hill Fair. Maybe it's because the cream is real — and hand whipped — the berries are local, and the shortcake biscuits are homemade. The Rebekahs get together and bake the biscuits (using the recipe on the Bakewell Cream can; see Maine's Own Leavening, page 213), split them, brush them with butter, and freeze them until the fair. One recent year the committee baked more than 315 dozen shortcakes.

"Working at the fair is fun," commented Betty Gray. "Until about ten o'clock at night. Even then, we always find something to laugh about. You'd be surprised at some of the things you see at the fair."

Best Wild Blueberry Pie

Not that you can't bake a wonderful pie with large highbush blueberries — in fact, you can — but until you've tasted a slice of pie made with the tiny lowbush Maine blueberries, you haven't *quite* lived a full and complete life — culinarily speaking, at least. Mainers don't tamper much with their wild blueberry pie filling, so this one is as pure and pristine as a cloudless Down East late-summer day, with the addition only of a smidgen of cinnamon and a little lemon juice to bring out the flavor of the berries. Because the deep purpley-blue of the berry filling is so gorgeous, this pie is especially lovely with a woven-lattice crust (see Note).

My Flaky Pie Pastry (page 235) or
   Old-Fashioned Lard Crust
   (page 236)

4 1/2 cups (2 pints) blueberries

3/4 cup sugar

2 1/2 tablespoons all-purpose flour

1   tablespoon lemon juice (juice of
   1/2 medium lemon)

1/4 teaspoon ground cinnamon

1/8 teaspoon salt

1   tablespoon unsalted butter, cut
   into several pieces

6 – 8 SERVINGS

1. Preheat the oven to 425°F.

2. On a floured surface, roll out one dough disc, working from the center in all directions until you have a 12-inch round. Fold the dough in half and ease it into a 9-inch pie pan with the fold in the center. Unfold the dough and fit the pastry into the pan.

3. Toss the blueberries with the sugar, flour, lemon juice, cinnamon, and salt in a large bowl. Scrape into the prepared pie shell and distribute the butter over the fruit.

4. Roll out the second dough disc to a 12-inch round and place over the fruit. (For a woven-lattice crust, see Note.) Trim the overhanging dough to 3/4-inch all around, fold the edges under the bottom pastry, and flute or crimp the dough to seal. Use a sharp knife to slash several steam vents in the crust.

Island Blackberries

I do like to think that our island berries are special. Of all the berries our island offers, the blackberry is my favorite to pick, and the challenge of picking them makes a full container all the more gratifying. Island friends tell me they put blackberries on cereal, ice cream, and yogurt. I know some people make blackberry cobblers and pies, jams and jellies. A neighbor makes blackberry wine. A blackberry shortcake — sugared, mashed berries over a warm biscuit or scone, with dollops of whipped cream — is by far my favorite way to consume the juicy and crunchy blackberry.

               — Jenna Webster, Vinalhaven, Maine, in *The Working Waterfront*

5. Bake for 30 minutes. Reduce the oven temperature to 350°F and bake until the crust is golden and the berry juices bubble through the vents, 25 to 35 minutes longer. Cool on a wire rack.

6. Serve slightly warm or at room temperature.

Note: *To make a lattice, roll out the top crust, cut it into ½-inch-wide strips. For a simple lattice, arrange dough strips over filling, spacing ¾-inch apart. Form lattice by arranging more dough strips at right angle to first strips, spacing ¾-inch apart. Trim ends to ¾-inch. Press ends of strips into edge of bottom pastry. Fold bottom pastry over strips. Seal and crimp edge. For an interwoven lattice, arrange strips over filling, then, starting in the center, interweave the strips into a lattice. (Consult a good reference, such as* The Joy of Cooking *[Scribner, 1997]). Turn the edges under and seal and crimp edge.*

Maine Wild Blueberries

Maine wild blueberries are lowbush blueberries. The plants grow only 6 to 18 inches high, as opposed to the much taller highbush cultivated blueberries. Wild blueberries are smaller and usually a little less sweet than cultivated blueberries, with a distinctive intense berry flavor.

One of North America's few native fruits (cranberries and wild grapes are two others), lowbush blueberries grow thickly on treeless sandy "barrens" in coastal Maine, particularly way Down East in Washington County. Blueberries are called an "assisted wild crop" because growers do not cultivate the plants per se, but they do irrigate, fertilize, spray, mow, and pollinate the crop. Some growers are trying mechanical harvesters, but most blueberry harvesting is still done by hand with a steel rake that is pulled through the tangled branches. Its teeth are close enough to catch the berries, but it takes a careful teasing movement to get them off without breaking their skins. After harvesting, they're canned or flash-frozen. Much of the crop is sold to companies like Sara Lee for pie fillings and muffin and pancake mixes.

In Maine, wild blueberries are picked and sold in their fresh state for a few brief shining August weeks, in heaping pints and quarts, from roadside honor stands and in local grocery stores. Then, in the Down East version of a bacchanal, they are eaten for breakfast, lunch, dinner, and snacks, slurped by the handful, scattered on cereal and ice cream, stewed into jam and jelly, and baked into breads, muffins, cobblers, cakes, puddings, and, of course, pies.

Blueberry-Peach Torta

Call it a tart, a torta (in Italian), a croustade or a cake — I couldn't resist including this fabulous open-faced, fruit-filled beauty in the book. The recipe is an adaptation of one that graced *Gourmet* magazine's cover a summer or two ago, but, not quite satisfied with the original, I changed things quite a bit (increasing the sugar, adding the cornmeal, and so on), much to the enjoyment of my dinner guests that summer, who quite happily ate any and all versions. Blueberries are, of course, emblematic of Maine summer, but, perhaps surprisingly, there are also some peach trees in the state and they produce some small, intensely flavorful fruit.

CORNMEAL TORTA DOUGH

1¼ cups all-purpose flour

⅔ cup sugar

¼ cup cornmeal

¼ teaspoon salt

½ cup (1 stick) cold unsalted butter, cut into about 8 chunks

1 egg

1 teaspoon pure vanilla extract

8 SERVINGS

1. To make the dough, combine the flour, sugar, cornmeal, and salt in a food processor. Pulse once or twice to blend. Add the butter and pulse just until most of the butter is about the size of peas.

2. In a glass measuring cup, whisk together the egg and vanilla. Drizzle the egg mixture through the feed tube and pulse until the dough clumps and begins to form a ball on top of the blades. (To make by hand, whisk the dry ingredients together in a bowl, work in the cold butter with your fingertips, add the egg mixture, and stir with a large fork to make a soft dough.) Turn out onto a board and knead several times to make a smooth ball.

3. Press the dough evenly into the bottom and about 1½ inches up the sides of a 9- to 9½-inch springform pan (see Note). Freeze for at least 15 minutes. (The torta shell can be made ahead and refrigerated up to 2 days or frozen for up to 2 weeks, wrapped in plastic.)

4. Preheat the oven to 350°F.

5. To make the filling, combine the sugar, flour, and cornstarch in a large bowl and whisk to combine. Add the peaches, blueberries, and lemon juice and toss to coat the fruit with the sugar mixture. Scrape into the torta shell and rearrange the fruit to make an even layer.

6. Place a sheet of foil over the torta and bake for 1 hour 30 minutes. Remove the foil and continue to bake for 15 to 20 minutes, until the longer peaches are soft and the blueberry juices are bubbling.

FRUIT FILLING

3/4 cup sugar

2 tablespoons all-purpose flour

2 teaspoons cornstarch

4 large ripe peaches (about 2 pounds), peeled and cut into thick slices

1 cup blueberries (1/2 pint)

1 tablespoon lemon juice (juice of 1/2 medium lemon)

Powdered sugar

7. Transfer to a rack to cool in the pan for 15 minutes. Remove the sides of the pan, leaving the torta on the pan bottom, and cool completely. (The torta can be made up to 4 hours ahead and held at cool room temperature.) Sieve the powdered sugar over the top before serving.

Note: *This dough is very malleable and shapes well. It's easiest to press into the pan by first flattening the dough into the bottom and then working it evenly up the sides, thinning the bottom in the process. I make a fist with my hand and press with my flattened first finger joints.*

—— Blueberry Tips and Lore ——

- A recent study found that blueberries are very high in healthful antioxidants.
- Blueberries are 85 percent water, and most of the flavor is in the skin. Since small, low bush blueberries have a greater proportion of skin, their flavor is more intense that larger high bush berries.
- When buying blueberries, check the sides and bottoms of the cardboard container for juice stains. Stains are an indication of over-ripeness, which can lead to mold.
- Store blueberries in the refrigerator in their original carton. If fresh, they'll keep this way for about a week.
- Rinse blueberries gently in cold water before using or serving.

- To freeze raw blueberries, first rinse and gently drain the berries and spread them out onto a paper towel-lined baking sheet. Place the baking sheet in the freezer until the berries are frozen through. Pour the frozen berries into freezer bags, and seal well. When they thaw in December, you'll have individual berries, not a lumpen mass. To use, rinse gently with warm water to remove ice crystals.
- Blueberries cooked with a little sugar for a few minutes to a thick saucelike consistency also freeze well.
- To remove berry stains from your white shirt, stretch the cloth over a bowl and pour boiling water down over the stain.

Graham-Cracker Cream Pie

One of the standout cream pies at Helen's Restaurant is this graham-cracker cream, which is simply a luscious egg custard nestled in toasty crumbs and topped with either shiny meringue (as in this recipe) or lightly sweetened whipped cream.

GRAHAM-CRACKER CRUST AND TOPPING

2 cups crushed graham crackers (from about 15 double graham crackers)

5 tablespoons unsalted butter, melted

1/2 teaspoon ground cinnamon

6—8 SERVINGS

1. Preheat the oven to 350°F.

2. To make the crust and topping, toss together the graham-cracker crumbs, melted butter, and cinnamon in a bowl. Remove and reserve 1/4 cup of the crumb mixture to use on the top. Press the remainder evenly into the bottom and up the sides of a 9-inch pie pan. Bake for 5 minutes, or until the crust just begins to smell toasty. Cool on a wire rack.

3. Reduce the oven temperature to 325°F.

4. To make the filling, whisk together the sugar, cornstarch, and salt in a medium-sized heavy saucepan. Slowly whisk in the milk and place the pan over medium-high heat. Cook, whisking constantly, until the mixture comes to a boil and is thick, about 5 minutes. Continue to cook for 1 minute longer, whisking until smooth.

— Fear of Piecrust Syndrome

Millions of otherwise accomplished cooks and bakers all across America suffer from Fear of Piecrust. Sure, the fillings are fun, and who doesn't love the idea of presenting a gloriously hand-crafted pie to a table full of admiring guests, but . . . oh, the angst when the stuff crumbles to bits while you're rolling it out, or glues itself to the board, or falls into pieces when you're lifting it into the pie pan. (Simply smush it all back together, flour the board liberally, and start again.) Or, if all this just seems like too much, there's absolutely nothing wrong with buying those already-rolled-out crusts in the refrigerated section of the supermarket. They taste fine, they fit into a standard 9-inch pie pan, and you can even crimp or flute the edges so the pie *looks* homemade. Since purchased crusts contain more sugar than homemade, they tend to brown more quickly, so subtract a few minutes from the cooking time.

CREAM FILLING

½ cup sugar

3 tablespoons cornstarch

¼ teaspoon salt

2 cups whole milk

3 egg yolks

1 tablespoon pure vanilla extract

MERINGUE (SEE NOTE)

3 egg whites

¼ teaspoon cream of tartar

5 tablespoons sugar

5. Lightly beat the egg yolks in a small bowl. Whisk about a third of the hot mixture into the yolks to temper them, then return the yolk mixture to the saucepan. Cook, whisking constantly, until the custard almost reaches a boil, 1 to 2 minutes. Stir in the vanilla.

6. Pour the custard into the prepared pie shell and press a sheet of plastic wrap directly on the surface to prevent a skin from forming.

7. To make the meringue, beat the egg whites with an electric mixer in a large bowl until foamy. Add the cream of tartar and beat until soft peaks begin to form. Gradually add the sugar and continue beating until the meringue is stiff, smooth, and glossy. Remove the plastic wrap from the custard. Beginning at the edges of the crust, spread the meringue over the custard. Sprinkle with the reserved crumb mixture.

8. Bake until the meringue is just touched with gold, about 12 minutes. Cool on a wire rack for at least 2 hours before serving.

Note: *If you prefer, substitute 1 cup of heavy cream whipped with 2 tablespoons sugar for the Meringue Topping. Spread it over the cooled custard and refrigerate.*

HELEN'S RESTAURANT

Helen's Restaurant, way Down East in Machias, has been a beloved local institution for more than a half century, and during that time the restaurant has been owned by only three families.

Helen's motto is "Almost Home," and current owners Gary and Judy Hanscom more than succeed in retaining the plain but comfy ambience and honest Maine food that patrons know. They have even expanded, opening a second Helen's in Ellsworth.

Seafood stews and chowders — haddock, lobster, crabmeat, and scallop — all made with fresh local seafood, are standouts. Fried seafood is a good bet, as are the comfort-food specials, such as roast turkey, pork chops, and liver and onions. And then there are the pies. Cream pies are my favorite type here — chocolate cream, banana cream, lemon meringue, and graham-cracker cream.

Rustic Summer Berry Croustade

This hand-formed tart, with its hidden sprinkling of sweet sliced almonds under the fruit filling, has the virtue of being simultaneously down-to-earth as well as sophisticated — a winning combination in my book. You can make it with whatever berries or other summer fruit is at its peak (see Note) and proudly serve it as the delectable finish to almost any summer meal you can think of.

PASTRY

1 1/4 cups all-purpose flour

2 teaspoons sugar

1/2 teaspoon salt

1/2 cup (1 stick) cold unsalted butter, cut into small pieces

3–4 tablespoons ice water

FILLING

2 1/2 cups blueberries (1 1/4 pints) or fruit combination (see Note)

1/2 cup sugar

2 tablespoons cornstarch

1 teaspoon lemon juice (juice of 1/8 medium lemon)

1/2 teaspoon ground cinnamon

1 egg beaten with 2 teaspoons water (egg glaze)

1/3 cup sliced almonds

1 tablespoon cold unsalted butter, cut into 3 or 4 pieces

Powdered sugar

Vanilla ice cream (optional)

1. To make the pastry, combine the flour, sugar, and salt in a food processor. Pulse to mix. Distribute the butter over the flour and process in short bursts until the mixture is about the size of small peas. Sprinkle 3 tablespoons of the ice water over the mixture and pulse just until no dry flour remains and the dough begins to clump together. If the dough is too dry, sprinkle on the remaining 1 tablespoon water and pulse again. (To make by hand, see page 236.)

2. Turn out onto a sheet of plastic wrap, gather into a ball, flatten to a 5-inch disc, and refrigerate for at least 30 minutes.

3. To make the filling, toss the berries with the sugar, cornstarch, lemon juice, and cinnamon in a large bowl.

4. Preheat the oven to 425°F.

5. On a lightly floured surface, roll out the dough, working from the center in all directions until you have a 13-inch round. Do not trim the edges, as they are supposed to be ragged. Fold the pastry in half, then transfer it to a large rimmed baking sheet, patching any tears by pressing the dough together with your fingers. Brush the pastry with some of the egg glaze and sprinkle with the almonds. Spoon the fruit filling onto the dough, mounding it slightly higher in the center and leaving a 2-inch border all around the edge. Fold the border in, pleating it as necessary to make an uneven 1½-inch-wide edge. Scatter the butter over the fruit and brush the edges of the crust with the egg glaze.

6. Bake for 15 minutes. Reduce the oven temperature to 375°F and continue to bake 25 to 30 minutes longer, until the pastry is golden brown, the fruit is soft, and the juices are bubbly. Transfer to a wire rack with a large spatula to cool.

7. Sprinkle with the powdered sugar and serve slightly warm or at room temperature, with scoops of the ice cream, if desired.

Note: *You can make this tart with just blueberries or other fruit combinations, such as blueberries and raspberries, blackberries and sliced peaches, or raspberries and rhubarb.*

Lemon-Peel Pound Cake for the Berries

This intensely lemony, nicely sliceable, tender-crumbed pound cake tastes wonderful on its own, but mainly it appears in this book because it's just the perfect vehicle for serving with summer berries and other fruits. Just stir the fruit — blueberries, sliced strawberries, raspberries, or sliced peaches or nectarines — with enough sugar to sweeten, set aside at room temperature for at least an hour to allow the juices to flow, and that's all there is to it. I like to keep this cake in the freezer all summer as berry insurance.

1½ cups plus 2 tablespoons cake flour

¼ teaspoon salt

⅛ teaspoon baking soda

¾ cup (1½ sticks) unsalted butter, softened

3 ounces cream cheese, softened

1½ cups sugar, plus ¼ cup for glaze

3 eggs

1 teaspoon pure vanilla extract

1 tablespoon grated lemon zest

6 tablespoons lemon juice (juice of 3 medium lemons)

Powdered sugar

AT LEAST 18 SLICES

1. Position a rack in the center of the oven and preheat the oven to 325°F. Grease a 10-cup nonstick Bundt pan with butter, sprinkle with 2 tablespoons of the flour, and knock out the excess.

2. Whisk together the flour, salt, and baking soda in a medium-sized bowl.

3. Using an electric mixer, cream the butter and cream cheese until fluffy in a large bowl. Gradually beat in 1½ cups of the sugar, and continue to beat for 3 minutes, scraping down the sides of the bowl once or twice. Add the eggs, one at a time, beating well after each addition. Beat in the vanilla, lemon zest, and 2 tablespoons of the lemon juice. Add the flour mixture in 3 batches and beat until just smooth. Spoon into the prepared pan, smoothing the top.

4. Bake in the center of the oven until the top is pale golden and a tester inserted near the center comes out clean, 40 to 45 minutes. Cool in the pan on a rack for 10 minutes. Unmold onto a rack set over a sheet of waxed paper.

5. In a small saucepan, heat the remaining ¼ cup sugar and the remaining 4 tablespoons lemon juice until bubbly and the sugar dissolves. Brush the syrup over the warm cake. Cool completely, wrap, and refrigerate for up to 2 days, or freeze for up to 1 month.

6. Sprinkle with the powdered sugar before cutting into slices, and serve.

Blueberry Cornmeal Cake with Toasted Nut Topping

Recipes similar to this one appear in most old Maine cookbooks. In Marjorie Standish's *Cooking Down East* (Down East Books, 1969) she puts Melt-in-Your-Mouth Blueberry Cake as the first recipe in her desserts chapter and says it was the "most popular recipe ever used" in her column, which ran in the *Maine Sunday Telegram* for 25 years during the mid-twentieth century. I have adjusted proportions a bit, and added some yellow cornmeal for its pleasantly crunchy texture and color. The cake can be used as a coffee cake or a snack cake or as a lovely, not-too-sweet dessert, especially if you make it in a round pan, cut it in wedges, and serve with a scoop of vanilla ice cream or a pitcher of heavy "pouring" cream.

1   cup plus 2 tablespoons all-purpose flour

3   tablespoons yellow cornmeal

1   teaspoon baking powder

½   teaspoon salt

½   cup (1 stick) unsalted butter, softened

1   cup plus 1 tablespoon sugar

2   eggs

⅓   cup whole or low-fat milk

1   teaspoon pure vanilla extract

½   teaspoon grated lemon zest

1½ cups blueberries (¾ pint)

¾   cup chopped pecans or walnuts

8–10 SERVINGS

1. Preheat the oven to 350°F. Grease a 9-inch square baking pan or 9-inch round cake pan with butter.

2. Whisk together 1 cup of the flour, cornmeal, baking powder, and salt in a bowl.

3. Using an electric mixer, cream the butter with 1 cup of the sugar in a large bowl. Add the eggs and beat until smooth. Beat in the milk, vanilla, and lemon zest. (It's okay if the mixture looks curdled at this point.) Add the flour mixture and beat on medium speed just until smooth.

4. Toss the blueberries in a bowl with the remaining 2 tablespoons flour to help prevent them from sinking to the bottom of the cake. Fold the blueberries into the batter, taking care not to mash them. Scrape the batter into the prepared pan, smoothing the top. Sprinkle evenly with the nuts and then with the remaining 1 tablespoon sugar.

5. Bake until the nuts look toasted and a tester inserted in the center of the cake comes out clean, 35 to 40 minutes. Cool completely in the pan on a wire rack. If not serving immediately, run a knife around the edges of the pan, invert onto a rack, and turn top-side up. (If nuts fall off, simply press them back into the cake.) Wrap in plastic wrap and refrigerate for up to 2 days, or freeze for up to 1 month.

6. Cut into squares or wedges to serve.

Gratin of Berries with Sweet Cheese Topping

Ripe summer berries (or other fruits, see Note) are topped with dollops of sweetened goat cheese and briefly baked in a hot oven. What could possibly be simpler? Or more delicious? If you have lots of fruit and need to feed more people, simply use a larger dish and increase the ingredients accordingly.

2   cups (1 pint) blueberries, raspberries, sliced strawberries, blackberries or a combination (see Note)

3   tablespoons half-and-half

2   tablespoons cream cheese, at room temperature

2   tablespoons fresh goat cheese, at room temperature

1   teaspoon granulated sugar

1   teaspoon pure vanilla extract

3   tablespoons dark brown sugar or granulated brown sugar

4 SERVINGS

1. Generously grease a 1-quart gratin dish or other shallow broiler-proof baking dish with butter. Preheat the oven to 450°F. Spread the berries into the bottom of the dish.

2. Combine the half-and-half, cream cheese, goat cheese, granulated sugar, and vanilla in a bowl and blend with a fork or small whisk until smooth. Spoon dollops over the fruit and then sprinkle with the brown sugar. (The dessert can be prepared up to several hours ahead to this point. Cover and refrigerate.)

3. Place the dish in the preheated oven and roast until the fruit starts to release its juices and the cheese begins to melt, 10 to 12 minutes. Serve warm directly from the baking dish.

Note: *This is also delicious with thinly sliced stone fruits such as peaches, plums, or nectarines, and also with sliced bananas or mangoes.*

Blueberry Heritage

The Passamaquoddy Indian tribe purchased Northeastern Blueberry Company in 1980. Manager Darrell Newell says that the tribe members have vowed never to use mechanical harvesters. "Picking blueberries is part of our heritage," he said.

Mixed Summer Fruit Cobbler

A cobbler is such a wonderful way to showcase summer fruits of all kinds. I have worked out the proportions of this recipe carefully so that the amount of biscuit topping is just right — not too cakey — for a one-quart dish. Its sweetness is pegged mainly to tart lowbush Maine blueberries, so if you use very ripe, sweeter fruit you might want to decrease the sugar by a tablespoon or two. But do experiment with a mix of any of the fruits suggested. You can't really go wrong, and the results will invariably be delicious.

FRUIT LAYER

- 4   cups fruit (blueberries; raspberries; blackberries; peeled and sliced peaches, nectarines, Italian prune plums; or any combination)
- 1/2   cup sugar
- 1/2   teaspoon grated lemon zest
- 2   teaspoons lemon juice (juice of 1/3 medium lemon)
- 1   teaspoon pure vanilla extract

COBBLER DOUGH

- 1   cup all-purpose flour
- 2   tablespoons plus 1 teaspoon sugar
- 2   teaspoons baking powder
- 1/2   teaspoon salt
- 5   tablespoons cold unsalted butter, cut into about 10 pieces
- 1/3   cup whole or low-fat milk

Lightly sweetened whipped cream or vanilla ice cream for serving

1. Preheat the oven to 400°F. Generously grease a shallow 1-quart baking dish, such as a deep pie pan or 8-inch square dish, with butter.

2. Place the fruit in the prepared dish, add the sugar, lemon zest and juice, vanilla, and stir gently to combine.

3. To make the dough, combine the flour, 2 tablespoons of the sugar, baking powder, and salt in a food processor and pulse to blend. Distribute the butter over the flour mixture and pulse until the butter chunks are about the size of small peas. With the motor running, pour the milk through the feed tube, stopping the machine as soon as the flour is moistened and the dough begins to clump together. (To make by hand, whisk the flour mixture together in a bowl, work the butter in with your fingertips, and stir in the milk with a large fork.)

4. Transfer the dough to a lightly floured board, knead a couple of times to bring the dough together, and roll or pat out into the approximate shape of the top of your dish. Trim the edges so the topping is slightly smaller than the dish, then crimp the edges with your fingertips or a fork. Place the dough over the fruit and cut several deep slashes to let steam escape. Sprinkle with the remaining teaspoon of sugar.

5. Bake for 20 to 30 minutes, until the topping is golden and the fruit is bubbly. Serve warm or at room temperature with whipped cream or ice cream.

Farm Stand Apple Crisp with Walnut-Oat Crunch

A crisp, which is even more casual and easier to make than a cobbler, seems to me perfectly suited to fall cooking. Sturdier, less sweet autumn fruits are blanketed by a layer of oaty, nutty topping that develops into a crunchy crust as it bakes, sending the perfume of cinnamon-scented apples out into the house.

WALNUT-OAT CRUNCH

- ¼ cup walnuts
- ½ cup packed light brown sugar
- ⅓ cup all-purpose flour
- ½ teaspoon ground cinnamon
- ⅛ teaspoon salt
- 5 tablespoons cold unsalted butter, cut into chunks
- ½ cup old-fashioned rolled oats or quick-cooking oats (not instant oatmeal)

APPLE FILLING

- 8 cups peeled and sliced medium-sweet apples, such as Cortland, Jonathan, or Macoun, or a mixture of tart and sweet such as Granny Smith and McIntosh (about 2½ pounds)
- ½ cup sugar
- 1 tablespoon lemon juice (juice of ½ medium lemon)
- 2 teaspoons pure vanilla extract

Vanilla ice cream

6—8 SERVINGS

1. To make the Walnut-Oat Crunch, pulse the walnuts in a food processor in short bursts until coarsely chopped. Remove and reserve. Combine the brown sugar, flour, cinnamon, and salt and process with long pulses to remove any lumps in the sugar. Add the butter and pulse in short bursts until most of the butter clumps are about the size of lima beans. Add the oats and pulse once or twice just to combine. Don't overprocess or the topping will be too uniform. Stir in the walnuts. (The topping can be made by hand by crumbling the flour and shortening together with your fingertips. It can be made ahead and refrigerated for up to 2 days, or frozen for up to 1 month.)

2. Preheat the oven to 350°F. Grease a shallow 2-quart baking dish, such as a 9-inch square pan.

3. To make the filling, toss the apples with the sugar, lemon juice, and vanilla in a bowl and spread in the bottom of the prepared dish. Sprinkle on the topping, spreading to the edges.

4. Bake, uncovered, until the apples are tender and the topping is browned, 50 minutes to 1 hour.

5. Serve hot or warm with scoops of ice cream.

   Note: *If the crisp has cooled to room temperature, reheat in a 400°F oven for about 10 minutes.*

U-Pick

Want to experience the prickly, dusty, buggy, thirsty work of picking your own raspberries, blackberries, blueberries, or strawberries? Despite the discomfort, it's fun, it's rewarding, it's money-saving, it's real — and the fruit tastes fabulous. The Maine Department of Agriculture's Web site, www.getrealmaine.com, has a great list of pick-your-own farms.

— Apples of Your Pie —

My apple pie recipe calls for a combination of sweet, juicy McIntoshes and tart, firm Granny Smiths. However, you may be able to substitute other apple varieties from your local farm stand or orchard for these pie apples commonly found in supermarkets:

Granny Smith (crisp, firm, and tart; sweeten with extra sugar or balance with a sweeter apple in pies) — substitute Greening, Pippin, York, Winesap

Macoun (medium-sweet, crisp, medium-juicy; good used alone in pies) — substitute Crispin, Gravenstein, Northern Spy, Rome Beauty, Cortland, Jonathan, Baldwin

McIntosh (sweet, aromatic, juicy; needs to be balanced with a tarter, firmer apple in pies) — substitute Golden Delicious, Gala, Fuji, Empire, Ida Red

Sedgwick Potluck-Supper Apple Pie

Even in Maine, which is considered, still, to be prime pie country, it's getting harder and harder — sad to say — to get a slice of real apple pie with a hand-crafted crust and made with sliced fresh apples. Some good old-fashioned places like Moody's Diner in Waldoboro still do it, and you can score the occasional slice of genuine apple pie at local public suppers. All that apple peeling, coring, and slicing is, indeed, labor intensive, which is why it's such a wonderful choice for a potluck supper (like the ones we have in my little town of Sedgwick) when the only thing the dessert maker has to do all day is bake the pie. Follow the suggested combination of readily available Granny Smiths and McIntosh, or use whatever local apples are fresh and good (see Apples of Your Pie, opposite).

---

1   cup sugar

2   tablespoons all-purpose flour

½   teaspoon ground cinnamon

¼   teaspoon ground nutmeg

¼   teaspoon salt

Pinch ground allspice

3   cups cored, peeled, and thinly sliced tart, crisp apples such as Granny Smith (about 1 pound)

3   cups cored, peeled, and thinly sliced juicy sweet apples such as McIntosh (about 1 pound)

1   teaspoon grated lemon zest

2   tablespoons lemon juice (juice of 1 medium lemon)

Old-Fashioned Lard Crust (page 236) or My Flaky Pie Pastry (page 235)

2   tablespoons unsalted butter, cut into chunks

Vanilla ice cream (optional)

6–8 SERVINGS

1. Whisk together the sugar, flour, cinnamon, nutmeg, salt, and allspice in a large bowl. Add the apples and lemon zest and juice and toss to combine thoroughly. Set aside for 15 minutes or so, until the apples begin to soften slightly.

2. Preheat the oven to 425°F.

3. On a floured surface, roll out one dough disc, working from the center in all directions until you have a 12-inch round. Fold the dough in half and ease it into a 9-inch pie pan with the fold in the center. Unfold the dough and fit the pastry into the pan. Spoon the apple mixture into the pie shell and distribute the butter over the apples. Roll out the second dough disc to a 12-inch round and place over the fruit. Trim the overhanging dough to ¾-inch all around, fold the edges under the bottom pastry, and flute or crimp the dough to seal. Use a sharp knife to slash several steam vents in the crust.

4. Bake for 30 minutes. Reduce oven to 350°F and bake until the crust is golden brown and juices bubble up through the vents, 25 to 35 minutes longer. Cool on a rack for at least 1 hour. Serve warm or at room temperature, with scoops of vanilla ice cream, if desired.

Bourbon Pumpkin Pie

Pumpkin pie is simply a custard pie made with pumpkin purée and seasoned with traditional sweet spices. After trying a couple of times to make pies with "from scratch" pumpkin purée (cutting, roasting, scraping, mashing), I concluded that it's really not worth the trouble — in fact, canned pumpkin is superior in some ways because the purée has been cooked down to a properly thick consistency. Just be sure not to buy pre-sweetened and spiced pumpkin-pie filling. This pie follows a rather classic formula, with a small slug of bourbon or rum added for interest (though it's fine, too, without the spirits).

My Flaky Pie Pastry (page 235) for single-crust pie

2 cups pumpkin purée (15-ounce can)

3/4 cup sugar

2 eggs

3/4 cup heavy cream

3/4 cup whole milk

2 tablespoons bourbon or rum

1 1/2 teaspoons ground cinnamon

1/2 teaspoon ground ginger

1/2 teaspoon ground nutmeg

1/4 teaspoon salt

Sweetened whipped cream

6–8 SERVINGS

1. On a floured surface, roll out one dough disc, working from the center in all directions until you have a 12-inch round. Fold the dough in half and ease it into a 9-inch pie pan with the fold in the center. Unfold the dough and fit the pastry into the pan. Trim and flute the edges and prick the crust all over with a fork. Freeze for at least 30 minutes.

2. Preheat the oven to 375°F.

3. Press a sheet of foil into the bottom of the pie shell. Bake for 20 minutes. Remove the foil and continue to bake for 5 to 8 minutes, until pale golden. If the pastry starts to puff up, press the bottom gently with a large spatula or oven-mitted hand to flatten. Fill immediately or cool on a rack.

4. Whisk the pumpkin purée with the sugar and eggs. Whisk in the cream, milk, bourbon, cinnamon, ginger, nutmeg, and salt in a large bowl. Pour into the pie shell.

5. Bake until the custard filling is set at the edges and a knife inserted near the center comes out clean, 40 to 50 minutes.

6. Cool on a wire rack before serving at room temperature. Serve with the whipped cream.

Grandpa Chose Pumpkin

Grandma liked to cook. Grandpa liked to eat. But they did not agree upon the relative merits of what she cooked and what he ate. Grandfather insisted that pumpkin is the king of pies. But Grandma chose squash. Grandfather gave his pumpkin patch special attention. On occasion, and without Grandma's knowledge, he poured skim milk on the soil around the plants. He gave the squashes no such preferential treatment.

— Esther E. Wood, *Country Fare*

Julia's Apple Cream Tart

Over her long and illustrious lifetime, Julia Child forged a couple of strong ties to Maine. She and her husband, Paul, spent many summer vacations at his family's home on Mount Desert Island, and then, in her later years, she often visited good friends on Deer Isle. In fact, one of the several 85th birthday parties that were given for her all across the country happened on Deer Isle. Like countless other late-twentieth century cooks, I was inspired by Julia's wonderful television show and her cookbooks. I like to think that she would approve this slight adaptation of her delectable Apple Cream Tart from *Mastering the Art of French Cooking* (Knopf, 1966). I also think she'd approve the use of local cooking apples, such as Macouns or Jonathans.

SWEET SHORT CRUST

1¼ cups all-purpose flour

1   tablespoon sugar

¼   teaspoon salt

5   tablespoons cold butter, cut into 5 pieces

3   tablespoons cold vegetable shortening, cut into 3 chunks

4   tablespoons ice water

6—8 SERVINGS

1. To make the crust, combine the flour, sugar, and salt in a food processor and pulse to blend. Add the butter and shortening and pulse until the shortening is about the size of small peas. Drizzle the water through the feed tube and pulse until the pastry begins to clump together. Turn out onto a sheet of plastic wrap, flatten into a disk, wrap, and refrigerate for at least 30 minutes. (To make by hand, whisk the dry ingredients together in a bowl, work in the cold butter and shortening with your fingertips, add the water, and stir with a large fork to make a soft dough.)

2. Roll the pastry out on a lightly floured surface, working from the center in all directions until you have an 11-inch round. Fold the dough in half and ease it into a 9-inch tart pan with removable bottom with the fold in the center. Unfold the dough, press it against the sides of the pan, and trim the edges. Freeze for at least 30 minutes.

3. Preheat the oven to 375°F.

4. Press a sheet of foil into the bottom of the tart shell. Bake for 20 minutes. Remove the foil and continue to bake for 5 to 8 minutes, until pale golden. If the pastry starts to puff up, press the bottom gently with a large spatula or oven-mitted hand to flatten. Fill immediately or cool on a rack. If proceeding immediately, leave the oven temperature at 375°F.

APPLE CREAM FILLING

3	cups peeled and sliced medium-sweet apples, such as Macouns or Jonathans (about 1 pound)
⅔	cup sugar
¼	teaspoon ground cinnamon
1	egg
3	tablespoons all-purpose flour
½	cup light cream
1	tablespoon rum or cognac
1	teaspoon pure vanilla extract

Powdered sugar

5. In a large bowl, toss the apples with ⅓ cup of the sugar and the cinnamon and spread into the bottom of the tart shell. Bake until the apples begin to color and are almost tender, 20 to 25 minutes.

6. Reduce oven to 350°F.

7. Whisk together the egg and remaining ⅓ cup sugar in a medium-sized bowl until well blended. Whisk in the flour, then the cream, rum, and vanilla. Pour the mixture over the apple mixture.

8. Bake until the top is pale golden and a knife inserted part way to the center comes out clean, about 20 minutes.

9. Serve warm or at room temperature. Sprinkle with the powdered sugar before serving.

— Finest Kind

"Finest kind" (sometimes spelled as all one word: "finestkind") is a Maine phrase indicating general approval and appreciation of top quality, or an expression of good news. "How's your boat building job going?" "Finest kind!" "What's your day been like?" "Finest kind!" "So, how's that walnut pie at Moody's Diner?" "Finest kind!"

Walnut Pie

When I took a poll, asking people to name their favorite menu item at Moody's Diner in Waldoboro, the answer among my (admittedly unscientific) sample was practically unanimous: walnut pie. With real whipped cream.

---

1 cup chopped walnuts (see Note)

My Flaky Pie Pastry (page 235) for a single-crust pie

3 eggs

1 cup dark corn syrup

3/4 cup sugar

6 tablespoons butter, melted

4 teaspoons all-purpose flour

1 teaspoon pure vanilla extract

1/2 teaspoon salt

1 cup whole milk

Softly whipped cream

8–10 SERVINGS

1. Toast the walnuts in a large skillet over medium heat, stirring often, until one shade darker, about 4 minutes. Set aside.

2. On a floured surface, roll out the dough, working from the center in all directions until you have a 12-inch round. Fold the dough in half and ease it into a 9-inch pie pan with the fold in the center. Unfold the dough and fit the pastry into the pan. Trim and flute the edges and prick the crust all over with a fork. Freeze for at least 30 minutes.

3. Preheat the oven to 375°F.

4. Press a sheet of foil into the bottom of the pie shell. Bake for 20 minutes. Remove the foil and continue to bake for 5 to 8 minutes, until pale golden. If the pastry starts to puff up, press the bottom gently with a large spatula or oven-mitted hand to flatten. Fill immediately or cool on a rack.

5. Whisk together the eggs, corn syrup, sugar, butter, flour, vanilla, and salt in a large bowl until blended. Whisk in the milk.

6. Spread the nuts into the bottom of the pie shell and pour the egg mixture over.

7. Bake until the filling is set around the edges but still jiggly in the center, 35 to 40 minutes.

8. Cool on a rack for at least 1½ hours, until the pie reaches room temperature. Slice into smallish wedges (this is rich) and top with the whipped cream.

Note: *Their recipe from* What's Cooking at Moody's Diner *(Dancing Bear Books, 2003) doesn't suggest toasting the nuts. This is my addition, but I like the way it tempers the sweetness of the filling and deepens its nutty flavor.*

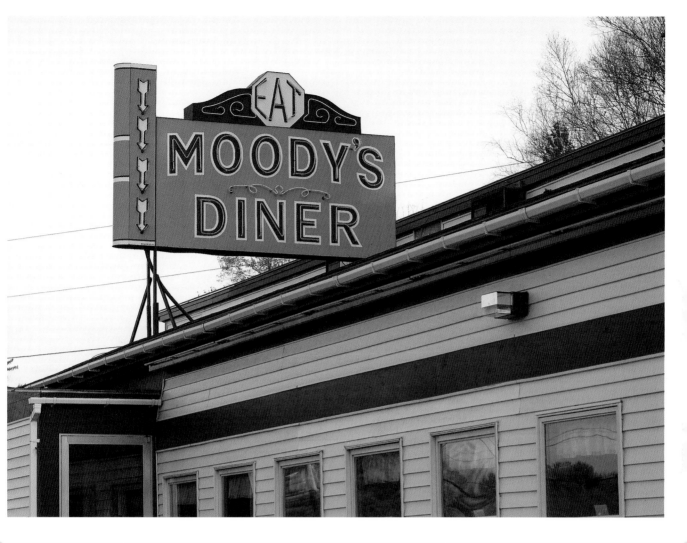

MOODY'S DINER

For most Mainers, Moody's Diner in Waldoboro needs no introduction. This quintessential '30s-style diner has become a destination itself for visitors to the state; for some, as obligatory as a visit to L. L. Bean, the clothing and outdoor equipment company founded in Maine in 1912.

Run by the same family since the late 1920s, the diner/gift shop/motel currently employs 31 Moodys. One of the secrets to Moody's success is that all customers are made welcome. As Nancy Moody Genthner puts it, "Locals aren't expected to go somewhere else during tourist season and tourists aren't taken advantage of."

The other trick is the food — which is really no trick at all, simply adherence to the tried-and-true formula of from-scratch ingredients cooked by dedicated cooks. Breakfasts, in true diner fashion, are preeminent, the home-baked goods (doughnuts, biscuits, pies, and so on) are legendary, and their famous daily special board — roast pork, lasagna, pot roast — is a roster of down-home, Down East cooking at its finest.

NE GROWN
RANBERRIES
PARROW FARM
4.99/lb.

Cranberry-Pear Crisp with Almond Topping

Pears and cranberries have one of those synergistic relationships in which together they surpass the sum of their parts. Tart, juicy cranberries offset firmer, sweeter pears, and the crunchy almond topping ties everything together. Served warm, topped with a scoop of good vanilla ice cream melting into rivulets, this crisp is an ideal finish to an autumn dinner.

ALMOND TOPPING

- ½ cup packed light brown sugar
- ½ cup all-purpose flour
- ¼ teaspoon salt
- ¼ pound (1 stick) cold butter, cut into several chunks
- 1 cup old-fashioned or quick-cooking rolled oats (not instant oatmeal)
- ½ cup sliced almonds

FILLING

- 5 cups peeled and sliced firm pears, such as Bosc or Bartlett (about 2 pounds)
- 2½ cups (8 ounces) whole cranberries
- 1½ cups sugar

Vanilla ice cream

1. To make the topping, process the brown sugar, flour, and salt in a food processor with long pulses to remove any lumps in the sugar. Add the butter and pulse in short bursts until most of the butter clumps are about the size of lima beans. Add the oats and almonds and pulse once or twice to just combine. Don't overprocess or the topping will be too uniform. (The topping can be made by hand by cutting the flour mixture and butter together. It can be made ahead and refrigerated.)

2. Preheat the oven to 350°F. Grease a shallow 2½- to 3-quart baking dish with butter.

3. To make the filling, toss the pears with the cranberries and sugar. Spread in the bottom of the prepared dish and sprinkle on the topping, spreading to the edges.

4. Bake, uncovered, until the pears and cranberries are tender and the topping is browned, 50 minutes to 1 hour.

5. Serve hot or warm with scoops of ice cream.

   Note: *If the crisp has cooled to room temperature, reheat in a 400°F oven for about 10 minutes.*

Dark and Sticky Gingerbread with Maple Whipped Cream

When Melanie Barnard, my long-time collaborator, and I set out to develop a gingerbread recipe, we decided that ideally the cake should be very moist — almost sticky — dark with molasses, and fragrant with spice. Finally, after much experimenting, we were delighted with the results, especially when we added chopped crystallized (also called candied) ginger to the cake to create a double hit of this pleasantly biting spice. When I'm serving this gingerbread as a dessert (as opposed to a snack cake), I like to bake it in a cake pan so it can be cut into wedges, which seems just a tad dressier than squares. The maple-spiked whipped cream is the crowning touch.

8—10 SERVINGS

- ½ cup (1 stick) unsalted butter, softened
- ⅓ cup packed dark brown sugar
- ⅓ cup dark corn syrup
- ⅓ cup molasses
- 1 egg
- ½ cup hot tap water
- 1½ cups all-purpose flour
- ½ teaspoon baking powder
- ½ teaspoon baking soda
- 1 teaspoon ground cinnamon
- ¾ teaspoon ground ginger
- ½ teaspoon salt
- ¼ cup chopped crystallized ginger
- 1 cup heavy cream whipped with 2 tablespoons pure maple syrup (optional)

1. Preheat the oven to 350°F. Grease a 9-inch round cake pan or square baking pan with butter and line with parchment if planning to unmold the cake (see step 4).

2. Using an electric mixer, beat the butter and brown sugar in a large bowl until light and fluffy. Beat in the corn syrup, molasses, and egg and beat until smooth. Slowly add the hot water, beating to blend.

3. Whisk together the flour, baking powder, baking soda, cinnamon, ground ginger, and salt in a bowl. Add to the butter mixture, beating on low speed until smooth. Stir in the crystallized ginger. Scrape into the prepared pan.

4. Bake until the top is springy and a tester inserted in the center comes out clean, about 30 to 35 minutes. Cool in the pan on a rack for 10 minutes. If unmolding, run a knife around the edge of the pan and invert onto a rack. Serve warm or at room temperature, plain or with maple whipped cream.

Maine Molasses

Molasses was once a major Maine import. Small Maine schooners took lumber and other sellable goods to the West Indies and brought back sugar and molasses stored in casks and hogsheads made from Maine wooden staves. Maine cooks used molasses to sweeten not just cookies but taffy, Indian pudding, gingerbread, doughnuts, even angel food cakes.

— Maine Maple Syrup —

Maine is the second largest producer (next to Vermont) of maple syrup in New England. Very early in spring the sugar maples are tapped — these days usually not with spouts running into quaint wooden or metal buckets, but with a system of plastic tubing that is gravity-fed into barrels at the foot of a hill — and the clear sap is collected. It looks like water (Native Americans called it "sweetwater"), but when it's boiled and boiled, usually over hardwood fires in small sugarhouses in the woods, the sap concentrates into amber ambrosia. The syrup is graded (I generally prefer Grade B, which has a more assertive maple flavor) and bottled, and you can use it with abandon on pancakes or waffles; in desserts; or in savory dishes, such as baked beans.

Best "Bangor" Brownies

Theories abound, but Jean Anderson, noted food historian, speculates that the story about brownies having been invented by a Bangor, Maine, housewife in the early twentieth century carries the ring of truth. It seems that the lady in question baked a chocolate cake one day and, when it didn't rise, instead of chucking it out (being a frugal Mainer) she cut the collapsed cake into squares and served it — to high praise. This recipe, which produces a brownie that is more on the fudgey side than it is cakelike, is based on one in another good old New England tradition, *The Fannie Farmer Baking Book* (Knopf, 1984), but I have added a "secret" pinch of black pepper, which is almost undetectable but serves to enliven the taste buds ever-so-slightly.

½ cup (1 stick) unsalted butter

2 ounces unsweetened chocolate

2 eggs

1 cup sugar

1 teaspoon pure vanilla extract

¼ teaspoon salt

⅛ teaspoon black pepper

½ cup chopped walnuts (optional)

½ cup all-purpose flour

ABOUT 16 SQUARES

1. Preheat the oven to 350°F. Grease an 8- or 9-inch square or 11-by-7-inch baking pan with butter.

2. Melt the butter and chocolate in a heavy, medium-sized saucepan over medium-low heat, stirring frequently, until both are almost melted. Remove from the heat and stir until melting is complete.

3. Whisk the eggs with the sugar, vanilla, salt, and pepper in a large bowl until well blended but not foamy. Gradually whisk in the melted chocolate mixture. Stir in the nuts, if desired. Sprinkle the flour over the top and whisk gently just until no white specks remain. Pour into the prepared pan, leveling the top.

4. Bake until a tester inserted about two-thirds of the way to the center comes out clean, 25 to 30 minutes. Cool the brownies in the pan on a wire rack for about 20 minutes. Cut into 16 or more squares and cool completely before serving. Store in the refrigerator for a day or so, or freeze for up to 2 weeks.

Spiced Hermit Bars

Sweetly spiced hermits are chewy, moist, raisin and nut-filled bar cookies that are good keepers. Some food historians think the name derives from that quality — they're even better when hidden away like a hermit for several days. Hermits are an old-fashioned favorite that probably originated in New England when clipper ships started bringing fragrant spices home from the Far East, and they are a delectable tradition well worth keeping alive.

2   cups all-purpose flour

1   teaspoon baking powder

3/4 teaspoon ground cinnamon

1/2 teaspoon baking soda

1/2 teaspoon ground nutmeg

1/2 teaspoon salt

1/4 teaspoon ground cloves

1/4 teaspoon ground mace

1/2 cup (1 stick) unsalted butter, softened

1/2 cup sugar

2   eggs

1/3 cup molasses

1   cup raisins, coarsely chopped

1/2 cup chopped walnuts

ABOUT 36 BARS

1. Preheat the oven to 350°F. Grease a 9-by-13-inch baking pan with butter.

2. Whisk together the flour, baking powder, cinnamon, baking soda, nutmeg, salt, cloves, and mace in a large bowl.

3. Using an electric mixer, beat the butter and sugar in a large bowl until smooth and creamy. Add the eggs and molasses and beat until smooth. Using a wooden spoon, stir the flour mixture into the butter mixture, then stir in the raisins and walnuts. Scrape the batter (it will be stiff) into the prepared pan, smoothing the top.

4. Bake for 15 to 18 minutes, until the edges are lightly browned and a tester inserted in the center comes out clean. Cool in the pan on a rack before cutting into 2-inch squares. Store in a tightly covered container for up to 5 days, or freeze for up to 1 month.

THE BURNING TREE

The Burning Tree, a welcome addition to an otherwise somewhat commercial and touristy Bar Harbor restaurant scene, is a simple farmhouse that owner/chefs Allison Martin and Elmer Beal have transformed into a cozy and stylish rendition of a country roadside restaurant. Good local art adorns the walls, a small French-style bar stands invitingly in one of the three dining rooms, and flowers grace the white-cloth draped tables.

The welcome is gracious and the service efficient and professional. And the food is consistently good. The Burning Tree's inventive, ever-changing menu emphasizes fresh seafood and chicken, and local produce — much of it grown right there on the grounds — plus there are always two or three vegetarian entrées. Some of the most popular starters are a white "hen" clam pasta made with chopped local clams in a garlicky sauce, mussels steamed with a spicy coconut broth, and a curried crabmeat salad to write home about.

Main-dish offerings are such delicacies as grilled Atlantic salmon with a mustard seed crust, oven-poached fillet of grey sole with lemon egg sauce on a bed of beet greens, lavender-roasted chicken, and, for vegetarians, ratatouille with sweet corn bread pudding or grilled vegetable stacks on a nest of peanut pesto noodles. Dessert listings are many and varied and include tarts, fruit crisps, a flourless chocolate cake, sorbets, and crème brûlée.

Orange Crème Brûlée

Crème brûlée is de rigueur on most white-tablecloth restaurant menus. The wonderful version at The Burning Tree is orange-liqueur–spiked and a fitting finish to one of the restaurant's consistently good meals.

1½ cups heavy or whipping cream

1 cup whole milk

½ cup sugar

2 tablespoons Triple Sec or other orange liqueur

7 egg yolks

2 teaspoons finely grated orange zest

⅓ cup granulated brown sugar (such as Sugar in the Raw) or light brown sugar

8 SERVINGS

1. Position a rack in the middle of the oven and preheat the oven to 350°F. Have ready eight 6-ounce ramekins (see Note) or one attractive shallow 1½- to 2-quart baking dish.

2. Combine the cream, milk, sugar, and orange liqueur in a medium-sized saucepan over medium heat. Bring to the scalding point, just until bubbles appear around the edges.

3. Lightly whisk the egg yolks in a medium-sized bowl until smooth but not frothy. Whisk in the orange zest. Slowly whisk the hot cream mixture into the yolks. Pour the custard into the baking dishes. Place the dish(es) in a large baking pan and fill the larger pan with hot water to come halfway up the sides of the dish(es).

4. Carefully transfer to the middle rack of the oven. Bake until the custard is set around the edges but still quivery in the center, or until a tester inserted near the center comes out clean, 25 to 35 minutes (the single large baking dish will require the longer baking time). Remove from the water bath, cool to room temperature, cover with plastic wrap, and refrigerate for several hours or overnight.

5. Before serving, preheat the broiler and position an oven rack about 3 inches from the element (see Note). Sprinkle the crème brûlées with a thin, even layer of granulated brown sugar (if using regular brown sugar, sieve a thin layer over the custards). Place under the element and broil until the sugar melts and caramelizes to a dark brown, 1 minute or so. Keep the oven door ajar and watch carefully. Cool for 5 minutes and serve. Use the back of a spoon to break through the hardened glaze.

Note: *You may use deep custard cups or shallow ramekins. The deeper dishes will require a slightly longer baking time. At The Burning Tree (and at most restaurants) they use a special culinary blow torch to caramelize the topping. If you'd like to purchase one, they're available through specialty gourmet catalogs.*

Crisp Ginger-Almond Wafers

This is a deliciously crunchy, not-too-sweet wafer cookie that comes via Linda Greenlaw and her mother Martha. (If by some chance you haven't heard of Linda, get a hold of any of her several books about life at sea and living and working on Isle au Haut.) Since ginger is a natural seasickness remedy, Linda touts these cookies as the ideal mid-morning snack aboard a fishing boat. I think they're delightful any time, but most especially at Christmas.

¾ cup sliced almonds

¾ cup (1½ sticks) unsalted butter

¾ cup sugar

½ cup molasses

2 cups all-purpose flour

2 teaspoons ground ginger

1 teaspoon ground cinnamon

¾ teaspoon baking soda

¾ teaspoon salt

½ teaspoon ground cloves

MAKES ABOUT 6 DOZEN COOKIES

1. Chop the nuts fine in a food processor. Remove and set aside.

2. Combine the butter, sugar, and molasses in the food processor and process, using long pulses, until the mixture is well blended. Add the flour, ginger, cinnamon, baking soda, salt, and cloves, and give the dry ingredients a stir with a fork to blend slightly. Process, using long pulses, until the dough begins to come together. Add the almonds and process until a ball of dough begins to form.

3. Turn out the dough onto two sheets of plastic wrap and shape into two compact logs about 1½ inches in diameter. Freeze for 40 minutes or longer.

4. Preheat the oven to 350°F. Slice the logs into ¼-inch cookies and place on ungreased baking sheets, spacing about 1 inch apart. Bake until the cookies just barely begin to color at the edges, 12 to 15 minutes. Remove to a rack to cool completely. (Cookies will crisp as they cool.)

5. Store in a covered container for a day or so, or freeze for up to 2 weeks.

Muster Cake

In the early 19th century, farm boys left their smaller outlying settlements and traveled to the nearest large town to take part in military musters once a month. To sustain themselves, they carried squares of hard gingerbread in their pockets and called it "muster cake."

Grape Nuts Pudding

Grape Nuts Pudding appears frequently on menus in classic New England eateries. This version from Cole Farms is velvety and egg-rich. It doesn't have the spices that some Grape Nuts puddings have, so its flavor depends on the quality of the vanilla. Be sure to use pure vanilla extract, not imitation vanilla. At Cole Farms they use a commercially available vanilla made by Schlotterbeck & Foss, a Portland company.

6 — 8 SERVINGS

6 eggs

1 cup sugar

3 cups whole milk

1½ teaspoons pure vanilla extract

¼ teaspoon salt

⅓ cup Grape Nuts cereal

Lightly sweetened whipped cream (optional)

1. Preheat the oven to 350°F.

2. Whisk the eggs with the sugar in a large bowl until blended. Gently whisk in the milk; mix in the vanilla and salt.

3. Sprinkle the Grape Nuts evenly over the bottom of a shallow 2-quart baking dish. Pour the egg mixture over the Grape Nuts. Place the baking dish into a larger baking pan and fill the larger pan with hot water to come halfway up the sides of the pudding dish. Carefully place the pan into the oven. (Or fill both pans while on the oven rack.) Bake for 35 to 40 minutes, or until a small knife inserted about two-thirds of the way to the center comes out clean.

4. Cool on a wire rack for at least 30 minutes. Serve the pudding warm, at room temperature, or chilled, topped with whipped cream, if desired.

COLE FARMS

Cole Farms is a sprawling establishment with homey varnished wood booths, affable waitresses, and a big contingent of relaxed local guys who sit at the counter dispensing Down East quips and folk wisdom.

Located in the quintessential New England town of Gray, halfway between Portland and Lewiston, Cole Farms draws loyal customers from the entire area. When we stopped late one morning it was on the cusp of breakfast and lunch, and so we sampled some of both meals: farm fresh eggs and huge blueberry pancakes, then on to fried haddock, from-scratch baked beans, some of the best coleslaw (vinegared, no mayonnaise) I've ever eaten, hot yeast rolls, and a few bites of velvety Grape Nuts pudding. Daily specials at Cole Farms include New England boiled dinner, chicken pot pie, roast pork, and turkey dinner with all the trimmings.

Hester's Delectable Lemon Pudding Cake

My mother, Hester White Maury, was an excellent cook, and this dessert recipe — one of her tried-and-true favorites — typifies the virtues of home cooking like hers. The pudding cake (also sometimes called sponge pudding in old cookbooks) is simple to put together, the ingredients are almost always on hand, and the seemingly straightforward batter magically separates as it bakes into a delicate sponge cake layer on top and a rich, lemony sauce underneath. This dessert is a perfect finish to a seafood meal (Maine Shrimp Linguine [page 125] or Baked Seafood-and-Herb-Stuffed Haddock [page 173] come to mind), or, for that matter, just about any supper at all.

2 tablespoons unsalted butter, softened

²/₃ cup plus 1 tablespoon sugar

3 egg yolks

3 tablespoons all-purpose flour

1 tablespoon finely chopped or grated lemon zest

¼ cup lemon juice (juice of 1 large lemon)

1 cup whole or low-fat milk

4 egg whites

⅛ teaspoon salt

6 SERVINGS

1. Preheat the oven to 325°F. Lightly grease a shallow 1½- or 2-quart baking dish, such as a 9-inch square dish, with butter.

2. Combine the butter and ²/₃ cup of the sugar in a medium-sized bowl and use an electric mixer or a wooden spoon to mix until crumbly. Add the egg yolks and flour and beat until quite smooth. Beat in the lemon zest and juice, then whisk in the milk.

3. Beat the egg whites and salt in a separate bowl until foamy. Sprinkle on the remaining 1 tablespoon sugar and beat until soft peaks form. Pour the lemon mixture over the beaten whites and use a large whisk to stir gently, just until no large lumps of egg white remain. Streaks are fine. (The lemon base is so light that it is difficult to fold the two mixtures together in the classic manner.)

4. Pour the batter into the prepared dish. Set the dish in a larger baking pan and add boiling water to come halfway up the sides of the pudding cake dish. (It's easiest to do this on the pulled-out oven rack.) Bake for 25 to 30 minutes, until the top of the pudding is lightly colored and springs back with lightly touched.

5. Cool the pudding cake in the water bath for 10 minutes. Serve warm, at room temperature, or even chilled.

Recommended Reading

Alex, Kyra, *Lily's Café Cookbook*. Thomson-Shore, 2001.

Anderson, Jean, *The American Century Cookbook*. Clarkson Potter, 1997.

Arlen, Alice, *The Maine Sporting Camp Cookbook*. Down East, 2004.

Behr, Edward, *The Art of Eating* newsletter, Summer 1994.

Brandes, Kathleen M., *Moon Handbooks — Maine*. Avalon Travel, 2001.

Carr, Sister Frances A., *Shaker Your Plate*. The Shaker Society, 1985.

Chase, Sarah Leah and Jonathan, *Saltwater Seasonings*. Little, Brown, 1992.

Child, Julia, *Mastering the Art of French Cooking*. Knopf, 1966.

Coffin, Robert P. Tristram, *Maine Cooking, Old-Time Secrets*. first published as *Mainstays of Maine*. Macmillan, 1944.

Cooney, Barbara, *Island Boy*. Viking Penguin, 1988.

———, *Miss Rumphius*. Viking Penguin, 1982.

Cunningham, Marion, *The Fannie Farmer Baking Book*. Knopf, 1984.

Doiron Paul, ed., Maine Writers and Publishers Alliance, 1998. *Eating Between the Lines: A Maine Writers' Cookbook*.

Dojny, Brooke, *Full of Beans*. HarperPerennial, 1996.

———, *The New England Clam Shack Cookbook*. Storey Publishing, 2003.

———, *The New England Cookbook*. Harvard Common Press, 1999.

Emerson Hospital Auxiliary, *Revolutionary Recipes: Concord à la Carte*. Wimmer, 2002.

Genthner, Nancy Moody, *What's Cooking at Moody's Diner*. Dancing Bear Books, 2003.

Greenlaw, Linda and Martha, *Recipes from a Very Small Island*. Hyperion, 2005.

Halliday, Fred, *Halliday's New England Food Explorer*. Fodor's Travel, 1993.

Jones, Judith and Evan, *The L.L. Bean Book of New England Cookery*. Random House, 1987.

Kimball, Christopher, *The Dessert Bible*. Little Brown, 2000.

Maine Coastal Cooking. Courier-Gazette, 1964.

McCloskey, Robert, *Blueberries for Sal*. Viking Press, 1948.

———, *One Morning in Maine*. Viking Press, 1952.

Meals, Maps, and Memories. Four-Town Nursing Service, 1977.

Miller, Amy Bess and Persis Fuller, *The Best of Shaker Cooking*. Macmillan, 1985.

Mosser, Marjorie, *Good Maine Food*. Down East, 1939.

Oliver, Sandra, *Joy of Historical Cooking*. Ongoing newsletter, not dated.

———, *Saltwater Foodways*. Mystic Seaport Museum, 1995.

Page, Katherine Hall, *The Body in the Lighthouse*. HarperCollins, 2003.

Portland Symphony Cookbook. Portland Symphony Orchestra Women's Committee, 1974.

Russo, Richard, *Empire Falls*. Vintage, 2001.

Sax, Richard, *Classic American Desserts*. Chapters, 1994.

Standish, Marjorie, *Cooking Down East*. Down East Books, 1969.

Stern, Jane and Michael, *Road Food*. HarperPerennial, 1992.

Thorne, John, *Serious Pig*. North Point Press, 1996.

Trillin, Calvin, *Alice, Let's Eat*. Farrar, Straus, and Giroux, 1994.

White, E.B., *Charlotte's Web*. Harper and Row, 1952.

———, *One Man's Meat*. Harper Collins, 1978.

White, Jasper, *Jasper White's Cooking from New England*. Biscuit Books, 1998.

———, *Lobster At Home*. Scribner, 1998.

Wood, Esther E., *Country Fare*. New Hampshire Publishing Co., 1976.

———, *Deep Roots*. New Hampshire Publishing Co., 1976.

Other Helpful Websites

Eat Local Foods Coalition of Maine
www.eatmainefoods.org
Information on eating local.

Maine Department of Agriculture
www.getrealmaine.com
Comprehensive site providing information on farmers' markets, apple orchards, Maine Maple Sunday, Open Farm Day, U-Pick farms, and much more.

Maine Cheese Guild
www.mainecheeseguild.org
Listings of Maine cheese makers and events featuring Maine-made cheese.

Public Market House
www.portlandmarkethouse.com
The Portland Public Market closed in 2006, but many of the vendors moved around the corner to this new venue on Monument Square.

Featured Restaurants

A-1 Diner
3 Bridge Street
Gardiner, ME 04345
207-582-4804
www.a1diner.com
Spicy Chicken Big Mamou, 160

Arrows Restaurant
Berwick Road
Ogunquit, ME 03907
207-361-1100
www.arrowsrestaurant.com
Trio of Autumn Greens, 91

The Bethel Inn
On the Common
Bethel, ME 04217
207-824-2175
www.bethelinn.com
Maple-Mustard Venison Medallions, 151

The Bradford Camps
P.O. Box 729
Ashland, ME 04732
207-746-7777
www.bradfordcamps.com
Pan-Fried Trout, 183

The Brooklin Inn
Route 175
Brooklin, ME 04616
207-359-2777
www.brooklininn.com
Milk-Poached Finnan Haddie with Hard-Cooked Eggs, 175

The Burning Tree
71 Otter Creek Drive
Otter Creek, ME 04660
207-288-9331
Orange Crème Brûlée, 271

Chase's Daily
96 Main Street
Belfast, ME 04915
207-338-0555
Chipotle-Roasted Winter Squash Tacos, 40

The Clam Shack
Route 9 at the Kennebunkport Bridge
Kennebunkport, ME 04046
207-967-3321
http://theclamshack.net
Fried Clam Rolls, 46

Cleonice
112 Main Street
Ellsworth, ME 04605
207-664-7554
www.cleonice.com
Paella Cleonice, 122

Cod End
(formerly Cod End Cookhouse)
Commercial Street
Tenants Harbor, ME 04860
207-372-6782
Mediterranean Seafood Stew, 109

Cole Farms
64 Lewiston Road
Gray, ME 04039
207-657-4714
www.colefarms.com
Grape Nuts Pudding, 273

Fore Street
288 Fore Street
Portland, ME 04102
207-775-2717
www.forestreet.biz
Pan Roast of Fish and Shellfish, 126

Francine Bistro
55 Chestnut Street
Camden, ME 04843
207-230-0083
www.francinebistro.com
Slivered Raw Asparagus Salad, 56

The Harraseeket Inn
Broad Arrow Tavern
162 Main Street
Freeport, ME 04032
207-865-9377
www.harraseeketinn.com
Harraseeket Market Pie, 42

Helen's Restaurant
28 East Main Street
Machias, ME 04654
207-255-8423
Graham-Cracker Cream Pie, 246

Henry & Marty
61 Maine Street
Brunswick, ME 04011
207-721-9141
Lobster Salad with Roasted Corn Salsa, 74

J's Oyster Bar
5 Portland Pier
Portland, ME 04102
207-772-4828
"Nude" Raw Oysters with Sauces, 31

The Maine Diner
2265 Post Road
Wells, ME 04090
207-646-4441
www.mainediner.com
Lobster Pie, 195

Moody's Diner
Route 1
Waldoboro, ME 04572
207-832-7785
www.moodysdiner.com
Walnut Pie, 262

Moose Point Tavern
16 Henderson Road
Jackman, ME 04945
207-668-4012
Venison with Cranberry-Chipotle Sauce, 148

Primo Restaurant
2 South Main Street
Rockland, ME 04841
207-596-0770
www.primorestaurant.com
Seared Halibut on Native Corn and Lobster Risotto, 177

Street & Co.
33 Wharf Street
Portland, ME 04101
207-775-0887
Mackerel with Caper and White Wine Sauce, 178

Featured Restaurants (continued)

Thomaston Café & Bakery
154 Main Street
Thomaston, ME 04861
207-354-8589
www.thomastoncafe.com
Dilled Fish Hash, 185

Thurston's Lobster Pound
Steamboat Wharf Road
Bernard, ME 04612
207-244-7600
Mussel Chowder with Colorful Vegetables, 105

See also Hidden Treasures listings:
Maine's Quintessential Clam Shacks, 54
Maine Pounds In-the-Rough, 196
Hot Dog Stands and Carts, 52
Maine's Food Festivals, 124

Mail-Order Sources

Aurora Mills and Farm
Linneus, Maine
207-521-0094
http://auroramillsandfarm.net
Makers of Maine-grown and -milled whole wheat bread flour

Bob's Sugar House
Dover-Foxcroft, Maine
207-564-2145
www.mainemaplesyrup.com
Maine maple syrup and maple sugar products

Boothbay Lobster Wharf
Boothbay Harbor, Maine
207-633-4900
www.boothbaylobsterwharf.com
Maine lobsters and other seafood

Bouchard Family Farms
Fort Kent, Maine
800-239-3237
www.ployes.com
Mixes for ployes, a French-American pancake

Bradshaw's Cranberry Farm
Dennysville, Maine
207-726-5065
www.cranberriesfresh.com
Fresh cranberries, cranberry sauce, cranberry spread

Harbor Fish Market
Portland, Maine
800-370-1790
www.harborfish.com
Seafood of all types

Maurice Bonneau's Sausage Kitchen
Lisbon Falls, Maine
888-453-5503
www.sausagekitchen.com
Smoked sausages and other meats

Morgan's Mills MOFGA Certified Flour Mill
Union, Maine
800-373-2756
Stone-ground organic flours and mills

Morse's Sauerkraut
North Waldeboro, Maine
866-832-5569
www.morsessauerkraut.com
Handmade sauerkraut

Nervous Nellie's Jams and Jellies
Deer Isle, Maine
800-777-6845
www.nervousnellies.com
Small-batch jams, jellies, preserves, marmalades, and chutneys

The New England Cupboard
Hermon, Maine
207-848-4900
www.newenglandcupboard.com
Bakewell Cream, Maine's unique leavening agent

Nezinscot Farm Store
Turner, Maine
207-225-3231
www.nezinscotfarm.com
Organic meats, cheeses, vegetables

Raye's Mustard Mill
Eastport, Maine
800-853-1903
www.rayesmustard.com
Stone ground mustards in several varieties

Sabbathday Lake Shaker Village
New Gloucester, Maine
207-926-4597
www.shaker.lib.me.us
Dried herbs of all kinds

Stanchfield Farms
Milo, Maine
207-732-5173
Cucumber pickles and other pickled vegetables

Stonington Seafood
Stonington, Maine
207-348-2730
www.stoningtonseafood.com

Townline Farm
Carmel, Maine
207-478-7360
townlinefarm@adelphia.net

Trenton Bridge Lobster Pound
Trenton, Maine
207-667-2977
www.trentonbridgelobster.com

W. S. Wells & Son
Wilton, Maine
207-645-3393
Belle of Maine fresh fiddleheads

INDEX

OTHER NEW ENGLAND COOKBOOKS
by Brooke Dojny

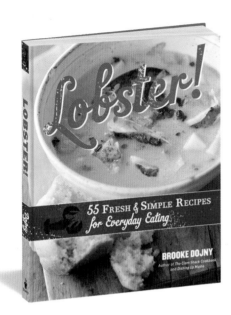

Lobster!

In Lobster!, cookbook author Brooke Dojny has taken her extensive knowledge of the northeast, paired it with her lobster know how, and compiled her favorite tips tricks and recipes. In these 55 mouthwatering recipes, readers will find renditions of all their favorites including bisques, salads and lobster rolls. The easy-to-follow recipes are satisfying for lobster lovers of all ages.

— *Houston Lifestyles & Home*

Can't get to the beach? Evoke the seaside at your backyard picnic with the sweet meat of what Dojny calls the "cardinal of the ocean."

— *Boston Globe*

144 pages. Hardcover with jacket. ISBN 978-1-60342-962-7.

The New England Clam Shack Cookbook, 2nd edition

Crammed with photos, vivid stories, and taxonomic information about local seafood, this masterpiece delivers a quick summer vacation in the dead of winter.

— *Village Voice*

Dojny has created a dependable travel guide for seafood lovers touring the Northeast while simultaneously offering mouthwatering recipes sure to torture those who have no access to fresh seafood or a decent deep fryer.

— *Publishers Weekly*

256 pages. Paper. ISBN 978-1-60342-026-6.